D1064319

HISTORY ON THE MARCH

Makers of the Americas
LANSING AND CHASE

Builders of the Old World
HARTMAN AND SAUNDERS

America—Land of Freedom
HARTMAN AND BALL

ALLAN NEVINS
General Consultant

Makers of the Americas

D. C. Heath and Company · Boston

AUTHOR

MARION LANSING

Educational Consultant
W. LINWOOD CHASE, Professor of Education, Boston University

General Consultant
ALLAN NEVINS, Professor of American History, Columbia University, New York

ILLUSTRATED BY
Frederick Trench Chapman

Maps by Beatrice and Leonard Derwinski

BOSTON NEW YORK CHICAGO ATLANTA
SAN FRANCISCO DALLAS LONDON

Printed in the United States of America 4 E 7

FOREWORD

If we could visit all the countries of the two Americas today, we should find there were more than twenty. And what a trip such a visit would be! We should begin with Canada, with its high western mountains, its broad prairies, its many cities, and its islands stretching out into the misty Atlantic. We should travel south across the United States, over the high tableland of Mexico, past the volcanoes of Nicaragua, across the canal that links the two oceans, and down into the rich tropical country of Brazil. We should turn to the west to see Ecuador, whose name means that it lies astride the equator, and Peru and Bolivia, with their herds of llamas and rich mines of copper and silver. In Rio de Janeiro we should marvel at one of the world's most beautiful bays, and in Buenos Aires at streets and parks as handsome as any on the globe. Argentina would show us fields of grain like those in Ohio and Kansas, and wide ranches with cowboys and cattle like those on our western plains half a century ago. Far down in Patagonia we should find ourselves once more in regions of snow and cold, facing the Antarctic as upper Canada faces the Arctic.

If you could go to school for a while in each of these lands from Hudson's Bay to Cape Horn, you would find the boys and girls studying their own history. You could tell your schoolmates a great deal about Washington, Lincoln, and the two Roosevelts. You would be amused if the Mexican children had never heard of the Pilgrims, and a little shocked if the Venezuelan youngsters did not know that Jefferson was a great President, and Edison a great inventor. But no doubt the school children scattered through other parts of the Americas would be as amused and shocked by many of the things you did not know about their great men. Just as we believe that Washington and Lincoln should be honored beyond our own land, so do Canadians believe that Sir John MacDonald ought to be remembered in other countries, and South Americans believe that other peoples should know about Bolívar and San Martín.

The two Americas were discovered at about the same time. They were settled under different conditions, and they grew up in different ways. But many parts of the story of Canada and the United States, where English is spoken, resemble parts of the story of Mexico, Brazil, and Argentina, where Portuguese or Spanish is spoken. We find the same sort of adventurers seeking for gold and silver. We find the lumbermen in South America felling mahogany, ebony, and logwood trees while the lumberjacks of North America bring down the great pines. We find the same struggle against the hardships of the frontier. We find Negroes brought as slaves into both the continents, and kindhearted men demanding that these slaves be set free. We find sturdy citizens in both the English colonies and the Spanish colonies deciding that they want to govern themselves, and catching up musket and sword to win their full freedom. We have the hunter, the fur trader, the rancher, and the plantation owner appearing in both the continents.

It is important that children in the United States know something of the wild, romantic, interesting story of the Latin American nations and of Canada, just as it is important that Canadian and Latin American children know something of our story. The people of the twenty-odd American countries have resolved to be "good neighbors." But they cannot feel a genuine and hearty neighborliness until they understand each other's history and ways.

This book is the story of the people, great and small, who made the New World what it is today.

ALLAN NEVINS

CONTENTS

UNIT VII. Americans on the Move 243

UNIT VIII. Democracy Gains in the Americas 289

I EUROPEANS FIND THE AMERICAS

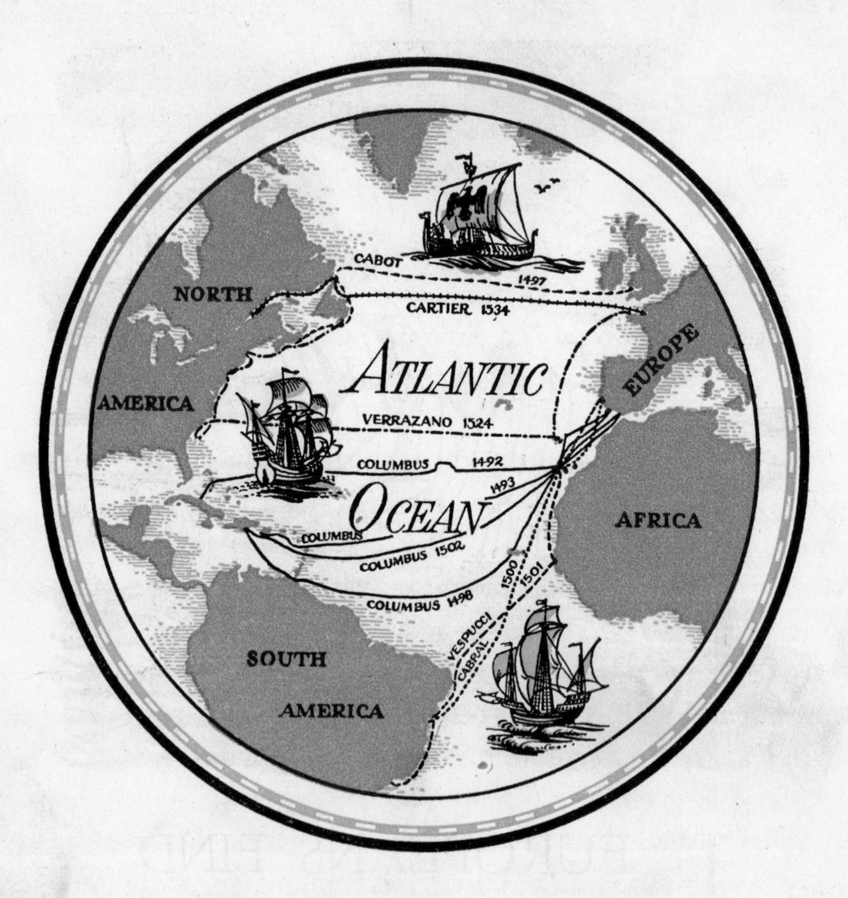

EARLY EUROPEAN VOYAGES TO THE AMERICAS

Five hundred years after the brief visits of the Norsemen to North America, Columbus made the voyage for Spain which opened the New World to exploration and settlement.

EUROPEANS FIND THE AMERICAS

VIKINGS SAIL WEST

Between Europe and America lies an Arctic land called Greenland. One summer nearly a thousand years ago a ship drew near its shores. This Viking ship was long and narrow, with a single square sail and long oars. The men who pulled at the oars were Northmen, or Norsemen, from Iceland.

A sturdy boy stood beside his father at the prow. His fair hair tossed in the wind, and his bright blue eyes gazed at the shores ahead. The fog had lifted and he could see a harbor and bare, flat land below the ice-covered mountains. He was eager to explore this new country which was to be his home.

The boy was Leif Ericsson. His father, Eric the Red, had discovered this new land. Eric was bringing his own family and several other families from Iceland to start a colony. He had called the country Greenland because he thought so pleasant a name would make men want to settle there.

Eric and the other Norsemen were daring sailors. Their ancestors had come from the northern parts of Europe that are now called Norway, Sweden, and Denmark. In their dragon-prowed ships they had sailed on many seas.

Eric's new colony flourished. In the following years other families came from Iceland. One autumn while Leif was still a boy, these settlers watched a Viking ship come into their harbor from the west. This was a surprise, for Norway and Iceland lay to the east. Everyone listened eagerly while the captain told of his voyage.

On his way from Iceland to Greenland a storm had driven his ship far off its course. After many days he sighted a land covered with woods. Sailing on, he saw other wooded shores, but he knew that none of them was Greenland, for Greenland has no forests. The captain did not stop to go ashore because he and his men were eager to reach Greenland.

Leif Ericsson never forgot this tale of new and unknown lands across the waters. He grew to be a tall, strong youth and a leader like his father. At last, in the year 1000, came the time when he could go out as captain of his own ship, to look for those western lands which others had seen from a distance. He had thirty-four men with him, all eager to go on this voyage with their brave young leader.

LEIF ERICSSON IN VINLAND

Leif followed as closely as he could the course which the captain had described years before. He and his men came at last to a pleasant land which they went ashore to explore. The more they saw of it, the more pleasing and comfortable it seemed to these men from the north. Leif decided to go no farther, but to build a house as a shelter for himself and his men.

The expedition was well managed. Leif did not yet know whether other men dwelt in this region. He kept one half of the little party near the house each day, guarding it against possible attack. Others went exploring or worked in the woods, cutting trees.

On an autumn day one of the men found vines with bunches of grapes hanging on them. That was a great delight and marvel, for no one but the old man who discovered the vines had ever seen this fruit. He had lived in the south of Europe in his youth. He showed the others how to press the juice from the grapes and also how to dry them to take back home.

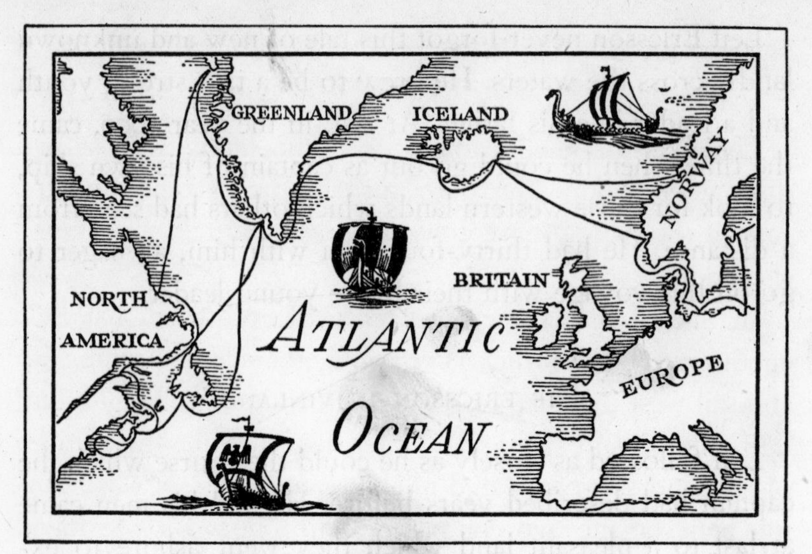

THE VIKINGS IN THE NORTH ATLANTIC

The men spent a busy winter. They fished and hunted and gathered wood, and they put in many hours of work on their boat. It had to be repaired before they started on their voyage home. Coming as they did from the bleak north, these men never ceased to marvel at the mild climate. There was little frost or snow. Winter in Iceland and Greenland had always been to them a time of constant snow and ice and bitter cold.

When the time came to go home, they loaded their boat with wood and dried grapes. Before they left, Leif named the place Vineland, or Vinland. That was the first name given by white men to the land along the Atlantic seacoast.

Just where this Vinland was, no one can be quite sure. Some think that Leif's house was built on Cape Cod. Others place it farther south, on Long Island.

Leif Ericsson never came back to this land which he had discovered. Soon after his return his father died, and the care of the struggling colony in Greenland fell upon Leif's shoulders.

In one of the Norse hero tales it is reported that Leif encouraged his brother, Thorwald, to take the same ship and sail west the next year with a crew of men. They found Leif's house and spent the winter near it. But some natives of the land soon appeared in skin canoes. There was fighting between the two companies, and Thorwald was killed by an arrow. Sadly the rest of the company loaded the ship with grapes and wood and sailed for home.

Within a very few years the Norsemen tried again to make a settlement in America. This time it was a woman who urged them on. Gudrid, who was a member of Leif Ericsson's family, listened to the tales of this fair new land and wanted to go there. Her husband, Thorfinn Karlsefni, was eager for adventure, too. A company of sixty men and five women sailed to Vinland and tried to start a Viking colony. They brought cattle and tools and clothing, as well as weapons with which to defend themselves.

The route to Vinland was by this time well known. When Leif's house was found, Thorfinn and Gudrid took possession of it. Others built cabins near by. For this company, as for those who had come before, life was pleasant. There were fish to be caught in the waters, and in the woods there were many small animals that could be hunted for food. In one of the tales it is reported that "wheat grew wild in the hollows, and vines were on every ridge."

Life went on peacefully in the little Norse settlement. Every once in a while during the spring and summer a long line of canoes would be seen on the water. The natives were coming to see these strange new people. They were always surprised at their light hair and blue eyes.

The settlers tried to make friends with the short, dark men. For a time there was barter. The natives often brought furs, heaped in great piles in their canoes, and were delighted to exchange them for pieces of red cloth. They returned again and again, and each time it seemed that there were more of them.

During the second year there was trouble with the natives. They had tried all along to buy some of the white

men's spears and battle-axes, but the settlers had never let them get hold of any of these weapons. One day a native tried to snatch a battle-ax, and was killed by the Norseman who held it. Other natives were killed when they made attacks on groups of two or three Norsemen in the woods. Finally the natives came in great numbers. In the battle which followed, many of them were killed. Those who survived departed in their canoes, carrying their dead. But Thorfinn knew that more would come. A company as small as his could not hope to hold out against such numbers.

Before the natives came back, Thorfinn and the other settlers loaded their boat and departed from Vinland, and made a safe journey to Greenland. The stories of their adventures, as told to their home people, were repeated again and again. After two hundred years these stories were written down, and are now known as sagas.

No lasting settlement was made by Norsemen in America, though Norse ships may have sighted these shores now and again on other daring voyages.

COLUMBUS, SAILOR AND MAPMAKER

A tall, red-headed Italian sailor by the name of Christopher Columbus came in the year 1477 to the busy seaport of Lisbon, Portugal. He was going to stay ashore for a while and earn his living with his younger brother Bartholomew by making maps to sell.

Maps were much in demand in the seaports of Europe. Sailing a ship had become, in that century, more of a science than it had ever been before. Men had better compasses than sailors of other times had used, and better instruments for measuring the height of the sun and stars.

Prince Henry of Portugal had set up, in the earlier part of the century, a school for seamen. He had encouraged exploration and sent out captains who had gone two thousand miles farther south along the coast of Africa than Europeans had ever gone before. Ships had passed beyond the borders marked on the old maps as the edge of the world.

A good mapmaker had to do much more than copy old maps. He must go to the wharves and listen to the talk of the seamen. A man who was an experienced sailor, as young Columbus was, could get much information by asking questions. Many sailors would tell him facts about winds and currents because they knew that he understood. After he had heard these reports, he would put down on his maps the information he had gathered, judging always as to what was true.

The family home of Christopher Columbus was in Genoa, a seaport of Italy, where his father was a clothmaker. Christopher had spent much of his childhood and youth in his father's shop, working with his brothers in the washing and combing of the wool which his father wove into cloth.

When he was fourteen Christopher, like many boys in seashore towns, became a sailor. He got his training as a seaman on short voyages in the Mediterranean Sea. Once he sailed to an island between Greece and Asia Minor, and probably more than once along the coast of Africa. Just before he settled in Lisbon, he made a trip northward to Iceland, and the ship touched at a port in Ireland on the way. There was much trade between Lisbon and some of these northern ports.

Aboard ship and in Lisbon he heard about new islands which had lately been discovered off the west coast of Africa. Voyages were also being made southward along the coast of that continent, where gold and ivory were obtained.

Among the islands which had been discovered and settled in Prince Henry's time were the Azores, which lie about nine hundred miles out in the Atlantic. This was the farthest western land that the Portuguese sailors had found.

"It was in Portugal that the Admiral began to think that if men could sail so far south, one might also sail west and find lands in that quarter," wrote the son of Columbus.

To a man who was listening for tales of these new lands and waters, there came strange and interesting news. The king's chief pilot, on a ship sailing far to the west of Portugal and beyond the Azores, had picked up "a log curiously carved, but not with iron, brought there by a westerly wind." Stories were told by other seamen about a kind of tree, not known in Europe, which came ashore on the Azores after a violent westerly storm.

REACHING THE EAST BY SAILING WEST

Kings and merchants of that day were eager to find better routes to the Far East. They called India, China, and all the lands near them the Indies. These eastern lands were rich in silks and spices. Gold was to be found there, too.

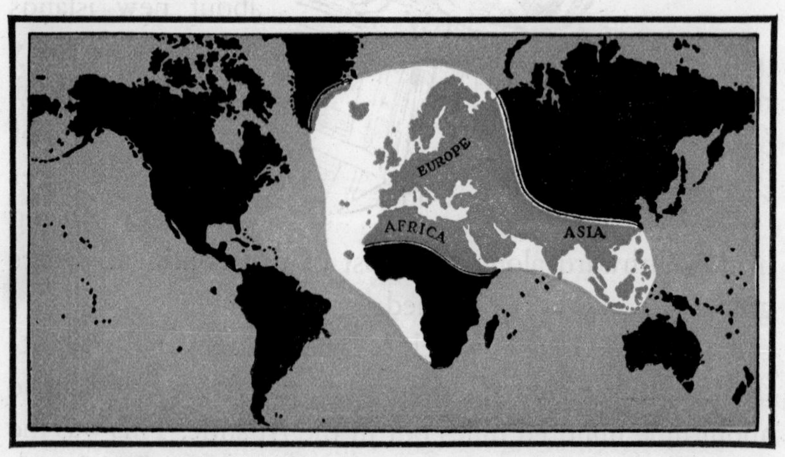

THE WORLD KNOWN TO EUROPEANS IN 1490

Land routes to these countries were long and difficult. Portuguese explorers were seeking a sea route around Africa. They hoped that it would be shorter than the land routes and also less expensive.

Christopher Columbus began to wonder if a new route to the Far East might be found by sailing straight west. As he asked the question, he became more and more sure of the answer. He believed the world was round, as ancient wise men had said. What could be more reasonable than to expect to get to the East if one sailed west long enough and far enough? One had only to trace a line around a ball to see how such a voyage could be made.

Christopher Columbus had not had much school life as a boy. He had been forced to pick up his education along the way. In Portugal, after his desire to explore came to him, he did a great deal of reading and studying.

Some of the books he read were in handwriting, the pages having been copied by the monks. But printing had been invented about the time Columbus was born.

He and his brother Bartholomew bought some of the early printed books, and read and reread them.

Two of those books were big volumes, somewhat like modern geographies. A third was a book which is known and read today—Marco Polo's account of his travels in the Far East. Marco Polo was an Italian who had returned in 1295 from a long stay in Cathay. That was the name by which China was then known. The tale of the marvels which Polo saw there became very popular. People found it hard to believe that he was telling the truth, but they liked to read about these wonders.

Columbus knew what was in this book before he owned his printed copy. He knew of the great "Ocean Sea" which washed the eastern edge of Asia, and of the islands near by. The most important of these islands was a very large one, which Polo said he did not visit because it was fifteen hundred miles from the mainland of Cathay. The name of this island was Cipango in those days, but it is now called Japan. Its king, according to Polo's account, had "a mighty palace roofed with the finest gold," and the floors paved with golden plate, each of these plates being "a good two fingers thick."

Columbus believed he could reach Cipango by sailing across the waters toward the west. Then from the island he would go to the mainland, to the court of the Great Khan, wealthy ruler of all those lands.

For a dozen years Columbus tried to get money and support for a voyage of western exploration. He was refused again and again at the courts of Portugal and Spain. He even sent his brother to the kings of France and England with his proposal, but he could get no help.

At last in Spain Columbus gained the needed support. Queen Isabella, with her husband, King Ferdinand, finally became enough interested in the venture to give him the

money he needed. Columbus was made admiral of the expedition and went quickly about the business of preparing for the voyage.

On Friday, August 3, 1492, in the early morning, the three ships set sail, the *Pinta*, the *Niña*, and the Admiral's own flagship, the *Santa María*. There were ninety men aboard. Among them were able captains and experienced seamen. But the undertaking was the plan of one man, the leader, Christopher Columbus.

Every night in his cabin Columbus wrote a report of the day. That daily record is called the log of the voyage.

The ships reached the Canary Islands in nine days and spent three weeks there, while the crew made repairs and rigged the masts with proper sails. Then they loaded the ships with supplies and set their course due west.

When Columbus was trying to get money for his voyage, there had been much argument as to how long it should take him to get to Cipango or, if he missed that island, to Cathay. He figured that he should arrive after sailing about three thousand miles. Learned men at the court of Spain thought that the distance would be greater.

Ashore, the exact distance did not seem very important. On shipboard, it was the chief interest. The sailors knew how far Columbus thought he would have to sail before he came to the first land. They kept watch, as he was doing. Day after day the ships drove briskly along, with favoring winds and currents. At first everyone was pleased. But when the men got farther and farther from home, these favoring winds disturbed them. The winds all blew one way, and that was away from Europe. "My crew dreaded," wrote Columbus, "lest they should never meet in these seas with a fair wind to return to Spain."

The ships were going farther than Columbus had expected, and still there was no land. As the days grew into weeks, Columbus tried to keep from the men the knowledge of how many miles they had covered each day. By October 6 he began to be disturbed. He thought that they must have passed some of the islands which he had expected to see. Yet there were, by this time, signs to make him think there must be land ahead.

Large flocks of birds were coming from the north and making for the southwest. Columbus remembered that the Portuguese had discovered the Azores by paying attention to the flight of birds. Watching their movements, he decided that he would turn more to the southwest and go in that direction for two days. If he had missed the islands, he might sail straight to the mainland of Cathay.

On October 8 the sea was like a river, and the air was soft and fragrant. Weeds floating on the water "appeared very fresh." The birds which the men saw flying past were land birds, some of which they knew. October 9 came and went. That night they heard through all the hours of darkness the sound of flocks of birds passing over their heads.

But the next day there was trouble. The men on the *Santa María* declared that they wanted to turn back and sail toward Spain. Columbus encouraged them as best he could, and then told them plainly that they must go on. He said that he had come out to reach the Indies and "so must continue till, with the help of God, he found them." The ships sailed on.

Thursday, October 11, the men saw sandpipers and found a green land plant like a rosebush floating on the water. Later in the day a stick carved by hand was picked up. "These signs made them all grow cheerful again," wrote the Admiral.

Then, two hours after midnight, in the first hours of October 12, a man keeping watch on the *Pinta*, which was ahead, saw in the moonlight a dark line of land. "Land! Land!" he shouted, and the news was passed to the Admiral. There had been false reports before, but there could be no mistake this time. There lay the land.

The men waited until dawn. Then they saw the land plainly and the strange people standing along the water's edge. Soon all the crews went ashore, and Columbus planted in the ground the banner of King Ferdinand and Queen Isabella. In the presence of his men and with his captains as witnesses, he took possession of this land and all lands near by in the name of Spain. The kneeling men gave thanks to God for having reached land, while the astonished natives looked on.

The island was one of the Bahamas, named by Columbus San Salvador. He described its people as a friendly, gentle, handsome people. He gave them little red caps and glass beads, and they brought him parrots and cotton thread and sharp-pointed sticks.

But Columbus was puzzled. He had brought along a man to talk one of the languages of Asia to the natives, but they could not understand him nor he them. The people looked different, too, from any described by other explorers. Their

foreheads were broad, their black hair was straight, and their eyes were large. They had skin of a dark copper color, sometimes painted with black, white, or red.

The Admiral was pleased to see that some of the natives wore ornaments of gold. When he pointed to these ornaments, they made signs that there was a king with much gold to the south.

For two days Columbus and his men explored this island to which they had come. Then he set out by ship to see

other islands. The natives had said over to him the names of at least one hundred. But the islands to which he came were not very different from the first one. "I am determined," he wrote, "to proceed on to the continent." There he hoped to deliver to the Great Khan the letters which he had brought for him from the king and queen of Spain. Although he had not found the kind of land and people he expected, Columbus thought he was in the Far East.

Two names are to this day a reminder of Columbus's belief that he had reached the Indies. He called the island people Indians, and the name remained for the natives of the Americas. The islands which Columbus discovered are now called the West Indies.

For three months Columbus and his men went by ship from island to island. When the Indians told him of a "very large island with much trade and having gold and ships," he was delighted. This must surely be Cipango. "According to the globes I have seen and the maps of the world, it must be somewhere in the neighborhood," he wrote. But what he found was Cuba. He declared it to be the "most beautiful island that eyes have ever seen," but there was no sign of the cities which Marco Polo had told about seeing in the Far East.

In January of 1493 Columbus sailed for home, leaving a colony of forty men on the island in the West Indies which he had named Hispaniola, or Little Spain. It is now known as Haiti. The *Santa María* had run aground on a coral reef and been pounded to pieces by the waves. In the two remaining ships, the *Niña* and the *Pinta*, the Admiral and the rest of the men set out. Columbus took with him several Indians, a few brightly colored parrots in cages, many small gold ornaments, and "other things never before seen or heard of in Spain."

He received a royal welcome. The king and queen greeted him as their "Admiral of the Ocean Sea, Viceroy and Governor of the Islands that he hath discovered in the Indies." No praise was too great for the man who had made this

marvelous discovery. The news of it was spread over all Europe.

In the fall of that year 1493, Columbus sailed again, this time with seventeen ships. Many persons were eager to sail with him to seek such treasure as might be found.

Columbus was distressed, on his arrival at Hispaniola, to find in ruins the little fort where he had left his men. There was no sign of them. He learned later that they had got into trouble with the Indians and been killed.

Near this place he started another settlement. This colony, which was later moved to a more healthful location on the same island, became the town of Santo Domingo, the first permanent European settlement in the Americas. From this point much of the later Spanish exploration started.

Things soon began to go badly with the Spaniards. The men who had come out on this second expedition quarreled among themselves and with Columbus. Worse still were their troubles with the Indians. The friendliness of the natives turned to hate as the white men tried to make slaves of them.

The Spaniards were disappointed in the islands. These were not the Indies of gold and quick riches and easy living which had been expected. When Columbus went back to Spain after this voyage, he had difficulty in getting colonists. He was not popular at court after he failed to find gold or reach the rich lands of the Far East.

Columbus kept right on looking for Cipango and the Indies. He landed on Puerto Rico, discovered Jamaica also, and went all along the southern coast of Cuba. On his third voyage he crossed the ocean from Spain by another route, a more southerly one. He came to South America and explored the waters off the coast of Venezuela. At first he thought this region was another island, but when he came to the mouth of the Orinoco River and found the waters fresh, he changed his opinion.

"I believe that this is a very great continent," he wrote, "which until today has been unknown."

This discovery of South America was made in 1498. His companions wanted to explore here, but Columbus did not stop. He was still searching for the water passage to the Indies.

On his fourth voyage he took a new route. No one had yet sailed farther west than Cuba. With a company of one hundred and thirty-five men and boys, among them his son Ferdinand, then thirteen years old, Columbus sailed west. He went into every inlet and stream and bay along the coast of Central America. It was a brave venture that deserved more success. The weather was against him from start to finish. Storms and the downpours of the rainy season continued week after week. He learned from

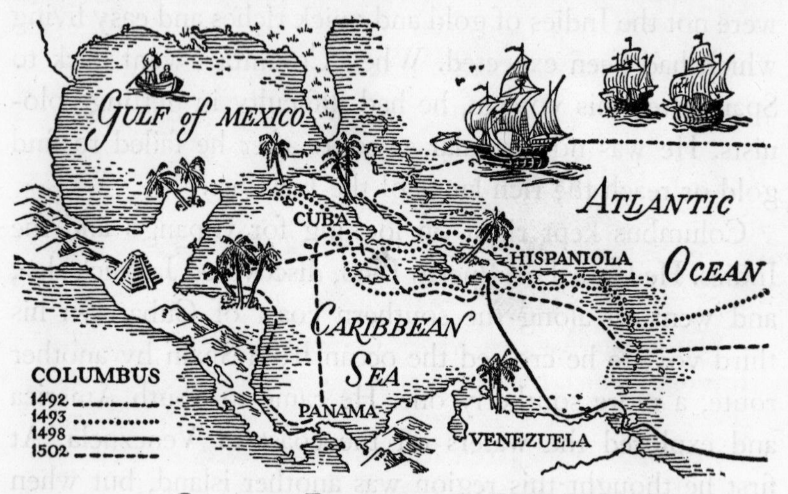

COLUMBUS EXPLORES THE CARIBBEAN

the natives of an ocean beyond their lands. He thought that must be the Indian Ocean, but he could not find a way to sail into it.

On Christmas Day of the year 1502, ten years after his first landing in America, Columbus anchored at a point within sight of the present entrance to the Panama Canal. So near did he come to the Pacific Ocean. But he turned back toward Spain, disappointed that he had found neither a water passage to the Indies nor the stores of gold which the natives kept promising him. Columbus died without knowing how close he had come to the great ocean which separates the Americas from the Far East.

JOHN CABOT, EXPLORER FOR ENGLAND

Two letters written in the year 1497 tell how an Italian made the first voyage from England to North America. The writers did not dream that their letters would be used as history more than four hundred years later. The letters were written by Italians living in London. They told how a third Italian, named John Cabot, had just returned from a voyage which he made for the English.

The first letter writer said:

> Our countryman, the Venetian who went with a ship from Bristol to search for new islands, has returned and says that seven hundred leagues from here he discovered mainland, the territory of the Great Khan. He went along its coast for three hundred leagues and landed. He saw no human beings, but has brought to the King some traps which had been set to catch small animals, and a needle for making nets. He also found some chopped trees, by which he judged there were inhabitants. This has greatly pleased the King.

The letter also said that Cabot had planted at the place where he landed a large cross and a pole bearing the flag of England. This was five years after Columbus had planted the Spanish flag in the West Indies.

The second letter about this discovery said that Cabot had only one ship, with a crew of eighteen men. These

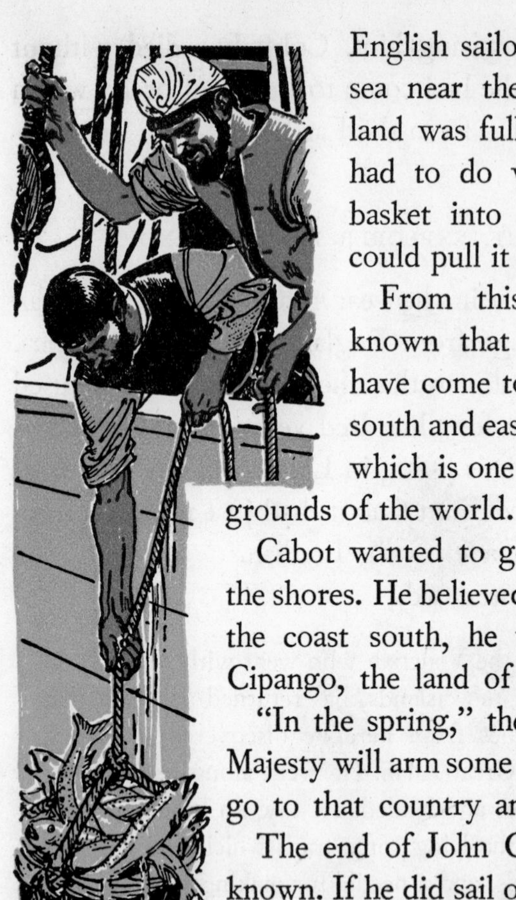

English sailors reported that the sea near the newly discovered land was full of fish. All a man had to do was to let down a basket into the water, and he could pull it up filled.

From this description it is known that John Cabot must have come to the Grand Banks, south and east of Newfoundland, which is one of the great fishing grounds of the world.

Cabot wanted to go back and explore the shores. He believed that if he followed the coast south, he would be opposite Cipango, the land of spices.

"In the spring," the letter ended, "His Majesty will arm some ships so that he may go to that country and plant a colony."

The end of John Cabot's story is unknown. If he did sail out, as the letter suggests, in the spring of 1498, there is now no record of the voyage. If, on this trip, he set up a colony on North American shores, that colony did not last.

On a map which was drawn fifty years later, the land opposite the St. Lawrence River is marked as having been discovered "by Juan Cabot, a Venetian, and by Sebastian Cabot, his son."

John Cabot had done great service for England. He had planted the English flag on North America. Many years later, England claimed lands along the North Atlantic coast because of his discoveries.

DISCOVERIES BY PORTUGUESE CAPTAINS

The king of Portugal was troubled when the explorer Columbus, whom he had refused to help, returned from a voyage with the news that he had found new lands for Spain. Portugal had been a leader in explorations since the days of Prince Henry the Navigator. A Portuguese sea captain by the name of Bartholomew Diaz had reached the Cape of Good Hope, the southernmost point of Africa. This discovery had encouraged Portuguese explorers to continue their search for the route to the Indies around Africa. Portugal had laid claim to all lands west and south of Africa "as far as the Indies." The king made up his mind that he was not going to let Spain get any more of these new lands than he could help.

The kings of Spain and Portugal disputed over this matter for some time. Then it was agreed that a line should be drawn from north to south on maps of the Atlantic Ocean. All lands east of the line were to belong to Portugal, while those west of it were to belong to Spain. The Pope, who settled such matters, approved this agreement between the kings.

The "Pope's Line," as it was called, was drawn in 1493. By it Spain was allowed possession of the lands which

Columbus had already visited. It was supposed that these new lands were near the Indies. No one yet knew that there was a South America. If, as some say, Portuguese seamen had visited it before Columbus ever crossed the ocean, they had put no records on their maps.

A Portuguese captain named Vasco da Gama sailed around the Cape of Good Hope and reached India in 1498. Two years later another captain, by the name of Pedro Álvares Cabral, was on his way to the Far East by this new sea route around Africa. His ship was driven far west of the usual route by a heavy storm, and Cabral saw from its deck an unknown land. He went ashore and claimed it for Portugal, thinking that it was a large island. He continued on his voyage to Cathay, but he sent one of the ships of his little fleet back to Portugal to report the discovery. On that ship was put some wood which had

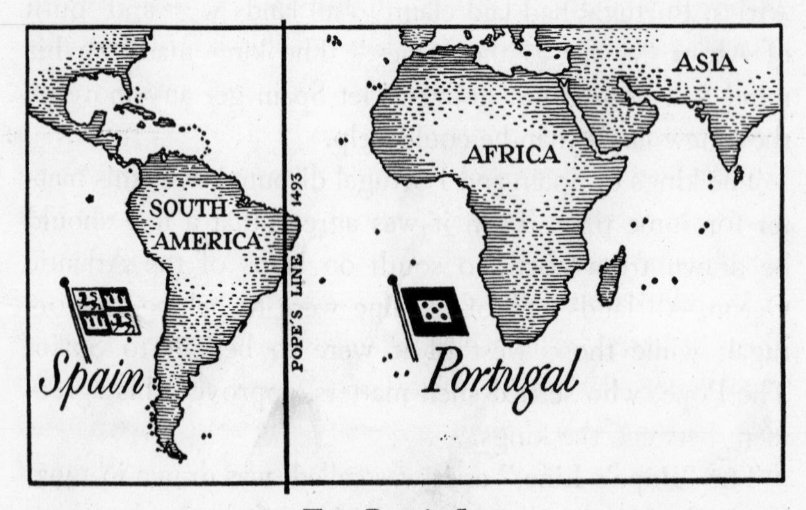

THE POPE'S LINE

been cut on the new land. It was a red wood from which red dye could be made. The Portuguese called this wood *brasil.* Cabral named the new land Santa Cruz, but this wood gave the country its later name of Brazil.

Now Portugal had a double claim on this region. It had been discovered and taken for the king by a Portuguese sea captain, and it lay east of the Pope's Line.

AMERICA—A NEW NAME ON THE MAP

Many explorers from Europe went out to the New World in the years immediately after the first and second voyages of Columbus. The names of most of these men are almost forgotten, but one man is well remembered. From him came the name America.

Amerigo Vespucci, who had been for many years a merchant in Italy, went, about this time, to live in Spain. There he became interested in the new lands. His first voyage to the west was made in the year 1497. Two or three years later he made another voyage in company with two well-known explorers of the time. The three sailed along the coast of South America, getting as far south as the part which is now Brazil.

Vespucci returned to Spain and wrote accounts, in the form of letters, telling of the lands across the sea. One of these letters fell into the hands of a famous mapmaker who was teaching in a French university. He read it with great interest, for he was making a new book of geography and trying to draw maps showing all the lands lately discovered.

When he got to the point of putting names on his maps, he put "Indies" on the regions which Columbus had discovered. The great explorer had called them that, thinking them to be a part of Asia. But this other land to the south, described by Vespucci, might be a new continent. When the mapmaker had drawn this region on his map, he wrote "America" on it, thinking from the letters of Vespucci that the Italian had discovered it.

Other mapmakers followed his example and marked "America" across this region, which was really Brazil. Later the name was used for the whole southern continent and then for the northern continent as well.

Vespucci held the high office of Chief Pilot of Spain for the last ten years of his life. "We may rightly call these lands a new world," he wrote in one of his letters, "because our ancestors had no knowledge of them, and it will be a new world to all those who hear about them."

The lands named America after Vespucci are still called the New World.

COLUMBUS, CABOT, AND CABRAL

The names of three men stand out in the story of the discovery of the Americas. In the short space of ten years they came to three parts of the Western Hemisphere.

Columbus was by far the most important of the three explorers. He was the great discoverer, and he followed his discovery of America by ten years of important exploration. He landed on many islands in the Caribbean Sea, explored the north coast of South America, and entered harbors along the coast of Central America and Panama. Columbus did more than discover and explore. He brought many Spaniards to the New World.

Cabot proved by his dangerous voyage across the Atlantic from England that there was a North America. Cabral landed on the eastern shores of South America.

These explorers planted on the Americas the flags of three nations. Columbus claimed the lands which he discovered for the king of Spain. Cabot left the flag of England flying on a lonely shore of North America. Cabral sent back word to the king of Portugal that he had discovered a great new island for him.

Slowly men began to realize that these explorers seeking a way to the Indies had discovered new lands. A mapmaker named those lands America.

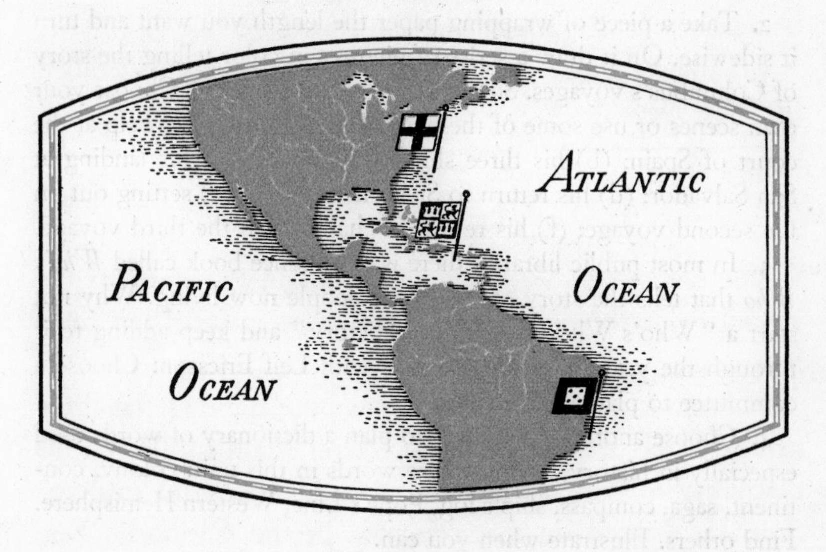

Talking Together

1. The discovery of a new world by the Norsemen caused no such excitement as its discovery by Columbus. Can you tell why?

2. Between the time of the Vikings and Columbus there were explorations and discoveries in other parts of the world. Where and what were they?

3. Why do maps change? How many places can you think of that have been named or that have had their names changed since 1900? Ask your parents to help you.

Interesting Things to Try

1. Uncertainty about what is going to happen helps to make a scene dramatic. Dramatize one of the following scenes:

a. Columbus's attempts to find backers for his expedition
b. Columbus dealing with the sailors afraid to go on
c. The worried wives of some of the sailors talking together as the news arrives of the return of the fleet

2. Take a piece of wrapping paper the length you want and turn it sidewise. On it draw a series of pictures in color telling the story of Columbus's voyages. Such a series is called a frieze. Choose your own scenes or use some of these: (a) Columbus seeking help at the court of Spain; (b) his three ships sailing west; (c) his landing at San Salvador; (d) his return to Spain in triumph; (e) setting out on the second voyage; (f) his return in chains from the third voyage.

3. In most public libraries there is a reference book called *Who's Who* that tells the story of important people now living. Why not start a "Who's Who in American History" and keep adding to it through the year? You might begin with Leif Ericsson. Choose a committee to plan about details.

4. Choose another committee to plan a dictionary of words used especially in history, such as these words in this unit: colony, continent, saga, compass, ship's log, Pope's Line, Western Hemisphere. Find others. Illustrate when you can.

The True Story of Christopher Columbus, by E. S. Brooks. Here is a whole book, instead of a few pages, about Columbus.

The Voyagers, by Padraic Colum. You will enjoy the stories of "The Children of Eric the Red" and "The Great Admiral."

The Story of Life in America, by Mary G. Kelty. Use the table of contents to find stories about the early explorers.

Great Moments in Exploration, by Marion F. Lansing. Look at the timetable of explorations in the back of the book and then read any of the stories that interest you.

The Romance of Discovery, by Hendrik Willem Van Loon. The stories are very short and the pictures are unusual.

LEARNING TO USE THE TABLE OF CONTENTS

Find the *table of contents* in this book. What is it called? In what part of the book is it? Is it found in the same place in all books? What does it include? How many units are there in the book? On what page does Unit III begin?

The table of contents in a book will help you to find out whether the book tells anything about a particular topic.

In *These United States and How They Came to Be*, by Gertrude Hartman, which chapter is likely to contain the story of Columbus?

Chapter		*Page*
I	First Families of America	1
II	Spices and a New World	19
III	In the Great Days of Spain	39

In Hillyer's *A Child's History of the World*, which story is probably about Columbus?

Story		*Page*
58	Off with the Old, On with the New	333
59	A Sailor Who Found a New World	337
60	Fortune Hunters	346

Quiz Yourself

I. Here are some statements about five of the following men: Eric the Red, John Cabot, Cabral, Columbus, Marco Polo, and Prince Henry. Number your paper from 1 to 5. After each number write the name of the man about whom the statement is true.

1. This Portuguese sea captain discovered Brazil.
2. This famous European spent his life encouraging the study of navigation.
3. This man founded a colony in Greenland.
4. This man claimed North America for England.
5. This Italian made his adventures in Cathay into a book.

II. Write in a column the numbers 1 to 12. After each number write the name of the continent where the place with that number is located. If the place is an island, name the nearest continent. Use maps to help you.

1. Genoa	5. Portugal	9. West Indies
2. Norway	6. Brazil	10. Newfoundland
3. Cape of Good Hope	7. Cathay	11. Venezuela
4. Cipango	8. Azores	12. Bahamas

III. On a sheet of paper copy the words in column A. Opposite each word write the correct meaning, found in column B.

A	B
century	a plan or suggestion
climate	trade by exchanging goods for goods
claim	a story of brave deeds
proposal	people living in a place, not visitors
barter	right to a thing
log	a journey for a special purpose, such as discovery
expedition	lasting; not for a short time only
permanent	the kind of weather a place has
saga	one hundred years
natives	the written daily story of a ship's voyage

II EUROPEANS CLAIM NEW LANDS AND SEAS

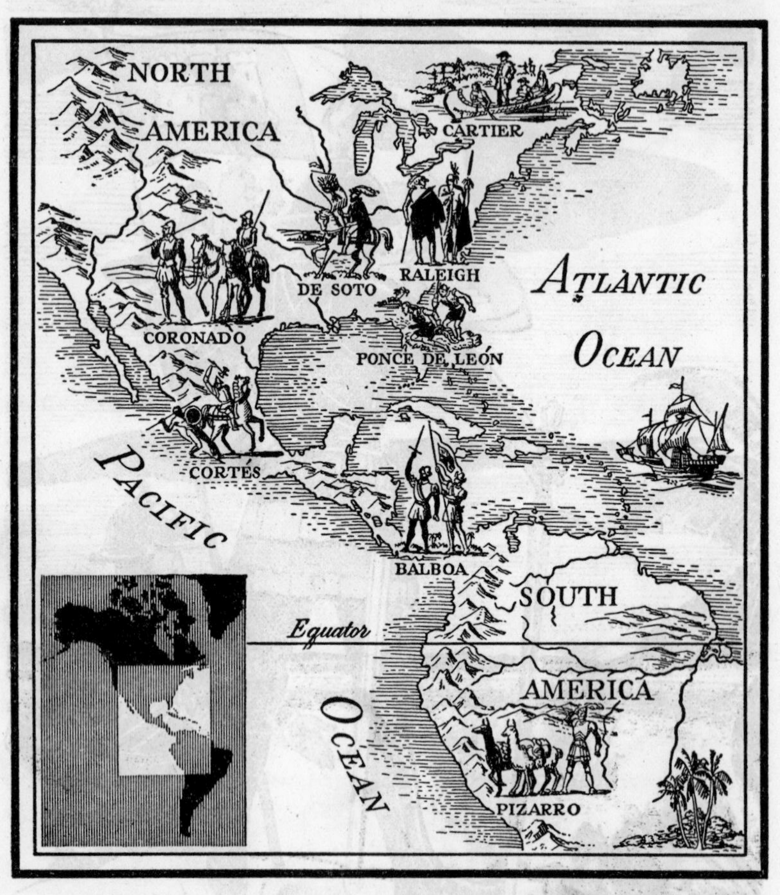

OPENING UP THE NEW WORLD. *Explorers from Spain were the first to claim land in the New World. Next came men from France to explore farther north. From England, Raleigh tried to found a colony. Though he himself never came to North America, he spent his fortune trying to start an English colony here.*

EUROPEANS CLAIM NEW LANDS AND SEAS

BALBOA, DISCOVERER OF THE PACIFIC

On a ship which sailed from the settlement of Santo Domingo in September, 1510, the sailors were startled to hear a loud knocking. It seemed to come from the barrels that made up the ship's cargo. The knocking became louder, and as they looked to see what it could mean, the top of a barrel flew up in the air, and a man and a dog pushed out their heads and shoulders.

Here was a Spaniard whom some of them knew by sight, a planter by the name of Vasco Núñez de Balboa. His only possessions there on shipboard were his dog Leoncico and the sword with which he had knocked off the top of the barrel.

Balboa was leaving the island as a stowaway on this ship because he was deep in debt. He had come out from Spain ten years before to seek his fortune in the New World. After some voyaging on ships that were exploring the Caribbean coasts, he had settled in Hispaniola. But he was no farmer. As time went on, he kept getting deeper and

deeper in debt. At last he was told that he could not leave the island until he had paid what he owed. Yet over on the mainland there was gold. If only he could get away, he might make a fortune and free himself from debt.

It was a great risk that Balboa took. The captain of the ship threatened to leave him on an island to starve. But the members of the crew liked him and pleaded for his life. In the end the captain let him stay aboard.

This ship was taking food to a colony of Spaniards reported to be starving on the coast of South America not far east of Panama. When the vessel arrived, these men were found to be not only short of food but ill with jungle fevers. They also were in the midst of hostile Indians, who attacked from the forests with poisoned arrows.

Balboa's knowledge of the region, which he had visited before, saved the day. He knew of a town not more than forty miles away, where they could find safety. He persuaded the colonists to move there. By the time the ship had come to this new place, Balboa was in command.

Balboa soon became governor of the entire region. The men chose him for that office in what has been called the "first town meeting in America." He had won the respect and devotion of these rough, hardy adventurers. As governor, he showed himself wiser in one way than many of the Spanish leaders. He made friends with the chiefs of the neighboring Indian tribes, and that helped him in his next great enterprise.

Balboa had come to the Isthmus of Panama, the region which Columbus had reached on his fourth voyage. As the Indians had told Columbus, so they now told Balboa, of a sea beyond the mountains. They told, too, of a kingdom to the south where gold was so common that men made their dishes and cooking utensils of it. Balboa did not hurry off at once on a wild chase for gold. It was three years before he made an attempt to reach that "sea."

On the first day of September, 1513, he started into the wilderness of the Darien jungles and mountains. With him were one hundred and ninety Spaniards, a thousand loyal Indians from the tribes with which he had made friends, and a pack of European hunting dogs. Trained dogs had been found useful in attacking hostile Indians in the jungles. Balboa's Leoncico, the dog that had escaped with him in the barrel, went along, with his name on the lists with the soldiers and drawing pay as if he were a man.

The soldiers were a picked group, the best and hardiest

in all the region. It was said of them that they were men "hardened to meet all sorrows, and able to bear labor, heat, hunger, and watching."

Enemy Indians attacked the marching men as they cut their way through the wilderness. Fever laid many of them low. But they were not men to turn back. Day after day they pressed on. At last, after more than three weeks, Balboa's Indian guide told him that, if he would climb to the top of the mountain just ahead, he could look over to that "other sea." Only a third of the Spaniards were strong enough to attempt the climb with their leader. But at break of day those men set out from the forests toward the bare mountaintop.

Balboa wanted to be first to view that "other sea." He halted his men, telling them to wait, while he went on alone. He climbed swiftly, and at the highest point of the mountain, looked off. There, beyond the forests and streams, lay an ocean, its waters shining in the morning sun. Reverently he dropped to his knees and gave thanks for being permitted to find this water and so do service to his king.

Rising, he called his soldiers, and they came rushing up the slope to gaze at the ocean. Together they chanted their thanks to God. Then Balboa spoke from that mountain height, taking possession of the sea, of the islands that were in it, and of all surrounding lands, in the name of the Spanish king. One of the company drew up a paper reporting the discovery, and all signed their names to it. Then a tree was cut down and shaped into a cross to be

left standing on the mountaintop. The Pacific Ocean had been discovered. Balboa called it the South Sea.

Four days later, after a hard journey, Balboa, with a few Spaniards and some Indian warriors, reached the shore of the ocean. There he repeated the ceremony.

Balboa did not hasten back across the Isthmus. He went by canoe along the coast to Panama Bay, where he was greeted by a powerful Indian chief. With eager eyes the Spaniards looked at the paddles of the chief's huge canoe, noting that the handles were set with small pearls. There were tales of gold, too, and of a kingdom rich in gold to the south. An Indian who described those lands made a drawing of the four-footed animal used as a beast of burden there. The picture was of a llama, which was shown to look like a sheep, but with the long neck of a camel. Some of the Spaniards had never seen such a creature; so they thought there could not be one.

One of the men who saw that picture was Francisco Pizarro. Years later when he came to Peru and saw llamas carrying loads, he remembered that drawing.

THE FIRST VOYAGE AROUND THE WORLD

The story of Balboa's discovery of another sea was carried across the waters to Spain and Portugal. There the old question raised by Columbus was still unanswered. Could Cathay be reached by sailing west? Explorers eagerly began to sail into every bay and up every river along the coast of South America, seeking a waterway from the Atlantic Ocean to the new sea which Balboa had discovered. Spain was especially eager to find such a route. After the Portuguese captain, Vasco da Gama, had found a way to India by sailing around Africa, the king of Portugal had promptly announced himself as "Lord of the Conquest, Navigation, and Commerce of India." Spain wanted a part of that commerce.

In 1520 the waterway to the other sea was found by a man from Portugal who went out with the support of the king of Spain. Ferdinand Magellan discovered, near the tip of the South American continent, the strait which has ever since borne his name. Sailing through, he came after many perils into the ocean which Balboa had reached so much farther to the north. Magellan called it the Pacific Ocean. He proved its great width by continuing across it for weeks that lengthened into months. Many of his men died of starvation. At last the survivors reached a group of islands which they named the Philippines.

By that famous voyage Magellan carried on the work begun by Columbus. He showed the world to be far, far

The Strait of Magellan

larger than anyone had ever dreamed. Magellan was killed by unfriendly natives of the islands, but one of his ships, the *Victoria,* finally circled the globe and reached Spain after an absence of three years.

At last Europeans knew that America was a land apart, truly a New World, lying between two oceans, the Atlantic and the Pacific.

PONCE DE LEÓN FINDS FLORIDA

From the West Indies went out the expeditions which further explored the two American continents. For this reason the West Indies have been called the "mother of America." With their harbors and little Spanish settlements, they made a convenient starting point for the ships.

Ponce de León was one of the first Spaniards to come to the New World to stay. He came with Columbus on his second voyage, when the island of Puerto Rico was discovered. Later Ponce de León became governor of that island. There he heard from the Indians much talk of a wonderful country to the north, where there was gold in abundance. More remarkable still, there was a Fountain of Youth. If one bathed in it, old age, gray hairs, and the weariness of years would disappear, and one would find his lost youth. Doubtless the Indians believed some of these stories. They may also have described the wonders of these distant lands in order to get the white men to go there. The only freedom for them was to send their masters off in search of better lands.

With three ships bought and fitted out with his own money, Ponce de León set sail toward the unknown north. After he had crossed wide stretches of water, he came in sight of a low, tropical coast, which he followed for a long distance. On a March day in the year 1513, he landed and took possession of this region in the name of the king of Spain.

He called the new land Florida from the name of the Spanish festival of flowers on the date of his landing. The day and name seemed fitting to all the company because of the beauty of the place, with its many flowers, its singing birds, and the abundance of plants and trees.

The country tempted the newcomers to stay, but from the first moment the natives were hostile. Whenever the explorers tried to land, the Indians fought them off.

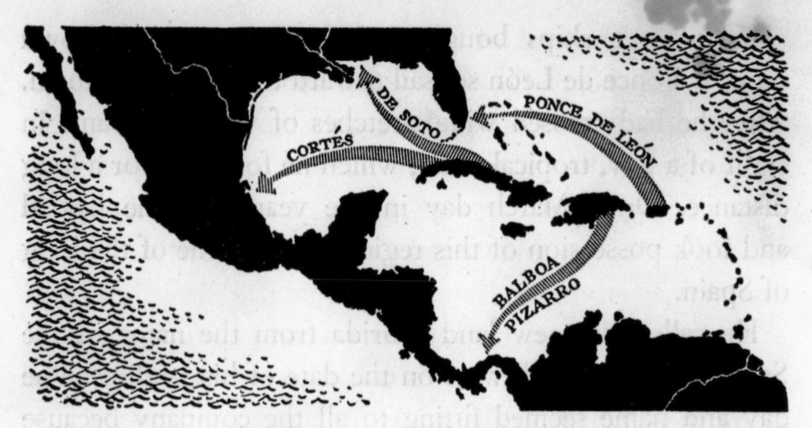

EARLY SPANISH EXPLORERS

After exploring the coast thoroughly, Ponce de León returned to Puerto Rico. He then journeyed to Spain to tell the king of the beauties of this land and thus to make his own claim to it more sure. He was given permission to start a settlement in Florida.

Ponce de León could not renew his explorations immediately on his return to the West Indies. There were Indian troubles in Puerto Rico for him to settle. Not until 1521 was he able to carry out his plan. This second expedition was not simply for exploration. He intended to found a colony, and took with him for that purpose a company of settlers, some churchmen to found Indian missions, and a goodly number of horses, cattle, sheep, and hogs. This was the first Spanish attempt to make such a settlement in territory which is now part of the United States.

The colonists landed on the coast of Florida and set about building houses. But the Indians would not let them alone. During one attack Ponce de León was wounded.

That was the end of all his hopes. Desperately ill, he was carried aboard the ship which had brought him there. The settlers all chose to go back with him. Many were sick, and, without their gallant leader, none of them had hope of defending themselves long against the natives. Ponce de León died within a few weeks in Cuba. It was part of his disappointment in his last days that he had never been able to find out whether this Florida was an island or was connected with the western lands which were being discovered along the Gulf of Mexico.

Other attempts to plant colonies in Florida were unsuccessful. It was not until 1565 that a permanent settlement was made at St. Augustine. Long before that, however, it had been learned that Florida was no island, but part of the continent.

CORTÉS CONQUERS THE AZTECS

In the first twenty-five years after the discovery of America, the Spaniards met only the Indians of the islands and nearby seacoasts. These natives were living as their ancestors had lived hundreds of years earlier. They had only the simple weapons, tools, and customs that belonged to such a life. Some tribes were quiet and peace-loving, others bold and fond of fighting, but none were rich.

Rumors came to the Spaniards of another kind of life on the mainland, far to the west or the south. There were tales of wealthy Indian cities, ruled by powerful kings and rich in gold. In Europe gold was very scarce at that time.

Everyone desired it. Explorers would endure any hardships to find a great supply.

In the Valley of Mexico, surrounded by towering, snow-capped mountain peaks, there was, at this time, a city beautiful beyond belief. For a thousand years one Indian people and then another had lived in this valley, each people building its own fine buildings and then being conquered by newcomers who were still more powerful. In 1500 the rulers were the Aztecs, a people with a proud past and rich possessions. Montezuma the Second had been emperor and high priest of the Aztec peoples for seventeen years when the Spaniard, Hernando Cortés, invaded the land.

Hernando Cortés had boldly sailed westward from Cuba with a fleet of eleven vessels, six or seven hundred men, eighteen horses, and a few cannon. On the shores of Yucatán, in the spring of 1519, he and his little army met a force of forty thousand Indians and put them to flight. In that conflict Cortés proved the power of his horses to inspire terror. When horses with men in armor on their backs

dashed through the ranks of Indian warriors, the natives fell back. They thought these mysterious four-legged creatures to be a new kind of god, half animal, half man, and feared them greatly.

Cortés received the Indian chiefs after that battle and graciously permitted them to make peace with him. He accepted kindly the presents they brought. All along the way to the distant Valley of Mexico he gathered in the chiefs of tribes which did not like the rule of Montezuma, the Aztec.

In his palace Montezuma heard of the coming of white, bearded men. He heard how they had arrived in houses that floated on the water. The Indian emperor had known of a tradition that white men or gods would come and take his throne. He sent messengers with gifts, and Cortés sent gifts back, but the white men continued their march toward the beautiful

valley city. Cortés met Montezuma and was entertained in his palace. The Spaniards marveled at the wonders of the city, the fine buildings, and the golden treasure. But they were horrified at the form of worship of the Aztecs and felt it a duty to try to turn them to the Christian God.

Montezuma was imprisoned by Cortés, and then after many months was released. In later fighting between Spanish and Aztec forces he was killed. Cortés was at one time defeated, and two thirds of his army was lost. He retreated and rebuilt his forces and returned to the fight. It took the Spaniards two years to win control of the Aztec city, and still longer to bring the surrounding peoples under their rule.

Cortés did not leave in the moment of victory. He was more than a fighter. He wanted to make Mexico part of a great Spanish empire in the New World. He brought thirty thousand Aztec families back to Mexico City. He knew how to get along with these Indians. The common people came to worship him almost as a god. Instead of giving the Indians only Spanish rulers, he kept many of their own leaders in office.

The Indians were good farmers. Cortés encouraged them to grow their own familiar vegetables and plants, and also new plants from Europe. "I beg Your Majesty," he wrote, "to order that no ship be allowed to sail without bringing a certain number of plants which shall help the prosperity of the country."

In ways like this Cortés strengthened the rule of Spain in the New World.

PIZARRO OVERPOWERS THE INCAS

The immense riches shipped from Mexico across the sea to Spain made every adventurer in the homeland and the colonies eager to go forth and discover other golden cities in the New World. Francisco Pizarro was a young man of eighteen or twenty, working as a swineherd in Spain, when Columbus passed through on his triumphant journey to the court. He made up his mind to join an expedition to the New World.

He was one of the soldiers who, with Balboa, reached the Pacific Ocean. At that time Pizarro heard the Indian stories of the rich nation to the south. After the conquest of Mexico by Cortés, he determined to go south to seek that empire. It took him seven years to gather money and support for that expedition.

In the year 1531 he sailed south from Panama with only one hundred and eighty men and twenty-seven horses. With this small force he surprised and conquered the Inca empire of Peru.

The Inca empire was well governed by an emperor and his nobles. It reached nearly fifteen hundred miles along the western part of the continent, and its parts were connected by narrow roads and bridges swung from one mountainside to another.

The Incas were an agricultural people. They used the steep slopes of their mountains for terraced gardens, made like staircases, with one narrow strip above another. On the high lands of the Andes were huge flocks of llamas and alpacas. These were the native animals of the region. Their thick coats supplied wool which the Incas wove into beautiful garments. These people were skillful in many arts and crafts.

The Incas had gold in such abundance as the Spaniards had never imagined. It was not used as money. The Incas loved its beauty and used it for decoration. The great Temple of the Sun, where they worshiped, was so rich in gold that it was often called the Gold House.

But this gold brought upon the emperor and his subjects their unhappy fate. The Spaniards imprisoned the ruler and held him for ransom. Even though his people supplied more than the gold demanded as the price of his freedom and safety, the Spaniards killed him.

Pizarro took control of the empire and founded the city of Lima, which is now the capital of Peru.

DE SOTO DISCOVERS THE MISSISSIPPI

A Spanish gentleman-explorer by the name of Hernando de Soto was with Pizarro when he conquered Peru. He returned to Spain with the wealth he had gained, but the desire to find other rich kingdoms in the New World sent him out again. De Soto obtained from the king of Spain the right to conquer and settle the great unknown region of Florida.

Many Spanish nobles and men of wealth were eager to join his expedition. Nine ships sailed from Spain to Cuba and then north to the shores of Florida. Six hundred men, many in shining armor, came ashore while wondering Indians looked on. De Soto had brought more than two hundred horses and also large numbers of pigs to supply meat. He had planned carefully and well.

For two years the Spaniards made their way slowly west. They found no gold, and they suffered much from sickness and hunger. In May, 1541, they came to the "great river," the Mississippi, of which Indians had told them. They built boats and crossed it, and then explored for another year.

Worn with their travels, they turned back to the Mississippi. In May, 1542, De Soto died. His followers buried him secretly in the river, for they did not want the Indians to know of his death. Then the three hundred and twenty men who survived began their long journey home by floating down the Mississippi to the Gulf of Mexico.

CORONADO SEEKS CITIES OF GOLD

While De Soto and his men were traveling west from Florida, other Spaniards were coming north and east from Mexico City. Indian tales of "seven golden cities" to the north led Coronado to set out in 1540 with a large army of Spanish horsemen and Indians. Because these men intended

to start colonies as well as to find gold, they took with them herds of sheep and cattle.

This expedition crossed what is now Arizona and New Mexico and reached the seven cities, which turned out to be only the yellow-white adobe buildings of the Indians. Hearing of other cities farther north, Coronado went on into the region that we know as Texas, Oklahoma, and Kansas. The Spaniards were the first white men to see herds of buffalo grazing on the western plains. One of the men returned after an exploring trip with a report of having seen the Grand Canyon. But Coronado, disappointed at finding no gold, went back sadly to Mexico City.

Spanish settlements in the Southwest began in 1598, and Franciscan missionaries came soon to teach the Indians.

For a time the missions were successful, but the cruelty of the Spanish soldiers led to a terrible Indian revolt. Hundreds of settlers were killed and many missions were destroyed. Though the revolt was at last put down, Spanish settlers were not so eager after that to come to settle in this region, and the government did not make any great effort to bring them. This was the outer edge of the great Spanish empire which slowly grew up in the Americas with its capitals at Mexico City and Lima.

FRENCH EXPLORERS IN NORTH AMERICA

No one knows the names of the first Frenchmen to see the shores of North America. Out from Saint-Malo, in northern France, small groups of fishing vessels used to start west across the wide waters of the Atlantic. Wives and mothers of the men aboard dreaded to see them go, for it would be months before they returned. These were the boats of the adventurous fishermen who were going across the ocean to the rich fishing banks off Newfoundland. Nova Scotia and Labrador had not yet been explored or named.

The men on these boats were content if they made a good catch and returned safely to their homes. They had no desire to explore the lands beyond the water or to stay there, but their trips back and forth made the western continent seem nearer to Europe.

Among themselves they talked of the best routes across the waters. There were winds and underseas currents that helped or hindered. In their minds the sea was mapped almost as if there were roads to follow. New men, sailing out, were told what routes were best. Explorers began soon to follow the fishermen.

King Francis I of France wanted to find out more about the New World and paid two explorers to go to America.

The first man sent out by King Francis was an Italian navigator by the name of Verrazano. In the year 1524 he sailed along the eastern coast of North America from North Carolina to Nova Scotia. He even entered New York harbor eighty-five years before Henry Hudson. In later years the French remembered this voyage. They said that because a French ship had been the first to visit these parts, France had first claim on them.

Ten years later King Francis sent another explorer to the New World. Jacques Cartier was a fearless sea captain who had been out to the fishing banks many times. The king ordered him to make a search for a northern water route to the Far East. After Magellan's discovery of the strait far to the south, men felt sure that a northern passage could be found. The search for a Northwest Passage was responsible for much of the northern exploration for the next two hundred years.

Cartier made three voyages between 1534 and 1542. On the first he explored the coast of Newfoundland and made his way into a great gulf to which he gave the name St. Lawrence. He made friends with the Indians, and put up, at one point where he landed, a tall wooden cross on which was written, "Long live the King of France."

When Cartier returned with tales of a large new land and of waters open to the west, the French king was pleased, though he was disappointed that there had been no sign of gold. Still, he was willing to pay for another expedition. This time there were three ships, and more than a hundred men. Cartier was told to explore, to trade with the Indians, and to start a colony.

This time the explorer went far up the St. Lawrence River, hoping that it would lead to China. When dangerous rapids blocked his way up the river, he named them hopefully Lachine (the China) Rapids, and so they are called to this day. From there the Frenchmen went on to a large

Indian town on an island mountain. Cartier called it *Mont Royal*, and the name has been Montreal ever since.

The Frenchmen marveled at the beauty of the country, the high cliffs, and the swift river. But the sharp northern winter caught them unprepared. They had no warm clothing, no houses, and little food. All suffered bitterly from the cold, and from the scurvy caused by lack of proper food. Twenty-five men died, and in the spring, when the ice went out of the river, those who survived turned gladly homeward.

Before he went, Cartier named the land, which he believed to be a great island, New France.

By this time the king had lost interest. Five years later, however, Cartier came back as captain-general of a larger expedition, paid for by a wealthy Frenchman. A colony was to be started. But the same story was repeated. Without enough supplies, and in the bitter cold, the settlers suffered great hardships. In the spring Cartier led his men home. When that brave venture failed, no one else came out from France to start colonies along the St. Lawrence River for more than fifty years. But there remained in France the knowledge of the new country, and the bold name New France.

ENGLISHMEN SEEK A PASSAGE TO THE INDIES

At this time Englishmen began to be disturbed because their little island kingdom was not sharing in the wealth of the Far East. Two new sea routes to the Indies were in constant use by Portugal and Spain, and England had no such route. Portugal was enjoying a rich Oriental trade as her ships came and went around Africa. Spain was sending vessels through the Strait of Magellan. There was also a steady stream of gold flowing from the mines of Mexico and Peru to the treasure houses of the Spanish king. England, meanwhile, was still poor.

A new sea route to the Indies was what Englishmen wanted most. So explorers started out in their ships, as Jacques Cartier had done for France, to seek a Northwest Passage to the Indies around the top of the world.

They made important discoveries. On one voyage Greenland, which had been forgotten for two hundred years in spite of the early Viking knowledge of it, was found. The Arctic waters off North America were explored. Lands and straits and bays in and near Canada and Greenland carry to this day the names of hardy British sea captains.

Still other English navigators, John Hawkins and his more famous nephew, Francis Drake, did the bold deed of going south into waters claimed by Spain. When they

were driven out, they struck back. Drake attacked Spanish cities and forts and captured gold and silver from the mule trains that carried treasure from the mines to the harbors on the coast. He did not dare to sail home with this stolen wealth by the usual route across the Atlantic for fear of being overtaken by Spanish vessels. Instead, he made his way south to the Strait of Magellan and through it to the Pacific. In 1579 he explored the western coast of North America, claimed California territory for England, and finally sailed home around the world in his *Golden Hind.*

By these and other voyages English seamen gave notice that they were not to be shut away from the trade and treasure of the world. War was bound to follow such exploits, and England and Spain were soon at war. A Spanish fleet of vessels, known in history as the Spanish Armada, attempted to attack and conquer England. It was defeated in English waters in the year 1588. That famous victory over Spain opened the seas to English ships. Before it happened, however, Englishmen had come again to the shores of North America.

RALEIGH SENDS OUT COLONISTS

In 1584 an Englishman, Walter Raleigh, sent two ships to explore the Atlantic coast north of Florida and the West Indies. They came to land which is now part of North Carolina.

Queen Elizabeth was on the throne of England at this time, and Raleigh was one of her favorite courtiers. He was a handsome man, always well dressed, always pleasant. Anyone seeing him at court might well have thought that his whole life and interest lay there. But that was not so. Raleigh had fought in England's wars, and had been on a dangerous exploring expedition in northern waters.

As Raleigh walked the streets of London, his thoughts turned to new lands across the ocean. He wanted to see an

English nation in the New World. He told the queen that England, if it was to rival Spain, must have colonies. Men and women and children must go out and live in the new country.

When Raleigh's two ships, sent out in 1584, returned, the men aboard them brought back glowing reports of the new land. "The air was as sweet as if in the middle of a garden." The trees were taller than any they had ever seen. The soil was "the most plentiful, sweet, fruitful, and wholesome of all the world," and the natives were "most gentle, loving, and faithful."

Queen Elizabeth promptly knighted Raleigh because of the success of this venture. The name Virginia was given to the new land in honor of Elizabeth, who was known as the Virgin Queen.

Sir Walter Raleigh would have liked to go himself to his new land, but the queen declared that he could not be spared from court. He sent out seven ships, with one of his friends in charge, and with colonists on board. They landed on Roanoke Island in what is now North Carolina, but the attempt to colonize failed. The men suffered many hardships. The Indians did not remain "gentle, loving, and faithful." The Englishmen forced them to supply food, and also burned their cornfields as a punishment for some unfriendly act. The colonists lived in terror of their lives before they were able to get away on ships bound for England. They took back, however, plants from the new land, potatoes and tobacco, and they told great tales of its richness.

One of the colonists took back to England sixty-three drawings of Indians and of native life, which he had made while the natives were still friendly. This artist, John White, went into the villages and talked with the people, making drawings of them while he talked.

He also drew a map of an Indian village, showing it carefully laid out along a main street. There were gardens, with plantings of young corn and ripe corn, and a watchman to protect them. There was a dancing ground and a feasting place and a place of prayer. White drew portraits of men and women at work, and of children. Englishmen could get from these pictures some idea of the inhabitants of the lands to which they were planning to go.

Under the leadership of White, and with the help of Raleigh, new colonists, a party of men, women, and children, sailed for the New World. They also landed on Roanoke Island and found the fort and houses left by the first colonists. Here a child was born, Virginia Dare, granddaughter of John White. She was the first child born to English parents in these lands.

After a time the colony felt the lack of supplies of food and other necessary articles. It was decided that White must go back to England and tell Raleigh of these needs. He went sadly, feeling it to be his duty, even though he was leaving his daughter and grandchild behind, along with more than a hundred other settlers. When he reached England, in the year 1588, the year of the coming of the Spanish Armada, the country was at war. Raleigh, who had already poured great sums of money into the colonial venture, sent two ships with supplies, but the Spaniards drove them back.

It was four years before White could return to the Virginia colony. He found Roanoke Island deserted. The word "Croatoan" was cut in the bark of a

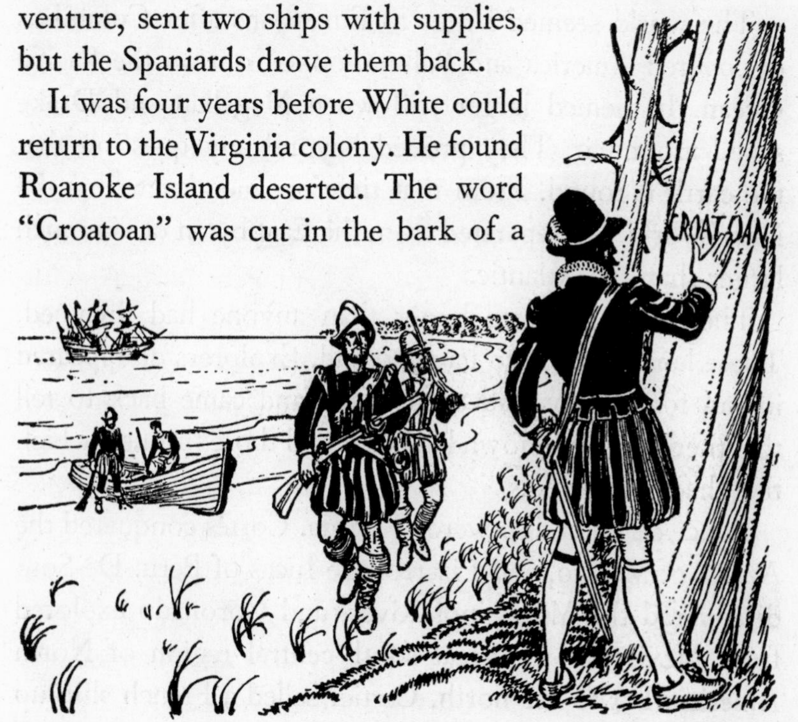

tree that formed part of the palisade around the settlement. This was the only clue to what had happened. It was the name of an island not far away to which the colonists might have fled. White was unable to go there at once, for the ship on which he had come was on a mission elsewhere, and he was obliged to go with it. Later, efforts were made to find the "lost colony," but in vain.

So, in spite of Sir Walter Raleigh's plans, the century ended with no English colony in America.

A LARGER WORLD

The world seemed larger to Europeans after Columbus discovered America and Balboa looked out on the Pacific Ocean. It seemed larger still when Magellan and Drake sailed around it. They proved beyond any question that the earth is round. From that time on, men knew that the New World was separated from the East by an ocean much larger than the Atlantic.

The Americas were larger than anyone had dreamed. These lands seemed to have no end. Explorers disappeared inland for months and even years, and came back to tell that there were unknown lands beyond those through which they had journeyed.

Ponce de León discovered Florida. Cortés conquered the Aztecs of Mexico, and Pizarro, the Incas of Peru. De Soto discovered the Mississippi River, and Coronado explored from Mexico to the great south-central region of North America. Far to the north, Cartier sailed a French ship up the St. Lawrence River, and English navigators explored the Atlantic coast. Raleigh made an attempt to start an English colony in North America.

Wonderful tales were told to the people of Europe concerning the wealth of this New World. Kings wanted to possess and rule these vast lands. Spain, Portugal, France, and England made their claims to the regions which adventurous explorers had made known.

Spain was far ahead of other countries in gaining possessions in the New World. It set up an empire, with cities in important places, and its ships crossed the ocean in a steady procession, bringing back treasure from the mines of South America. But toward the end of the century England defeated Spain in a great sea battle. Spain no longer controlled the seas. The time had come when adventurous men of other countries were eager to acquire and occupy new lands.

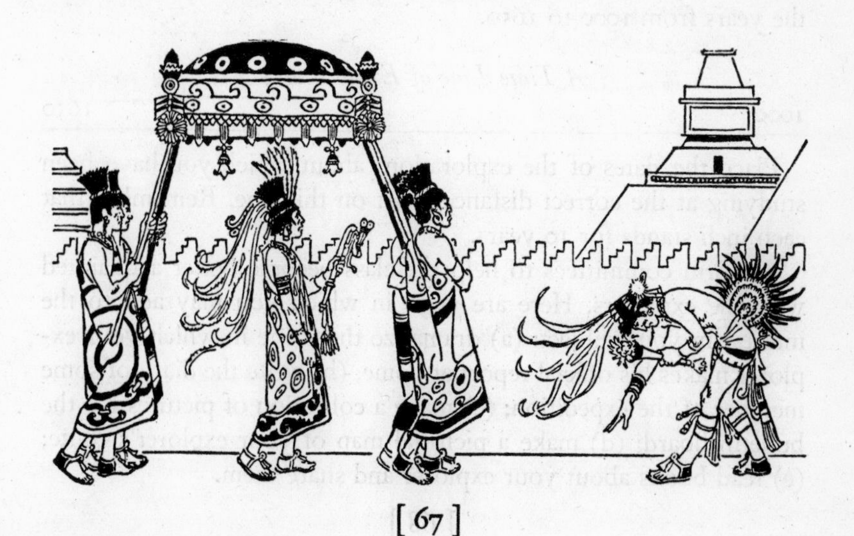

Talking Together

1. Explorers and discoverers do not work alone. In what ways do other people help them prepare for an expedition?

2. Explain the difference between (a) traveling and exploring; (b) discovering and exploring; (c) exploring and settling.

3. How do you account for the fact that Italian sea captains explored for France and Spain and England? How many examples can you find of men of one country exploring for another country?

Interesting Things to Try

1. A pictorial map has little pictures to mark important places and events. On a large map of the Western Hemisphere draw (a) a Viking ship near Greenland; (b) Balboa wading into the Pacific Ocean; (c) Cortés arriving in Mexico City; (d) Pizarro in the Incan empire. What other pictures can you add?

2. Add more stories to your "Who's Who in American History" and more words to your history dictionary.

3. Make a *time line*. Let 1 inch = 10 years. On the blackboard or on a long piece of paper draw a line 65 inches long to represent the years from 1000 to 1650.

A Time Line of Explorations

1000 — 1650

Place the dates of the explorations about which you have been studying at the correct distance apart on this line. Remember that each inch stands for 10 years.

4. Form committees to help the class become better acquainted with the explorers. Here are ways in which you may add to the interest in your subject: (a) dramatize the scene in which your explorer makes his official report at home; (b) write the diary of some member of the expedition; (c) make a collection of pictures for the bulletin board; (d) make a pictorial map of your explorer's route; (e) read books about your explorer and share them.

Let's Read

Ten Boys Who Lived on the Road from Long Ago to Now, by Jane Andrews. You will want to read about Sir Walter Raleigh.

Pueblo Boy, by Cornelia J. Cannon. Coronado failed to find the "seven golden cities," but this book tells what he did find.

Pathfinders by Land and Sea, by Elmer Green. The stories "Around Africa to India," "How America Was Named," and "First Around the World" will give you further information about Vasco da Gama, Vespucci, and Magellan.

New Found World, by Katherine B. Shippen. You will seem to be marching with Cortés and Pizarro as you read about them here.

Those Who Dared, by Carrie Willis and Lucy Saunders. Many boys and girls recommend the stories by these authors.

Learning How to Use the Index

The *index* of a book is at the back. It lists all the important places, people, and subjects in the book and gives the page numbers where they may be found. An index, like a dictionary, is arranged in alphabetical order. Here is a sample:

Balboa, 37–41
Boats: of the Vikings, 3; of Vinland, 7; of Columbus, 15. *See also* Shipping
Boone, Daniel, 219–222
Bradford, William, 81, 82, 83, 85, 86
Brazil, 29

On what pages can you find something about Balboa? A dash between two page numbers means that the subject is treated on those two pages and the pages between. Find another dash.

There are several topics under the heading "Boats." Each is called a subheading. If you wanted to find out the names of Columbus's ships, where would you look?

"*See also* Shipping" is a *cross reference*; that is, a reference from one heading across to another. The cross reference here means that you will find more about boats under "Shipping."

Find the index in this book and look up topics in Unit II.

Quiz Yourself

I. As you study history, it helps you to remember what you have read if you locate on the map all places mentioned in the text. Let us see how well you remember what you have already read in this book. Draw or trace an outline map of North America and do the following things:

1. Put a figure 1 where Florida is located.
2. Write the word *Mexico* in the right place.
3. Put a figure 2 on Cuba.
4. Write the words *Pacific Ocean* in the right place.
5. Write the words *Atlantic Ocean* in the right place.
6. Put a figure 3 at Montreal.
7. Put a figure 4 on Newfoundland.
8. Put a figure 5 on New York Harbor.
9. Draw a line across Panama.
10. Put a figure 6 at the mouth of the Mississippi River.

II. Here are some statements about eight of the following explorers and colonizers of the New World: Cortés, Balboa, Vasco da Gama, Verrazano, Pizarro, Magellan, Cartier, Vespucci, Ponce de León, John Cabot, and Raleigh.

Number your paper from 1 to 8. After each number write the name of the man about whom the statement is true.

1. One of his ships sailed around the world.
2. The Aztecs were his victims.
3. This Frenchman discovered and explored the St. Lawrence.
4. He was the first to try to establish an English colony in North America.
5. This Spaniard conquered the Incan empire.
6. He discovered Florida.
7. He discovered the Pacific Ocean.
8. He was the first to reach India by sailing round the tip of Africa.

III NEW HOMES IN A NEW WORLD

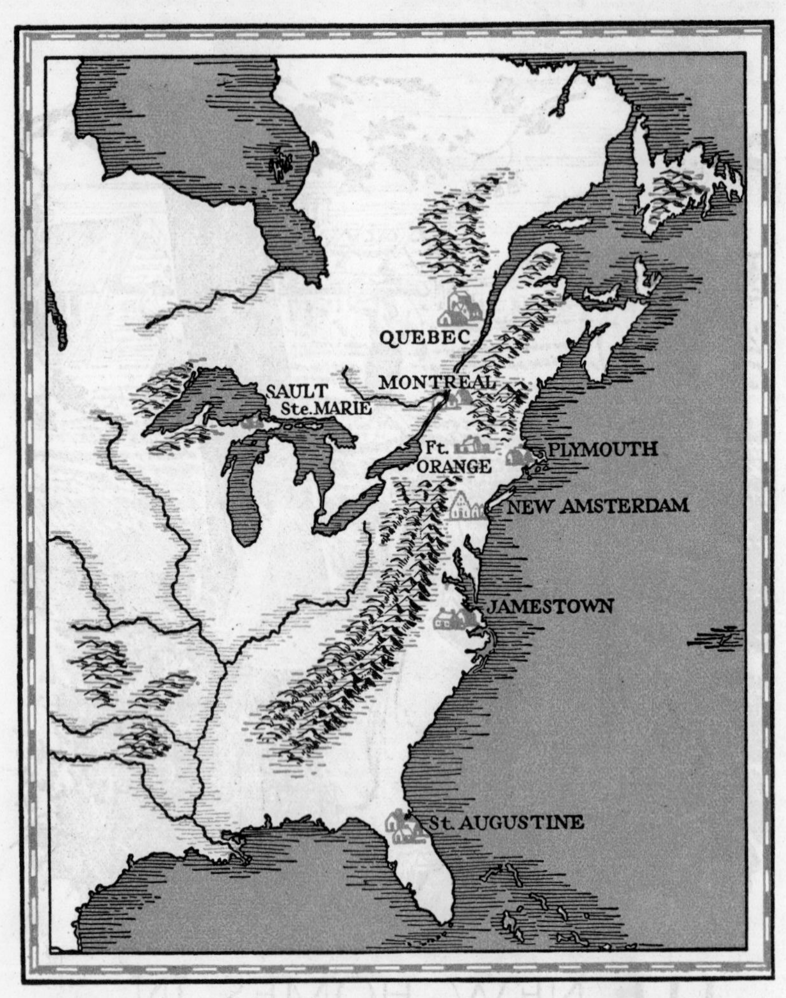

First Settlements. *Spain, England, France, and Holland all had settlements in eastern North America by the early seventeenth century.*

NEW HOMES IN A NEW WORLD

ENGLISHMEN IN VIRGINIA

The year 1607 is one that stands out on the calendar of America. In that year three ships, the *Sarah Constant* and two smaller vessels, came into a great bay, later called the Chesapeake. The money for a new colony had been provided by the London Company, a group of English merchants, who hoped to make good profits.

The colonists came with careful instructions. Captain Newport, an experienced explorer, was in charge. He was to seek, along the coast, the widest river mouth he could find. The river should be one up which he could sail, a river bending toward the northwest. It was the idea in London that this Virginia, as they called America, was a fairly narrow strip of land. They believed that any wide river might be a strait leading to the Pacific Ocean, and that the Pacific would lead directly to the riches of the East.

Having found a river, Captain Newport was to select a place for the settlement, land his party, and put them to work. Some were to build a storehouse; others were to prepare the ground and plant corn; and still others were to watch the water for attack from the sea by an enemy fleet. The English knew that their presence in these parts would not please the Spaniards.

Besides exploring and starting a settlement, the colonists were to look for gold and silver mines. When any high lands or hills were seen, one of the captains was to take twenty of the company and go out with pickaxes, trying to find minerals. The final instruction was about the Indians. The settlers were to take great care not to offend them, and it was hoped that they could be converted to the Christian religion.

Twenty or more men went ashore first to explore the country and were delighted with it. But at twilight, as they were returning to their ship, "there came Savages creeping upon all fours, from the Hills, like Bears, with their Bows in their mouths."

Within a couple of days the sailors put together a boat which they had brought with them in sections aboard the large vessel. In this they set out to explore the bay. Soon they came to the mouth of a deep river which they later named the James River. As a place for the settlement they chose a peninsula far up the bay. It was chosen because it was protected from attack by fairly deep water on three sides. In other ways it was a bad place for their village. The land was low, with marshes and pools near by. There was no spring of fresh water, as there would have been on higher ground. In May blossoming flowers made the place beautiful. In summer mosquitoes and other insects were to rise from those marshes.

Late in May, to the sound of trumpets, all came ashore from the boats and began their settlement. They named the place Jamestown in honor of their king.

THE SETTLEMENT AT JAMESTOWN

Captain Newport explored many miles up the river in his boat until he was stopped by rocks, rapids, and falls. At the point where the city of Richmond now stands, a friendly chief entertained the Englishmen. On an island near there Captain Newport put up a cross. As he did so, he proclaimed "James, King of England, to have the most right unto the river."

When the exploring party returned to Jamestown, they found that a large number of Indians had attacked the settlement. A dozen men had been wounded and a boy had been killed. The colonists went to work to finish their fort and build a high fence around it.

When Captain Newport sailed for England near the end of June, he took with him a cargo of timber which the settlers had cut. Wood was one thing which the London Company wanted. England was becoming a shipbuilding country with great need of wood, but it did not have many forests. Every explorer who had returned from the New World had told of the forests of tall trees which lay just back of the coast.

The troubles of the settlement began in the first summer. Many of the men became ill with fever and died. There was need of someone to act as leader. Fortunately the colony had an excellent leader among its members.

One of the Jamestown colonists was John Smith, a man who had already had many adventures. He had left his father's farm in England and started off for Europe when he was only seventeen. There he fought for three years in wars that were going on in the Netherlands and against the Turks in eastern Europe. For a long time he was held as a prisoner, but he escaped to Russia, and finally got back to England. There he heard of the prospect of colonies in the New World. Such an undertaking in a new country attracted him. He was twenty-six years old when he sailed on the London Company's expedition.

On the long voyage across the ocean Smith got into trouble with some of the men who were leaders in the company. At the time of the landing in Virginia he was being held as a prisoner, chained to a beam in the ship's hold. At this point the men who were punishing him had a surprise. Captain Newport had in his cabin a sealed box in which was a paper with the names of the men who were to make up the ruling council of the colony. The officers of the London Company had prepared this list and placed it with the other instructions for the starting of the settlement. Orders were given that the box was not to be opened until the ship reached Virginia. When it was opened, the name of John Smith was on the list of seven men chosen to rule the colony.

During the first weeks John Smith did not take a leading part in the community life, but as the months went by and the hardships increased, he began to show his ability as a leader. To him was given the charge of building the little settlement. The report of the colony says:

> By his own example, good words, and fair promises, he set some to mow, others to bind thatch, some to build houses, others to thatch them, himself always bearing the greatest task for his own share, so that, in short time, he provided most of them lodgings, neglecting any for himself.

Next, Smith began to search the region for food. The supplies brought from England were fast disappearing. He went on long exploring expeditions, hunting for precious minerals and a passage to the South Sea. He also traded with the Indians in their villages and brought back food to the starving colonists. On one of these expeditions he and two others were taken prisoner. His companions were killed, but he was pardoned by the chief and set free.

John Smith was a strong leader. He saved the colony from starvation by forcing the men to do the hard work that was needed. "If you do not work, you shall not eat," he said. "The sick shall not starve, but everyone else that does not gather as much food every day as I do shall be set down across the river, to live there or starve."

After two years of hard work misfortune came to John Smith. He was severely burned in a gunpowder explosion and went back to England, never to return to the colony in Virginia.

JOHN ROLFE AND POCAHONTAS

That same year five hundred new settlers arrived at Jamestown. The London Company had spread news all over England about the wonderful new country, and offered land, houses, and orchards to those who would go to it. Among the new colonists was John Rolfe. He took up land on the shore of the river.

Tobacco had been brought to England in the time of Raleigh and Drake and was becoming popular there. Most of it was imported from Spanish possessions in America. That which was grown by the Indians along the James River was of poor quality. Rolfe, who was experienced in farming, found ways of improving it. The tobacco which he sent to England began to sell at good prices. Fifteen years later, half a million pounds of Virginia tobacco were sold in London. This crop alone made the Virginia colony a success.

John Rolfe married an Indian princess, Pocahontas. She was a daughter of Powhatan, head chief of the tribes along the James River. It was Powhatan's warriors who captured John Smith on one of his exploring expeditions. Long afterward in London, Captain Smith told a tale of having been saved from death at that time because the chief's daughter pleaded for his life.

As a child, Pocahontas was known to the Englishmen, for she came often to the fort at times when Chief Powhatan was friendly with the white men. When she was older, she spent a long time there as a hostage while the governor was trying to make her father keep some of the promises he had made to the Englishmen. At that time Pocahontas learned many of the English ways.

When John Rolfe saw her, he fell deeply in love with her. But he felt that it was a strange thing for him, an English gentleman, to marry an Indian. Pocahontas was ready, however, to learn the white man's ways. She took the name of Rebekah, and the two were married in 1614 in the Jamestown church, with Englishmen and Indians looking on.

When Rolfe was called to England to make his report as secretary of the colony, he took with him his wife, Rebekah Rolfe, and their baby boy. In England she carried herself with the dignity becoming a princess and won the respect and affection of those who came to know her.

The Rolfes were preparing to sail for their home in Virginia when Pocahontas was taken ill and died. John Rolfe returned sadly to America, bringing his child with him. That child lived and prospered. His descendants proudly trace their family line back to Pocahontas.

PILGRIMS TO NEW ENGLAND

In England, in these same years, a fine-looking boy of fifteen or sixteen might have been seen any Sunday morning walking across the fields to the tiny village of Scrooby. He was going to church in the house of William Brewster, postmaster. Other people from all this region were coming to this house where, in a large room, a minister was to hold a church service.

These people worshiped in this place because they did not agree with the ways of the Church of England. Young William Bradford went there because he liked the preaching of the minister. He liked to hear him say that every man had a right to worship God in his own way. That was what William believed. He was a lad who had had to be independent and think for himself because he had been left an orphan when he was a baby. Now he was living with an uncle.

It took courage to go to this church. The king said that everyone must go to the Church of England and follow its ways. Before long the minister and some of the leading men of the church were brought before the courts to answer for their disobedience. Some of them were put in prison. Payment of a fine usually got them out soon, but before many weeks passed there would be trouble again. William heard the men talking of what they should do. They felt that soon they would not be allowed to hold any meetings.

"We must leave England," they said. "We must go to Holland, where there is religious freedom."

Before long many of the Scrooby people, among them William Bradford, escaped across the English Channel. Because they were going secretly, they went in small groups. Friendly sea captains hid them on their ships.

For some years these English folk lived in cities in Holland, earning their living by practicing trades which were new to farming people. William Bradford learned to be a silk weaver. Then some of them began to talk of moving again. Though they were free to worship as they pleased, they felt that it was not good for them to stay in a foreign land. They were not willing to have their children grow up speaking the Dutch language and following Dutch ways. Besides, it was hard to make a living in the crowded parts of Holland, and there was always danger of war. William Bradford said they felt like "pilgrims and strangers upon the earth."

"We must find a place where we can start an English settlement of our own," some of them said. Soon their thoughts turned toward America.

It took these Pilgrims three years to get everything arranged so that they could go. They had little money, and ships and supplies cost a great deal. Finally men were found who were willing to put up the money for an expedition in the belief that the colony would make a profit for them.

When the time for going drew near, many of those in Holland who had come over from England decided not to risk this new adventure. Only thirty-five returned to England to sail. Among them were William Bradford, William Brewster, and Myles Standish. Captain Standish was a soldier who had joined the company in Holland after fighting in wars in Europe. A large number of others of their own religious faith joined them in England.

There were to be two ships to take the colonists across the ocean. One of them proved to be leaky and even when it had been repaired it still was not safe. In the end all who could find room crowded aboard the *Mayflower*, and twenty who had meant to come stayed behind. There were one hundred and two Pilgrims in all.

When the *Mayflower* finally sailed, about the middle of September, 1620, it was much too late in the season to start. The colonists should have been getting to the new land in the summer or early fall, to have time to start their homes before winter.

They had a hard two months' voyage across the Atlantic, with storms and high seas. Then when they sighted land, they were off a coast far north of the Virginia region where they had intended to settle. After seeking a safe place to land, they came into a quiet harbor and gave thanks to God for their safety. Their first harbor in America was at the tip of Cape Cod, at the place now known as Provincetown, Massachusetts.

THE MAYFLOWER COMPACT

The London Company had granted to the Pilgrims rights to set up a colony and a government within the borders of Virginia, but these rights did not hold outside that area. A few men on the ship had been heard to say that when they got ashore they would do as they pleased, for "no one would have power to command them."

The Pilgrim leaders realized that trouble might follow unless some orderly form of government was agreed upon before they landed. They therefore drew up an agreement, or "compact," as it was called. This compact gave the colonists a foundation on which to build their government, and power to make laws for the good of all. Forty-one men signed the agreement as the ship lay at anchor.

The Mayflower Compact was an early step toward self-government in America. After it had been signed, John Carver, one of the group who had lived in Holland, was elected governor. Carver died the following April, and William Bradford was chosen to take his place, although one of the younger men of the company. Bradford was re-elected by the voters each year until he had held the office of governor for thirty-one years.

A HARD WINTER AT PLYMOUTH

For five weeks parties of men from the ship explored the region. They found signs of Indians and once had a brief fight with thirty or forty of them. They came upon fields in which corn and beans had been planted, and carried away about ten bushels for use as seed the next spring. It was well they did so, for this was all they had for planting when that time came. Six months later, when they had become acquainted with the Indians, they paid for this corn.

The Pilgrims searched anxiously for a place to settle, for the weather was getting cold. Journeying along the coast in a small boat, the men at last found a place. On December 26, 1620, they brought the *Mayflower* into Plymouth harbor. The next day being Sunday, they stayed on the ship. In the next week they chose the place where they would live and went to work building houses.

The little band of settlers suffered greatly in that first winter. More than half of them died from illness, hunger, and cold. William Bradford was one of those who were dangerously ill. His diary tells that "in the time of most distress" there were only six or seven well persons to take care of all the sick.

During the winter Indians were seen. They took some tools left by men working in the woods, but none of them came near the settlement. One day in March a tall, fine-looking Indian marched boldly down the street, stopped at a house, and said, "Welcome."

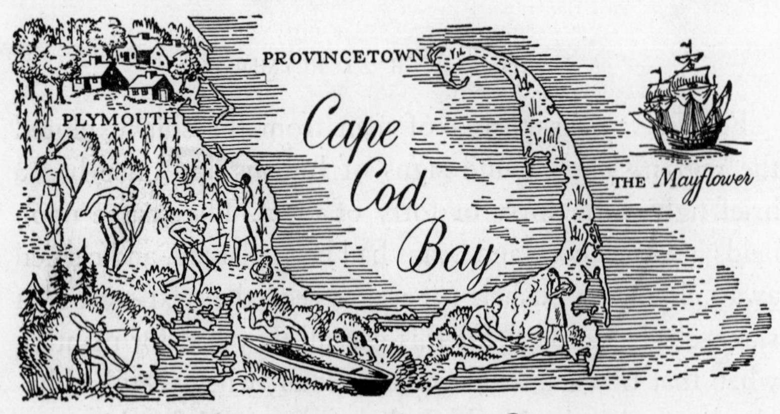

PLYMOUTH, THE PILGRIM COLONY

His name was Samoset, the Indian told them. He had learned English from captains of fishing vessels along the coast. His home was in the part of New England which is now Maine. He promised to bring another Indian named Squanto, who could talk better English than he.

That was the beginning of friendly relations with the Indians. Soon Squanto came and lived in the settlement, showing the people how to plant corn and where to catch fish and find other foods. He also acted as pilot on their exploring trips. Squanto was a faithful friend to the English and stayed with them as long as he lived.

On the day when Squanto first came, he and Samoset reported that the Indian chief Massasoit was near with his men. Very soon Massasoit, with sixty men in his train, appeared at the top of a nearby hill. There he stayed, watching the Pilgrims and being watched by them. Yet no move was made on either side.

Then Squanto went to talk with the chief, and on his return, Englishmen went over to the Indian camp. They agreed to stay there as a pledge that no harm should come to Indian warriors if they, in turn, would venture into the settlement to make a treaty of peace.

Captain Standish, with half a dozen armed men, met these Indians when they came to the brook and took them to a half-finished house. The governor came to this house and there an agreement was made by which neither red men nor white should harm one another. This agreement was kept for Massasoit's lifetime. It was the first New England treaty with the Indians.

The *Mayflower* sailed back to England in April, bearing a small load of beaver skins obtained from the Indians. In this way the Pilgrims began to pay back the debt the colony owed. The company of men who put up the money for ships and supplies had driven a hard bargain. They claimed all the earnings of the colonists for their first seven years.

All summer the people worked, and in the fall they gathered in their harvest. Twenty acres of Indian corn, planted in the spring, gave a good crop, as did the fields

of barley and peas. Wild geese returned with the fall days, and there were wild turkeys and deer in the woods.

Governor Bradford appointed a time of thanksgiving, and sent four men out to hunt deer and turkeys for the feasting, while others fished in the bay. King Massasoit was invited and came with ninety men, bringing gifts of deer. White men and Indians feasted together, and the Pilgrims gave thanks to God for their blessings.

Only fifty remained of the hundred and two people who had come out the fall before. The men had been able to build only seven dwelling houses, besides four community buildings, though others were started. Thirty-five more people had just arrived on a boat from England, but they had brought no supply of food to carry them through the winter, no bedding or pots or pans, and not much clothing. Yet, with Governor Bradford leading them, the Pilgrims gave thanks for their blessings and went on bravely into the next year.

This little Pilgrim settlement prepared the way for the coming of many Englishmen to nearby parts of the Massachusetts coast. Later, the colony at Plymouth became a part of the Massachusetts colony.

HENRY HUDSON DISCOVERS A RIVER

In September, 1609, a Dutch ship called the *Half Moon* came into a beautiful bay for which its captain had been searching. It is now known as the harbor of New York. Captain Henry Hudson was an English explorer who was sailing this ship for a group of Dutch merchants. They wanted him to find a waterway to the Pacific. The explorer John Smith had written to Hudson that he thought there might be a great sea inland from about this point on the Atlantic coast.

The Indians who saw the *Half Moon* sail into the harbor might well look at it with surprise and fear. Its bow was painted green, red, and yellow. Other parts were a rich blue. There were also pictures on its sides and on the flags which flew from its masts. The red men came out in their canoes to gaze at this queer floating house, and Hudson made them gifts and traded with them. He stayed in the bay for several days. "This is a very good land, a pleasant land to see," he told his companions.

He found a large river flowing into the bay from the north and started up it, in the hope that it was a way to the Pacific. The leaves of the trees along its high banks were bright with autumn colors in the September sunshine. The captain and his men agreed that this was the finest country they had ever seen.

Hudson went on for one hundred and fifty miles up the river which now bears his name. Then the banks came nearer together and the water became more shallow. The explorer had to turn back, disappointed at not finding a way to the Pacific.

The report which Hudson sent back to Holland pleased the merchants who had hired him. They were particularly interested in his story of the furs which the Indians offered to him. Furs were in great demand in Europe.

The Dutch at this time were carrying on trade with all parts of the world. Spain had been defeated, and the seas were free. Dutch merchants now controlled the trade with the Far East and were growing rich by it. That was why they wanted to find a shorter route to those distant lands.

Soon men from Holland came out to this region which Hudson had explored and began to trade in furs. They set up trading posts where they could meet the Indians. One was far up the river near the place where the city of Albany now stands. This was the gateway of the region controlled by the Iroquois Indians. Another was at the mouth of the river.

The Dutch had long had an East India Company for trade with the Far East. In 1621 the Dutch West India Company was formed. It was given by the government the right to trade in America and plant colonies there, as well as to trade in the West Indies and other parts of the world. One of the first acts of this company was to bring colonists to its American lands.

In the spring of 1624 a fine new ship was ready to carry the first colonists across the ocean. It was the *New Netherland*. This Dutch ship was different from the English ships of the time. It had a "tower," two stories high, with two rows of portholes, or small round windows. The passengers lived in this tower, where they were far more comfortable than the passengers on the *Mayflower* or the *Sarah Constant*. Captain Cornelius May, who was in command of this ship, had sailed up and down the Atlantic coast for years. Cape May, New Jersey, bears his name.

Thirty families sailed with him. As they went on board the ship, anyone looking at them would have thought them Dutch. Their children spoke Dutch to the sailors, and the older people could speak that language, too. But the Dutch called them Walloons, a name meaning "foreigners." They had come to Holland from northeastern France and the region which is now Belgium. They, like the Pilgrims, had left their homes to find religious freedom in Holland. Now they, too, wanted to set up homes for themselves in the New World.

The Dutch West India Company was fortunate in finding these colonists. Holland was very prosperous at this time, and its own people were not eager to leave their comfortable homes for adventure in a wilderness.

When the ship came to the American coast, a few of the colonists landed at the mouth of the Hudson River. Some of them stayed at the trading post there, and others went into Delaware and nearby lands. But the larger number went up the Hudson River to the trading post there. In 1624 they built a fort which they called Fort Orange. This was the first settlement in New Netherland.

The second settlement was founded on Manhattan Island in July, 1625. It was named New Amsterdam, and later became New York. Here a large fort was built, with a street connecting its two gates. There was a market place, and within the walls were the offices of the company, the houses of its officers, and the storehouses for the precious loads of furs which came down the river.

Peter Minuit, the first director-general of the colony, lived at New Amsterdam. In 1626 he purchased the island of Manhattan from the Indians for the sum of sixty Dutch guilders. In modern United States money this would be twenty-four dollars. To the Dutch this was a small amount, but to the Indians it looked large. They measured it in the articles which it would buy from the white men—the iron pots and copper kettles, the beads and mirrors and pieces of brightly colored cloth.

The director-general began at once to plan for the comfort of the colonists. He gave them seeds brought from Holland so that they could plant gardens and orchards, and he had four ships sent to the colony with horses, cows, sheep, and pigs. He also started the industry of shipbuilding.

To the Dutch people who came to live in New Netherland, the country seemed a good deal like their native land. The climate and seasons were much the same. Climate made a great difference in the success of a settlement. Men from sunny France nearly died of cold in the winters of Canada, and the settlers of Virginia found the first hot summers very hard to bear because they were so different from those in England. New Amsterdam suited the Hollanders.

Fur trade was the chief business of the colony. To get settlers, the West India Company offered large sections of land to rich men in Holland if they would bring colonists to them. These landowners were called patroons. They were to start little colonies of fifty or more people. These wealthy men, living in Dutch cities, began to rule overseas as if they were lords who had servants living on their American lands and working for them. All that they wanted was furs and more furs, for furs meant money in their pockets. But few independent, self-respecting Hollanders would come to the colony on such terms.

One of the wiser patroons, named Van Rensselaer, who owned all the country around Fort Orange, made a better offer. A settler and his family would be provided with a house and barn, horses, cows, and pigs, for which he could pay in a few years by his labor on the land and by fur trading. Settlers liked this offer, and the Van Rensselaer lands were quickly occupied.

CHAMPLAIN IN NEW FRANCE

While settlements were being made along the Atlantic coast, a great French explorer became interested in the New World. Samuel de Champlain was captain of a Spanish trading vessel which sailed between the West Indies and Spanish ports on the Caribbean Sea. He even went inland as far as Mexico City, and also visited Panama. When he went home after these travels, the French king made him his own geographer and mapmaker.

Returning to the New World, Champlain did much exploring along the Atlantic coast. He entered Plymouth harbor fifteen years before the Pilgrims arrived, and mapped the entire coast before any Englishmen came. In 1608 he

Quebec in 1610, after a Drawing by Champlain

came to America to stay. On the St. Lawrence River he built a fort which was the beginning of the present city of Quebec. This was the first permanent settlement in what is now Canada.

From there Champlain did much exploring. He made a voyage by canoe to the lake between northern New York and Vermont which bears his name. On this trip into the wilderness he traveled with a big Indian war party. Within the next few years he went west as far as Lake Huron and, returning, explored the eastern end of Lake Ontario.

He came to the New World in that early period when every North American explorer had the hope of finding a short route to the Pacific and so to the East. With this purpose he went up the rivers and out on the lakes, questioning his Indian guides and listening eagerly to their tales of great waters beyond. Being a mapmaker, he drew maps of the territory he covered. At the same time he made careful written reports to the king. The knowledge of the New World increased very fast in France because of these reports, which only a man of Champlain's learning and skill could have made.

Champlain brought from France French priests, who went out into the Indian villages to preach and teach. These priests were the first of many black-robed French missionaries in this heroic service.

Most of the French settlements were only trading posts, where the traders could gather furs from the Indians. Champlain, however, wanted permanent settlements, where French families would come and live. If he had had support from France, he could have done much to build up such colonies. But the king and his courtiers did not care. They wanted only the profit that they could get out of the new land.

FRIENDSHIP WITH THE INDIANS

Champlain quickly learned how much the Indians could help him in exploring the wilderness. He lived with the Indians, traveled with them, and even fought for them. Because he got on well with them, he was able to show other Frenchmen how to deal with them.

In a book which he wrote, Champlain told about one way in which he helped both Indians and Frenchmen to understand one another better.

"I had with me," he wrote, "a young lad who had already spent two winters at Quebec, and who wanted to go with the Algonquins to learn their language."

Champlain decided that it would be a good idea to let this French boy return with a certain tribe to their own region. The boy could see what the Indians' country was like, and could report on his return about the rivers and the "great lake" of which these people told.

The Indian chief, who was a friend of Champlain's, took kindly to the idea. He said that he would be pleased to take the boy until spring and would treat him as his own son. Some of the chiefs objected, fearing lest some harm might come to their young guest and they might be blamed. Champlain explained that if, through accident or the fortunes of war, harm did come to the boy, this would not break the friendly relations between the Frenchmen and the tribe.

Then the Indians came to Champlain with their plan.

"Sire," they said, "since this is your desire, we will take him, and treat him like one of ourselves. But you shall also take one of our young men in his place, to go to France with you. We shall be greatly pleased to hear him report the fine things he will have seen."

Soon the French governor went home to Paris with a young Indian lad as his guest, while the Indian chief paddled to his winter quarters, taking the French boy with him. All went well on both sides, and in the spring both boys returned to their own people. Champlain had agreed on a meeting at a certain place near a waterfall. To that spot came two hundred Indians in their canoes. The French soldiers in thirteen boats waited to meet them.

"We were greatly pleased to see them," wrote Champlain. "I went to meet them in a canoe with our savage. When they were near, approaching slowly and in order, they all began to shout together."

One of the chiefs made a long speech, praising Champlain for meeting them at this place as he had promised. At the end of the speech they "raised three shouts, all two hundred of them joining." The Frenchmen, desiring to do them honor, fired the guns they had with them in salute.

Next, the Indian lad told how well he had been treated in France and described some of the wonderful things he had seen. The French boy was then brought to

Champlain's boat. While he was still in his Indian dress he told his friends how good the Indians had been to him.

All the Indians went away quietly, stopping nearby for the night. On the following day Champlain held important talks with the chiefs and elders of the tribe. They liked and trusted this "great chief" of the French. He had proved himself to them. But they were troubled to see so many Frenchmen with guns.

Champlain's friendship with the Algonquin tribes did much to open up the Great Lakes region to the French. Unfortunately the Algonquins were at war with the powerful Iroquois tribes of the region that is now New York State. By joining in this war, Champlain turned the Iroquois people against the French.

For twenty-five years Champlain worked hard for New France, of which he was made the governor. Always he believed in its future. He said in a letter which he wrote home: "The beauty and richness of this land cannot be praised too much. Everything stretches out its arms to you."

FRENCHMEN FOLLOW THE GREAT LAKES INLAND

The wealth of New France was in furs. At first the Indians brought to the settlements on the St. Lawrence enough furs to meet the Frenchmen's needs. Fleets of canoes carrying furs appeared each fall at Montreal. Then times changed. Indian nations went to war with one another. There were some years when no fur fleet came to the French settlements. It became plain that traders must go far into the interior and find out more about the lands from which the Indians brought the furs.

An explorer by the name of Jean Nicolet traveled with Indians to Lake Michigan in 1634 and came ashore at Green Bay in what is now Wisconsin. Other Frenchmen came to Lake Superior within twenty or twenty-five years.

It was in 1671 that Daumont de St. Lusson took possession of the region for his king. The place which this soldier-explorer chose for his ceremony was near Sault Sainte Marie, where the waters of Lake Superior rush into Lake Huron. At this spot there was already a French mission station as well as an Indian village. For months the French and Indians prepared for this event. Messages of invitation were sent to all the tribes living within three hundred miles. On the morning of June 14, when members of fourteen tribes had arrived, St. Lusson declared himself ready.

Priests, explorers, soldiers, traders marched in solemn procession up the hill, with a throng of Indians following.

Near the top the long line halted and those in the lead stepped forward to take their places beside a huge cross that lay on the ground. The Indians stood silent, waiting to see what the "white faces" would do. At a sign from St. Lusson the wooden cross was slipped into the opening prepared for it. Beside the cross was placed a cedar pole to which was nailed a metal plate engraved with the royal arms of France. While the flag was being raised, the Frenchmen chanted words from the Twentieth Psalm: "In the name of our God we will set up our banners."

St. Lusson made a speech in which he took possession in the name of the French king of "all these lakes, straits, rivers, islands, and regions stretching to the sea at the north and at the west, or on the opposite side extending to the South Sea."

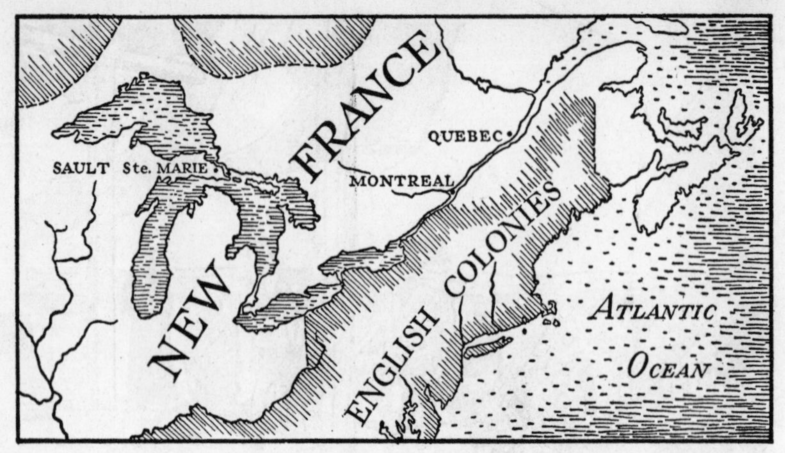

THE BEGINNINGS OF NEW FRANCE

The Frenchmen shouted "Long live the King!" Guns were fired. The Indians cried out in delight.

Another such claim was made eight years later. That summer Daniel Du Luth made a tour of the country which is now Minnesota. At the end he held a great council of Indian chiefs on the shores of Lake Superior, near the site of the present city of Duluth, and made a treaty of peace. After ten years among the Indians he entered a written protest, still kept in the records of Canada, against the sale of whisky and brandy to the natives. There is also in French records the brief report which the governor of Canada sent to the king in the year 1710: "Captain Du Luth died this winter. He was a very honest man."

The French were the only white settlers in the whole Great Lakes region until nearly the time of the American Revolution. Towns and cities there owe their founding to French explorers, priests, and fur traders. These men could reach this country because they could go by water from the St. Lawrence River to the waterways in the center of the continent. Frenchmen were taking possession of this region at the time when the English were planting their colonies on the Atlantic seacoast.

MARQUETTE AND JOLLIET FIND THE UPPER MISSISSIPPI

As French traders and priests pushed farther and farther west in the Great Lakes region, they heard from the Indians of a great river which flowed southward, and hoped that it would bring them to the Pacific. The Indians called this river the Mississippi, or "Father of Waters."

At a mission station near Lake Michigan two men sat together on long winter evenings and drew maps and discussed where they would go to reach this river. Father Marquette was a priest who was teaching the Indians there. His friend was Louis Jolliet, a fur trader and explorer.

On May 17, 1673, the two men with five helpers started out to find the great river. "We were fully resolved," they said, "to do and suffer everything for so glorious an undertaking." They launched their two birch-bark canoes in front of the little chapel and paddled into the wide waters of Lake Michigan. They then crossed Green Bay and went up the Fox River. Near its source they stopped and carried their canoes on their shoulders across the country to the Wisconsin River. For seven days they traveled down that stream until they found on June 17 that its waters flowed into a wide river. They knew that they had found the waters which they were seeking. The point where they entered the Mississippi is near the northern boundary of the present state of Iowa.

For a month they followed the great river downstream. Hills and forests were left behind, and they looked out on wide, flat lands. Sometimes they saw large herds of buffalo. The weather was pleasant, and there were no falls or dangerous rapids, such as they were used to in the rivers of the north. Once in a while they met Indians, and Father Marquette preached the Christian faith to them. It was easy to go on, but they had come hundreds of miles and the journey upstream would be hard. After a month, when they had reached the mouth of the Arkansas River, they decided to turn back. They knew now that the great river flowed into the Gulf of Mexico. If they went farther, they would be in a region claimed by Spain.

They returned by way of the Illinois River and Lake Michigan, and probably passed near the present site of Chicago. Their discoveries roused great enthusiasm when reported in France. Frenchmen gained some idea of the vast empire which they might build in America.

SETTLERS FROM MANY LANDS

In 1600 there were no English settlements in North America. Within a few years Europeans found they could survive and make homes on the edge of the wilderness. From 1607 on, the Englishmen who crossed the ocean came to the New World to stay. So did the Dutch who landed on the banks of the Hudson River, and the French who came to the St. Lawrence Valley. The Englishmen who came were seeking homes. They desired to create a "New England," and the wisest Englishmen at home did everything they could to encourage the establishment of colonies along the Atlantic coast. The Dutch West India Company sent colonists because it wished to get wealth by trade in furs. Its businessmen had no particular interest in developing the country which furnished this wealth. The king of France and his advisers were also chiefly interested in the wealth obtained by the fur trade of New France. But the great French explorers had a vision of starting a colonial empire. Champlain led the way. Marquette and Jolliet explored the upper Mississippi.

While governors and explorers made bold plans, the colonists who started settlements went quietly ahead making homes for themselves and their families. Because they did this, more and more people came to live in America.

Talking Together

1. If a sea captain had sailed along our Atlantic coast in 1600 and then again in 1625, what changes might he have noticed on the second trip?

2. The colonists had troubles of many kinds. What were some of them? Could any of them have been avoided?

3. Describe an experience of someone living in a certain colony which would be true only for that colony. Pretend that you are that person and make the experience as real as possible. Let the class try to name the colony.

4. Why were no English settlements started during the early years in regions away from the rivers and seacoast?

Interesting Things to Try

1. Thirty-four boys and girls came to Plymouth on the *Mayflower*. Pretend that you were one of them and write a letter to a boy or girl left behind in England.

2. Collect pictures of Jamestown, Plymouth, New York, and Quebec that show how they look today. Perhaps someone who has visited those places will tell the class about them.

3. Read the poem "The Landing of the Pilgrims," by Mrs. Felicia Hemans. Copy this poem in the center of a poster and draw illustrations for it around the edge.

4. Where do most of our furs come from today? Use an encyclopedia to get information.

5. Dramatize a scene that might have taken place in Jamestown in the spring of 1610. Two of the colonists are talking. One is discouraged and wants to return to England; the other is sure that better times will come.

6. Make a pictorial map called "English Settlements in the New World." What places will you put on it?

7. Write the diary of the French boy whom Champlain left to spend a winter with the Algonquin Indians.

Let's Read

Our Nation Begins, by E. C. Barker, W. E. Dodd, and W. P. Webb. Use the index to locate more stories about the colonies and explorers discussed in this unit.

The First Thanksgiving, by Lena Barksdale. When Hannah came by boat from Maine to visit her grandmother nearly three hundred years ago, she heard about the first Thanksgiving.

André, by Bertha B. and Ernest Cobb. The story of a boy who sailed with Champlain and had exciting adventures with his Indian friends.

America Builds Homes, by Alice Dalgliesh. This book will tell you how people lived in the early colonies of Virginia, New England, and New Amsterdam.

And There Was America, by Roger Duvoisin. Both the stories about our early history and the illustrations are delightful.

Wooden Shoes in America, by Lois Maloy and Alice Dalgliesh. This is interesting reading about boys and girls in New Amsterdam.

America's Old World Background, by Gertrude and John Southworth. The maps in the last two chapters, pp. 454–507, will help to give you a background for the unit you are studying.

Learning How to Hunt for Information

If you are asked to make a special report on some topic, you will want to find really good material on that subject. There are many sources to which you can turn. Here are some:

1. Other history and geography books in your classroom. Use the index in these books to help you find material on your particular topic.
2. Encyclopedias, such as the *World Book Encyclopedia*, *Compton's Pictured Encyclopedia*, and the *Book of Knowledge*.
3. Magazines and books in your home or in the library. In your library look up the books mentioned under "Let's Read." Ask the librarian to show you how to look for them in the *card*

catalogue. See if you can find there the names of other books on your topic. Then make use of index and table of contents to gather material for your report.

4. Interviews with persons who may have special knowledge of your topic. If, for example, your topic is "Plymouth," see if you can find someone to interview who has visited the town. Include in your report what you learn in this interview.

Make a *bibliography*, that is, a list of books you have found useful in preparing your report. For each book give (a) the name of the author; (b) the title of the book; and (c) the page numbers on which you found material. Arrange the list alphabetically.

Choose a topic from this unit and prepare a bibliography.

Quiz Yourself

I. Arrange these places in order of their position on the map from north to south. Do this without referring to a map. Write on your paper the place that is farthest north, then the one that is next farthest, and so on: Plymouth, St. Augustine, Quebec, Jamestown, New Amsterdam, Chesapeake Bay, Lake Champlain.

II. Number your paper from 1 to 5. After these numbers list the following places in the order in which they were founded: Quebec, St. Augustine, Plymouth, New Amsterdam, Jamestown.

III. Here are some statements about five of these seven men: Peter Minuit, William Bradford, John Rolfe, Myles Standish, Henry Hudson, Champlain, and John Smith. Number your paper from 1 to 5. After each number write the name of the man about whom the statement is true.

1. His explorations showed the best route from the Atlantic into the interior of North America.
2. This English sea captain explored for a Dutch company.
3. He served for many years as governor of Plymouth Colony.
4. He successfully cured Indian tobacco for the English market.
5. He bought the island of Manhattan from the Indians for about twenty-four dollars.

IV THIRTEEN GROWING COLONIES

THE THIRTEEN ENGLISH COLONIES

THIRTEEN GROWING COLONIES

THE MASSACHUSETTS BAY COLONY

The year 1630 was a good year in America, a year of promise for the future. It was the year when a fleet of eleven ships crowded with colonists arrived in Massachusetts Bay, not many miles from the place where the Pilgrims had settled in 1620. These ships were the first of nearly two hundred vessels which brought over twenty thousand passengers to New England before 1643.

Eagerly the people crowded into these ships, seeking homes in the New World. A writer of the time says that the people who came to the new colony were "people of all sorts."

They were people who wanted land and homes in America. The men were accustomed to work. They were farmers, carpenters, men skilled in all the trades. When they arrived in the new country, they knew how to build houses and to care for the cattle and sheep which they had brought along and to take up lands for farming. In the New World they could be landowners. That was what was pulling them to America. Up and down the highways and byways of

England, and at markets and fairs and inns, there had been talk of the offer of land which the Massachusetts Bay Company was making.

"One hundred acres of land for each settler," one man would say, while a group listened to his words.

"That can't be," someone would object.

But from those who knew, the answer was sure. In this new colony each settler was to have one hundred acres. The Massachusetts Bay Colony was the only one which offered this amount of land to everyone at the start.

The colonists were allowed to bring their own possessions with them, as they would have done if they had been moving from one home to another in England. Each family could have a certain amount of space on the ship. They were leaving the homes and villages where they had always lived and were coming to an uninhabited shore. Therefore they must think carefully what they would bring.

A minister who came with the first settlers in 1630 wrote to friends who were planning to come: "When you are once parted with England, you shall meet neither markets nor fairs to buy what you want." He gave a careful list of things they would need, even to pans and kettles.

Many a Massachusetts housewife was grateful to him when she unpacked her belongings in the little house which her menfolk had built. For the making of such houses the men were told to bring "all manner of carpenters' tools, a great deal of iron and steel to make nails, glass for windows, and locks." Other articles which could be had only by bringing them were meal for bread, malt for drink, woolen and linen cloth, and leather for shoes.

Before these people left England, their leaders had made careful plans for this colony. In August, 1629, a dozen Puritan gentlemen had met in Cambridge, England, to make plans for starting this colony in the New World.

It was to be a Puritan colony. The Puritans were persons belonging to the Church of England who did not approve of its ways and wished to reform it. They wanted simpler forms of worship, and they wanted all church members to lead better, purer lives.

The Puritans leaving England were about to try an experiment in government. They were setting up a church-state. The law of God was to be the rule of government, and the men at the head were to decide what that rule was.

They talked of the land which the king would grant them, of settlers, and of the charter they must get from the king. This would be a paper giving them the right to start and manage a colony.

These men were not simply putting up their money and sending out colonists. They were going to "adventure" themselves, and they declared that they would take their charter with them. That would make them a free and independent colony under the king.

Before that famous meeting ended, these twelve men signed their names to a paper. In it they agreed to sail within the year, on condition that they take their charter with them.

JOHN WINTHROP, GOVERNOR

One of the twelve men at that meeting was John Winthrop. He was a lawyer, a man "brought up among books and learned men." He was also a landowner who had long managed his own and his father's large estates in the country. He was chosen governor of the colony.

John Winthrop proved himself a leader in the new colony. Some of these Puritans were so strict and stern and long-faced that we feel sure we should not have liked them. Governor Winthrop was a serious man, as his portrait shows, but his eyes were kindly and his smile was friendly. He began to win the people to him in the first dreadful winter, when two hundred of the colonists died before the end of December.

Every able-bodied man had to help in building shelters to get the people under cover from the winter storms. Governor though he was, Winthrop did his full share of digging and other work. He looked far ahead, too, and planned for his people. As soon as he arrived with those first settlers, he became fearful lest the food run out, and sent a boat back to England to get more provisions. Its return early in February, 1631, saved the colonists from starving.

He won the Indians by his friendliness, entertaining the chiefs at his own table. From that same table it was his custom to send gifts of food to neighbors who might not have enough to eat. He was wise and generous in his

friendship with Roger Williams, a young minister who came to the colony during its first year and was always in trouble with some of its other leaders.

PURITAN WAYS

As more and more colonists came, the towns grew. Among them were Salem, Boston, and Newtowne, which is now Cambridge. The Puritans believed in education and began to plan for it almost as soon as they landed on Massachusetts shores. In 1636 they started Harvard College. A few years later they passed a law that every town of fifty families must have a teacher of reading and writing for its children, and each town of one hundred families, a grammar school.

These public schools helped toward democracy. In England children went to different schools according to their fathers' wealth, occupation, or office. Here the children of the minister sat on the school benches with the children of the fishermen. Farmers and mechanics as well as government officials paid taxes to support such public schools and were proud of them. New England made a great contribution toward the American way of life by encouraging public education.

In the name of their religion the Puritans did good things and also dreadful things. They lived honestly and soberly and worked hard. They kept order in their towns and punished severely those who did wrong. But they were dreadfully harsh in their treatment of a few persons whom they believed to be witches.

In the early years of the colony the Puritan leaders were very severe also in dealing with persons who refused to accept the rule of the church-state. They wanted everyone to believe and to worship in the Puritan way. Persons who worked against their plans must be banished. One who suffered this punishment was Mistress Anne Hutchinson, a woman of great ability. She felt and taught that a person must obey the "voice of God" as it came to him in his own heart and mind. Another person who could not accept the Puritan rule was Roger Williams, whose banishment led to the founding of the Rhode Island colony.

Roger Williams came to Massachusetts because he had to leave England. If he had stayed, he would have been imprisoned because of his religious and political beliefs.

"The state has no right," he declared openly, "to say to any man, 'Go to the religious service which we provide, or be punished.' "

Young Mr. Williams, then about twenty-eight years old, was welcomed in Massachusetts for a while. Soon it was discovered that he did not agree with the leaders of the Massachusetts church. Then Williams went to neighboring settlements at Salem and at Plymouth, where he was allowed to teach in the churches.

In Plymouth his real American life began. He was given his own land, and learned what it was to pioneer in the wilderness and how to run a farm. At a later time he described this experience.

"I wrought hard at the hoe for my bread. I know what it is to study, to preach, to be an elder, to be applauded; yet also what it is to tug at the oar, and to dig with the spade and plow."

At Plymouth he came in close touch with the Indians, and was eager to convert them to Christianity. In order to learn their language, he spent many hours with them in their wigwams. He learned their speech while he was winning their friendship.

At a time when Winthrop was not serving as governor, the other leaders brought Roger Williams before the General Court to answer for acts and words which were against the rules of the colony. It was decreed that he should be banished to the wilderness, but he was allowed to stay at Salem with his family until spring.

Later the leaders decided that the only way to silence him was to send him back to England. A ship was sent down the harbor to get him. When the captain reached Salem, he found that the young minister had been gone three days. Williams said later that he had been warned of his danger of being sent back to England "by the loving private advice of that much honored soul, Mr. John Winthrop."

Williams had set out from Salem ill, alone, on foot, in a driving snowstorm. Finally he came to the camp of his Indian friends, who gave him food, clothing, and shelter. In spite of his sufferings he did not blame those who had banished him. They were doing what they believed to be right, even as he was.

Soon he started again on his wanderings. In the month of June, 1636, he and five companions paddled up a river which flows into the northern end of Narragansett Bay. They landed at a spot where there was a bubbling spring of clear water near the river's bank. The story says that as he and his men stepped from their canoes, Indians met them and invited them to a meal of succotash and boiled bass, which was then cooking over their campfire. On this point of land Roger Williams built his house beside the bubbling spring. The place is now a part of the city of Providence, in the state of Rhode Island.

There Roger Williams started the colony of his dreams. It was to be a state which claimed authority only in things that belonged to community life, not in those which had to do with the church or religion. By his plan all men were to have equal rights. It was another step toward American democracy. The willingness to let other people hold such beliefs as they pleased was becoming a part of the American way.

A MIGRATION TO CONNECTICUT

On the last day of May, 1636, John Winthrop of Massachusetts wrote in his diary:

> Mr. Hooker, pastor of the church of Newtowne, and most of his congregation, went to Connecticut. His wife was carried in a horse litter; and they drove one hundred and sixty cattle, and fed of their milk by the way.

He tells the number of cattle, but does not say that there were about one hundred people—men, women, and children. They were going to a place with fertile land and plenty of space for themselves and their cattle in the valley of the Connecticut River.

As they journeyed through the wilderness, traveling only seven or eight miles each day and then camping for the night, the members of the Hooker party were the first of a long line of people moving west. In the years which followed, thousands of New England families made journeys like this

to points farther and farther west, helping to open up the entire continent.

The minister of this group, Reverend Thomas Hooker, had come from England to the church at Newtowne, as

Cambridge was then called. There he had been displeased by the narrow ideas of the Massachusetts leaders. He was a wise, farseeing man, the son of an English farmer. He had come to the new country with dreams of a democratic society. In it the people should govern themselves. There should be a free church in a free state.

When Hooker's people complained because they did not have room for themselves and their cattle in the village on the banks of the Charles River, he advised that they all move farther into the wilderness. They chose a spot in the fertile Connecticut Valley, and there they founded the town of Hartford.

In a few years the freemen of Hartford and two other "river towns" set up a government of their own. A constitution was written with "orders" as to how their affairs should be managed. They were to elect their own officials. Thus they carried out their leader's belief that government belonged in the hands of the people.

Here in Connecticut was the founding of a free state by free men under a constitution. Here were signs of the American democracy of the future.

NEW HAMPSHIRE AND BORDERING SETTLEMENTS

From the earliest colonial days there were fishing settlements and trading posts along the coast of Maine. New Hampshire also had groups of a few farms and fishing villages in several places. As the Massachusetts colony grew, many moved from its lands into these regions. Some of these people left the colony because they wanted to get away from its strict Puritan ways. Fur trade, farming, and fishing were the occupations of these pioneer settlers.

Massachusetts claimed all this territory. New Hampshire remained part of the Massachusetts colony for many years. It became a separate province in 1679, but for a long time New Hampshire and Massachusetts had the same governor. Maine was joined to Massachusetts in 1652 and did not become wholly independent for many years.

The lands of Vermont lay between New France and the English colonies. This territory was fought over for many years by French and English. New Hampshire and New York claimed parts of its lands. Boundaries between the English colonies in America were much disputed in those years. Vermont finally succeeded in setting up a separate government of its own.

LIFE IN NEW ENGLAND

New sounds came in the wilderness with the coming of the white men. The Indians must have listened to them and wondered. There was the sound of the ax and the saw, followed quickly by the crash of falling trees. The Indians' only cutting tools were made from stone or shell or the bones of animals. The white men brought tools of iron and steel. With these they cut wood for building their houses.

To the sound of the ax and saw in the woodlands there was soon added the cheerful ring of hammers, both in the

villages and on the water fronts. The white men began at once to build ships.

In the pastures around the new settlements there were the sounds of sheep bleating and of cattle mooing. These were new sounds for the Indians, who had heard only the calls and cries of wild animals. The English wanted to raise their own mutton and to have their own wool. The women wanted milk for their children.

As years passed, the newcomers arriving on every boat did not all stay in the first settlements. The lands beyond tempted them. As they followed rivers and Indian trails, they came to many pleasant places for the location of new villages.

There grew up the system of having in the center of every village a "common," a piece of land belonging to all. Here anyone might bring his cows to feed. Beside this

common the meetinghouse was built, and around it were the first houses. Each settler had his own piece of land within the village, the amount depending on what he was able to cultivate. Outside the village were the woodlands, of which each settler always had his share.

The men of the village or town took the responsibility of dividing the land, of building houses, and protecting them from Indian attack. The business of carrying on community life was done in a town meeting. Here men came together to manage town affairs. From these town meetings representatives were sent to an assembly for the entire colony. The town meetings and the assembly gave men practice in managing affairs in a democratic way. As the members became more independent in their ideas, they gave much trouble to the Puritan leaders and the royal governors. From these independent gatherings, where all could have their say, came the men who had an active part in starting the American Revolution.

Many of the colonists who came to New England had been farming people in England. In a more fertile region they would naturally have continued their farming. They soon found, however, that all of them could not get their living from the land, where rocky, hilly pastures lay back of the fertile valleys and orchard slopes. They must turn from the land to the sea for their living, and this they gladly did.

From Gloucester, on the seacoast north of Boston, men went out to the Newfoundland Banks for cod, starting an industry which has continued to this day. Salted fish found a ready market in England and the West Indies, as well as in some of the other American colonies.

New Englanders also cut their forests and sent much

lumber to England, but they had no single product like the tobacco of Virginia and other Southern colonies. Besides lumbering and fishing, they turned to building ships for sale in England and in their own and other colonies. Also they sailed the ships up and down the coast and to the West Indies with cargoes for trade.

Within fifty years, more than seven hundred ships were built in Massachusetts alone, and hundreds more in the other New England settlements. Sometimes they were built by the seashore or on nearby river banks. Often they were made in the forest and rolled on tree trunks to the edge of river or ocean.

From Maine to Florida the sea and the rivers were the highways of those times. Land travel was difficult. The sea was the chief connecting link between the colonies.

NEW NETHERLAND BECOMES NEW YORK

In New Netherland the Dutch settlers, during the early colonizing years, were farming and trading in furs. They had been wise enough to make friends with the powerful Iroquois Indians. Up the Hudson and on toward Canada fur trading was the chief business.

The Dutch were home-loving, industrious people. They took up lands and cultivated them, making fine farms around their towns. They were also good at trade. Their leaders became merchants in the wilderness regions, or, if they lived around New Amsterdam, owners of trading ships. New Amsterdam was growing into a city.

The colony was, however, neglected by the Dutch West India Company. It sent over directors who cared little for people's comfort, and refused to allow any form of self-government or any popular assembly. One of these was Governor Peter Stuyvesant, who had lost a leg in his soldier days and stumped about on a silver-tipped peg. He was always in trouble with the colonists. He bullied them according to his own impatient notions. Some of the New Netherlanders said that they wanted a government like that in the neighbor colonies of New England. They were promptly told that they deserved to be "hanged on the tallest tree in the land."

Many New Englanders began to move into the region claimed by the Dutch. A large number settled on Long Island. New Englanders did not want the Dutch to control these lands which were so near their own borders.

England was at war with Holland at this time, and that was a good excuse for seizing Dutch lands in America. In 1664 the English king, Charles II, granted to his brother, the Duke of York, proprietor's rights in all the land between the Connecticut and the Delaware rivers. The Dutch in New Amsterdam knew nothing of this grant until three British ships appeared in their harbor with the duke's orders to surrender their fort and town.

When the British ships had anchored in the harbor, the British commander sent the governor a letter. In it he offered easy terms of surrender. Governor Stuyvesant read the letter scornfully and tore it into bits. Some of his people, however, pieced the letter together. When they saw what it offered, they forced the governor to yield. They had no desire to fight the English for the sake of a trading company which had done little to deserve their loyalty.

The name New Amsterdam was changed to New York, in honor of the English Duke of York. The Dutch people did not leave their homes. They merely came under English rule. For a century New York and the towns up the Hudson River were in appearance and in ways of life Dutch towns. But gradually the Dutch and the English began to think alike. These people, like all the other colonists, were becoming American.

WILLIAM PENN AND PENNSYLVANIA

William Penn, son of a British admiral who had been knighted by the king, belonged to the Society of Friends in England. He wanted to found a colony in America. Admiral Penn had loaned money to the king, besides helping him in other ways. William suggested after his father's death that this debt be paid in land in America. Since the debt amounted to a large sum of money, King Charles was delighted to agree.

The Friends, or Quakers, had been going to America in small companies, but were having unhappy times in most of the colonies. Their religious beliefs made them unwelcome both in America and in England. When wealthy young William Penn joined them, everyone was astonished. The English king and his government officials were all glad to see this bold Quaker leave the country.

They were annoyed by the behavior of the Quakers, who not only believed that all men were equal before God, but acted on this belief. They refused to take off their hats to any man, even the judge of a court. They addressed everyone, whatever his rank or office, by the familiar "thee" and "thou."

But there was much more to the Quaker belief than this idea about men being equal. Quakers believed that each person should follow his own "inner light" in matters of religion. Also they were opposed to wars and refused to help support armies.

William Penn dreamed of a land where there should be no fighting and no violence. That was the Quaker ideal. He stood also for religious freedom. His colony was to be a refuge for all who were persecuted for their beliefs.

When it came to choosing a name for the colony, Penn suggested Sylvania, which means "woodland." The king insisted on the name Penn, not for the son but in honor of the admiral who had been his friend. The result was our familiar Pennsylvania.

William Penn came to his lands in 1682. One of his first acts was to lay out a capital city on the banks of the Delaware River. This was named Philadelphia. In this, as in his other acts, Penn showed that he was looking far ahead. He did an excellent job of what would today be called city planning. Space was reserved in the center for public buildings, and streets crossed one another in a regular pattern of squares.

Penn at once made friends with the Indians. When he sat down in council with them he talked of "the Great Spirit who made me and you." He sat with the Indians on the ground, ate their roasted acorns and hominy, and joined in their games of running and jumping. When he got ready to make his famous treaty with the Indians he

wrote into it his hopes for peace and friendship between white men and Indians in his colony.

> We will be brethren, my people and your people, as the children of one father. All the paths shall be open to the Christian and the Indian. The doors of the wigwam of the Indian shall be open to the Christian. The Indian shall not harm the Christian nor his friend; the Christian shall not harm the Indian nor his friend; but they shall live together as brethren.

Penn was a good advertiser. He wrote an "Account of the Province of Pennsylvania," which was distributed all over the British Isles. It was also translated into German, Dutch, and French for people in Europe.

Those were years of great suffering in Europe. Kings and princes, dukes and barons, were constantly at war with one another. Their armies swept back and forth across the farm lands of the people, destroying the crops and ruining the villages. There was persecution because of religion as well. Before William Penn came to America he had traveled in Europe and had seen the terrible sufferings of these people. He saw, too, that they were the kind of people he wanted for the development of his new lands.

He described carefully the needs of the colony, telling that he wanted carpenters, farmers, weavers, shoemakers, masons, and mechanics. Above all he wanted men seeking the religious freedom which they had lost at home.

Families by thousands came at the call. Unfortunately the boats were overcrowded, and the refugees were ill-treated by the shipowners, who packed them in with no care for their comfort. The people were mostly poor and unable to pay for food for the voyage. Many died on the way, but those who reached the new lands rejoiced and wrote home of the rich soil and other advantages.

A stream of people followed, moving through Philadelphia into the lowlands and highlands of Pennsylvania

and the regions north and south. They started the great Pennsylvania Dutch farm communities of that section. The name Dutch comes, in this case, from the word *Deutsch*, which is another name for German. Scotch-Irish emigrants from the British Isles read the advertisements and came too, seeking to escape oppression and poverty.

Penn's own years in his colony were few. He was called back to England by his affairs there. He had done, however, the important work of setting America before the world as an open door. Through his lands men of all kinds and from many places were invited to enter.

DELAWARE AND NEW JERSEY

Delaware Bay was known to early English explorers. It was named for a governor of Virginia, Lord de la Warre. Dutch sea captains also visited this region. One of them was Captain May, who brought the first colonists to the Hudson River in 1624.

The Dutch were the first to make a settlement in Delaware. It was destroyed by the Indians. Next, Swedes tried to start a little New Sweden. The Dutch objected to having these people on lands which they claimed, and the fort and settlement of the Swedes were captured by men from New Amsterdam led by Peter Stuyvesant. The Duke of York acquired all this territory when he seized New Amsterdam. Later William Penn was given Delaware because it was just across the river from his own growing colony. For a long time it was connected with Pennsylvania.

New Jersey, which was next to the Dutch colony at New Amsterdam, had many Dutch settlers. To it came also many Quakers fleeing from England and from New England, where they were being roughly treated by the Puritans. William Penn bought the western section of New Jersey and helped the Quakers to make homes there. To its eastern section came many other settlers from New England. The whole of New Jersey finally became a royal colony under the king of England.

New York, New Jersey, Pennsylvania, and Delaware were often called the middle colonies because they lay between New England and the Southern colonies. These four colonies were alike in many ways.

Delaware, which was owned by the Penn family until almost the time of the American Revolution, gave to Pennsylvania the seacoast which it lacked. Ships could go from Delaware Bay up the Delaware River to the growing port of Philadelphia, and to the western section of New Jersey. Northeastern New Jersey and New York had good harbors along New York Bay and the Hudson River. These connecting waters were important to the early colonists, for settlers did not go far inland for many years. Travel by boat was easier than through forests, where trails were narrow and the few roads were rough.

Since these middle colonies were easily reached from the sea, they received many immigrants from the Old World, who scattered over the river lands. Dutch, Swedes, Germans, Swiss, Scotch-Irish, and English came to the ports of New York and Philadelphia and then moved inland. Unlike New England, where the colonists came chiefly from England, the middle colonies had groups from many countries.

At first these groups lived apart from one another in separate villages and on farms. People continued to speak the language of their homeland. But exchange of goods brought them together. They were neighbors in a new land and they all had the same tasks of clearing land, building houses, planting crops, and starting a new life.

These colonies had rich soil. The small farmer from Holland could get a comfortable living from his piece of land, and the patroons could lay out huge estates along the Hudson. Germans who came in large numbers from the Rhine region of Europe went inland from the banks of the Delaware River and found rich, level lands which reminded them of their old homes.

Small farmers lived much the same life in all these colonies. Each had his house, garden, orchard, and fields, and his horses, cows, sheep, hogs, and poultry. Within the house were spinning wheels and the loom on which the women made cloth for clothing the family. Every man must be skillful enough to keep his farm tools in order. Boys and girls helped with the farm work and grew up with a habit of depending on themselves. Often these same young people became, in a few years, pioneers who moved out from the family home to clear new land and start new farms farther from the coast.

Many artisans, or men skilled in handicrafts, came to these colonies. Some settled in the towns and cities. Others lived on the big farms or set up their own little shops. A blacksmith might choose a crossroads where people passed on their way to market as the place for his shop. A shoemaker would build his house near the church and courthouse.

Maps of those early days seldom have the names of the colonies or their boundaries. Changes came too often. But

the names of port cities stand out. The life of the middle colonies centered in Philadelphia and New York.

Philadelphia, begun as a Quaker city, soon became a shipping center even larger than New York. Its merchants and leading citizens were well to do. The streets were broad, the houses fine, and the appearance of the city was one of comfort and prosperity. Many of the houses were built of brick in the style of London houses of that time. Others were of timber. Independence Hall was built by 1741, and other public buildings were later constructed near it. Here was a city which visitors from abroad admired.

New York kept for a long time the appearance of a Dutch town. Its buildings were in the Dutch style. In the earliest days a canal ran where Broad Street now is. There were windmills, houses with gardens and orchards, and small parks called "greens," where young and old gathered for recreation. Bowling Green of today has kept its name from that time. In the early days a boatman was always ready at the water's edge to row passengers to Brooklyn, the Dutch town on Long Island.

New York grew slowly, but its merchants were prosperous. Their ships came and went in the harbor, and men from many ports walked the streets. A traveler in 1643 told of hearing eighteen languages spoken there. Often a merchant would speak four languages, English, Dutch, German, and French. The city began early to be a meeting place for many peoples.

In both town and country the middle colonies were becoming truly American because people from many different nations lived and worked together. The forms of government were English, but the kinds of life were as varied as the places in the Old World from which the people came. Life was more free and less strict than in New England.

THE CALVERTS ESTABLISH MARYLAND

The rulers of European countries owned the lands of America. They could give lands to whom they chose—to companies, as in Virginia and New England, or to single persons. King Charles, who made a grant of land to William Penn, also made one to the Calverts. They were to be proprietors, that is, "owners in charge," always under the king. Before William Penn made beginnings in Pennsylvania, the Calverts started the Maryland colony.

George Calvert was eight years old in that famous year, 1588, when England won the great battle with the Spanish Armada. The boy grew up in the midst of talk of adventure in the New World. While he was still a young man, the Virginia Company, which colonized Jamestown, was started. Calvert put money into that venture, and was interested in other colonizing companies.

George Calvert was an important man in England and held high positions at court, but he resigned his offices when he became a Catholic. He asked then for a grant of land in Newfoundland, and took his family and forty other settlers there, intending to start a Calvert colony. But the winter was so cold that he wrote to the king, asking for a new grant of land in the south. Without waiting for an answer, he sailed southward.

In Virginia the royal governor welcomed him cordially as a guest, but others of the colony were less willing to admit the Calvert group because they were Catholics. Calvert, therefore, returned to England. There the king gave him a grant of land north of the settled part of Virginia.

When the charter was written, the question of a name for the grant came up. Calvert, who had been made Lord Baltimore, went to the king.

"Let us name the place in honor of the queen," said King Charles. After some talk the two agreed on Mary's Land, which later became Maryland.

Calvert died within a few months, before the charter could go into effect. His illness was partly the result of that dreadful winter in Newfoundland. His son Cecil, who became the second Lord Baltimore, took over the rights to the new land and went about the business of setting up the colony. Cecil never came out himself to his lands in America, but he did an excellent job of planning and managing the colony.

The Calvert who did come to Maryland with the first settlers was Cecil's brother Leonard. It was late in March, 1634, when he and three hundred colonists in two boats, the *Ark* and the *Dove*, arrived at the beautiful banks of the Potomac River. They put up a wooden cross in sign of taking possession, and started their government.

Here there was to be religious freedom. Such had been the wish of the first Lord Baltimore, and such were the instructions given by his son Cecil Calvert to the leaders before they started. On board ship and on land after they arrived, the colonists were to be silent concerning matters of religion "in order to preserve peace."

Maryland's beginnings were favorable. The Indians were friendly. There was food in plenty, with abundance of wild game in the forests. Tobacco proved to be an easy crop, so that there came to be the saying that in Maryland there were "toleration and tobacco." Within the first year there were, according to one of the colonists, "comfortable houses, surrounded by cattle, hogs, and poultry, and fruit trees brought from England and Virginia."

People poured into the little colony from other American settlements until it was soon more thickly settled than the other new colonies.

When some of the groups quarreled over their religious differences, the assembly passed a law called the Toleration Act. It granted freedom of worship to all Christians and was adopted by the colony in 1649.

Maryland people did not care to live in towns, as people did in New England. The city of Baltimore was not settled until nearly one hundred years after the colony was founded. Even then people were slow to take up the city lots, though these were offered at low prices. They preferred to live on their farms. Not till shipping made Baltimore one of the leading ports on the Atlantic coast did it become a large city.

In Maryland, as in other colonies, the people demanded early the rights of self-government. The proprietor system did not come to an end until the time of the American Revolution, but even under that system democracy won its way. As in all the so-called "tobacco colonies," the richer men had large plantations while the less wealthy lived on small farms. These farmers enjoyed their new independence. As time went on, they took more and more share in the government of the colony.

THE GROWTH OF VIRGINIA

The colonists of Virginia, from the beginning, had the task of conquering the wilderness. In the early days of the colony the Indians turned unfriendly, and there was a terrible massacre. After that Virginians learned, as they began other settlements, to protect them by building strong palisades and blockhouses. As the years went by, they also began to clothe themselves suitably for wilderness life. In winter they fitted themselves out, as their Indian neighbors did, in skins and furs. There came into being the American frontiersman, with his coonskin cap, his coarse shirt, and his deerskin breeches.

Virginia led the colonies in self-government. There, as early as 1619, met the first representative assembly ever to be gathered in America.

It was only a little gathering in that first year of self-government. Word had come from the London Company in England that the people of each small settlement should meet and elect two burgesses to send to a general assembly at Jamestown. The name "burgess" was used in England for a freeman of a borough, or town district.

On July 30, 1619, the burgesses met in a little wooden church at Jamestown. There were present the governor, the councilors, and twenty-two burgesses representing eleven places. The sessions were opened with prayer. After the burgesses had taken an oath of loyalty to the king, the colony business was discussed, and votes were taken. On August 4, the little legislature adjourned because of the extreme heat.

England had given to these colonists the rights which they would have had in the home country. They could choose men from their own number to represent them and

make their local laws. The custom continued even after the London Company ended and the colony was controlled directly by the king.

The House of Burgesses continued to meet as long as Virginia remained a colony, though the capital was moved from Jamestown to Williamsburg. Gentlemen planters sat in the assembly beside frontiersmen in their coonskin caps and deerskin garments. Together they settled the problems of government. Many leaders of the American Revolution had their training in this democratic assembly.

Virginia was the oldest and, for a long time, the most prosperous of the Southern colonies. To it came from England men who had been important in the home country. They made of it for many years a "little England" in the New World.

On tobacco plantations there was much hard work to be done. It was difficult for the owners to find enough workers. As the years passed, the colonists who came out to Virginia to become servants of gentlemen planters became themselves independent farmers. Free land was there. After serving their term of four or five or six years as laborers in the fields of others, they would take up their own patches of ground. The planters sent to England for more servants, and they, in turn, became independent.

Then the planters began to buy slave labor. In 1619 a ship reached a Virginia port with a cargo of Negroes. They had been brought from Africa to be sold as slaves. There were only a few of them, but many more followed. The tobacco colonies began to use all the slaves they could get.

NORTH AND SOUTH CAROLINA

In 1653 a group of Englishmen went from Virginia into the wild, unknown region to the south. They wanted more freedom than they were getting under the leaders of the Virginia colony, just as the people who settled Connecticut, Rhode Island, and New Hampshire wanted more freedom than they could have in Puritan Massachusetts.

These pioneers liked the country to which they came. The soil was good and the climate pleasant. For food they could shoot deer and wild turkeys in the woods. They built cabins in the forests and made a living by selling lumber, tar, and pitch to ships which came from the Northern colonies. That was the beginning of North Carolina.

Then the king of England took notice of this great stretch of territory which lay between Virginia and Spanish Florida. In 1663 King Charles made a gift of all this land to eight of his friends. He wished to reward them for help they had given him in wars which were just over. Several years passed before these men sent out any settlers.

Then in 1670 a group of Englishmen crossed the Atlantic and started a village which they called Charles' Town. They had chosen a fortunate location. Their settlement grew rapidly and became the important seaport of Charleston, South Carolina.

The Carolinas, as the whole region was called, attracted many settlers. Colonists from farther north and newcomers from many parts of Europe joined the pioneers in North

Carolina. They did the hard work of clearing the forest and making farms. By 1700 there were five thousand people living in this region.

To what is now South Carolina there came many Frenchmen. They were seeking freedom from the religious persecution which they were suffering in their own country. They found the climate like that of southern France, and planted orchards and vineyards. Scotch immigrants came, too, and also Englishmen from the West Indies. These brought Negroes to work on their plantations.

The new colonies were not well governed. The nobles tried to rule from England, and quarrels arose constantly between the settlers and the English governors. Finally the nobles grew weary of the whole undertaking and sold their lands to the king. In 1729 he divided the region into the two royal colonies of North Carolina and South Carolina.

GEORGIA AND THE WORK OF OGLETHORPE

The last English colony to be started along the Atlantic coast was Georgia. It was founded by General James Oglethorpe, an English soldier and member of Parliament. He wanted this colony to be a refuge for a group of people who were greatly in need of help at that time. These were debtors. Because of very severe laws, a man who owed money could be thrown into prison and kept there with no chance to earn money to pay his debt. The prisons were crowded and horrible.

In 1732 Oglethorpe and some other men persuaded the king to grant a charter for a colony to which poor debtors and others in distress could go. Oglethorpe himself led the first company of settlers to Georgia in 1733, and began the town which became Savannah, Georgia. There were some English debtors in this company, but also a number of Germans and Scotchmen. Many of these colonists started small farms. For a time slavery was not allowed in Georgia, and religious freedom was the rule.

The king was glad to have a colony in this region. It would give him a stronger hold on lands which the Spaniards of Florida also claimed. South Carolina willingly gave up its claim to these lands. Settlers there would be a protection against the Spaniards and hostile Indians of the back country. Spaniards did attack the colony, and it was saved because General Oglethorpe

was an experienced soldier and knew how to defend it. The war lasted four years, however.

With the establishment of Georgia, English colonies occupied the Atlantic seacoast between Spanish Florida and the French colonies in Canada.

LIFE IN THE SOUTHERN COLONIES

The colonies of Virginia, Maryland, the Carolinas, and Georgia were alike in many ways. The first settlements were along the seacoast or the many waterways which led inland from the Atlantic. Chesapeake Bay was like an inland sea, serving Virginia and Maryland and reaching to within a few miles of North Carolina. Broad rivers here and farther south were open for long distances to ocean-going vessels. All along them were private wharves from which the products of the plantations were sent direct to England. The ships which took these crops returned with supplies of clothes, books, and furniture which the planters had ordered in London. These people never lost touch with their home country.

Eastern Maryland, much of Virginia, and part of North Carolina were tobacco-growing regions. Here there were plantations rather than villages. The nearest neighbor might be two or three miles away from the great house where the owner lived. Planters built fine mansions and imported hundreds of Negro slaves to work on their lands. There were also smaller plantations of fifty or one hundred acres, whose owners were prosperous and independent. Doctors, lawyers, and preachers with homes along the river banks or in the towns, and many merchants and men skilled in crafts made up the rest of the population.

Children in the planters' families were taught at home by private tutors until they were ready for college. At first the boys went to England to finish their education. But in 1693 King William and Queen Mary gave permission and money for the founding of a college in Williamsburg, Virginia. This college was named William and Mary College in their honor. Its first class was graduated in 1699.

South Carolina, part of North Carolina, and eastern Georgia had great rice plantations in their low country. Soon after 1690 a ship brought to Charleston bags of rice from the island of Madagascar. The governor of South Carolina sowed the seed in

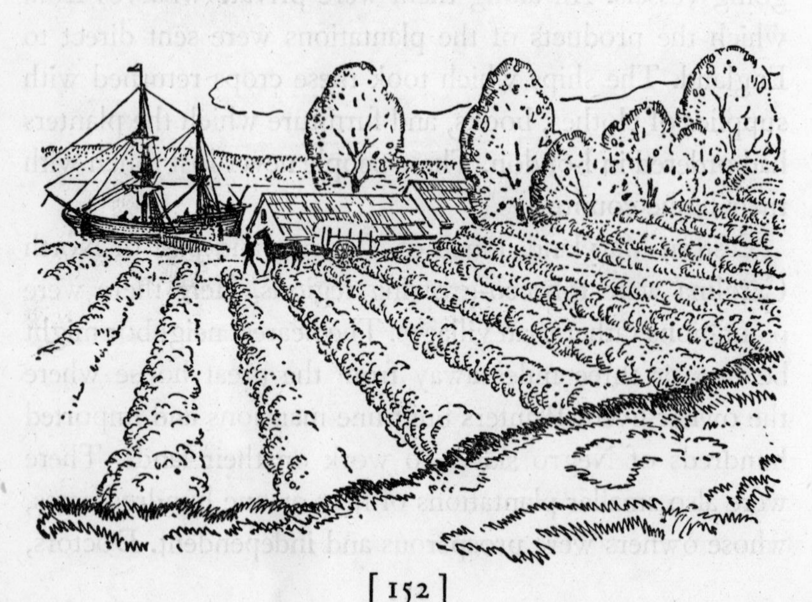

his garden, where it grew so well that he tried it in his fields. After the governor's success rice was widely sown and became the chief crop of the region. The work of planting, tending, and harvesting rice was hard, and there were not enough laborers among the colonists to do it. The planters, therefore, brought in thousands of slaves.

Another successful crop which was widely grown was indigo. About 1740 a sixteen-year-old girl, Eliza Lucas, experimented with this plant from which blue dye was made. She found that it could be raised on her South Carolina plantation, and others soon followed her example.

There was a great demand for indigo in Europe and England. At one time the colonies were shipping a million pounds a year. Cotton also grew well, especially in South Carolina.

Ports along the coast or on the inland waterways grew into flourishing towns and cities. Norfolk, Virginia, and Charleston, South Carolina, were centers for exchange of native products and imported goods. Beautiful homes were

built along the streets of these towns, and fine public buildings were erected. Williamsburg, which became the capital of Virginia in 1699, was another important city of the South, with government buildings and many fine homes.

Back from the coast in South Carolina, North Carolina, and Virginia was a region called the pine belt. Here men cut timber and gathered the pine products so useful in shipbuilding. The smell of tar, pitch, and turpentine greeted the buyer who came into the woods for shipbuilding supplies and lumber. The life was hard, and the workers, with their tiny huts deep in the forest, were poor, but these settlers of the pine belt had their part in the clearing of the land and the growth of the colonies.

THE FRONTIER

Slowly the frontier moved westward. The frontier was the border line of settlement along which homes were few and scattered. The people who lived on the frontier were folk who had made the venture into the new lands to gain more independence and freedom. Beyond was the wilderness, which would some day in turn become the frontier.

Neither Virginians nor Marylanders nor the people of the colonies north or south were content for long to live only along the seacoast or on the river lands. They pushed back into the uplands which lay west. At first they took up small farms on which the family did the work with only a servant or two to help in the fields. Germans, Swiss, and Scotch-Irish moved into these lands and lived there as they would have lived in their home countries, keeping many of their native customs and arts and crafts.

Also to these frontier settlements came planters who had worn out their tobacco lands. This crop exhausted the soil after a few years. The sons of wealthy planters often chose to take twenty or more slaves and go to new land and start plantations of their own.

Along the frontier these young planters met the immigrants from other regions and countries. Out of this meeting grew a new kind of American, a man independent, self-reliant, and tolerant of the ways of other people. To him the chief business was the opening of new country. He wanted roads along which hogsheads of tobacco could be taken to market. He went to the assemblies and demanded such roads, and then returned and helped his neighbors build them. He and his neighbors invented new kinds of boat-rafts on which their products could be floated down the streams. The frontiersman was always looking west toward the mountains and the rich lands beyond.

While the Americans who stayed on the seacoast felt very close to the Old World, these frontier settlers began to dream of a new nation which would rise in the New World.

ENGLISH COLONISTS GROW MORE INDEPENDENT

Most of the colonies along the Atlantic coast were begun by people from England. Newcomers from many lands also came as settlers, but they accepted the fact that these were English colonies.

As the years went by, the colonists became more and more independent. Three thousand miles lay between them and England, and it took ships many weeks to cross the ocean. Most of the colonies were under royal governors who came out from England to represent the home country. Each colony elected its own assembly. These governing bodies frequently quarreled with their British governors. Their members were loyal to England, but they wanted to settle local affairs for themselves.

Within the colonies there were great differences. In some there were people from many nations. In all there were the people of the cities and towns and those of the frontier. Along the seacoast the pioneer way of life passed as towns and cities grew. But the people of the cities found that they could not manage the independent farmers and hunters of the back country. Questions which came up were discussed and voted upon in the popular assemblies. Democracy was beginning. Religious and racial differences were recognized and respected. During a century and a quarter the colonists in the different regions worked out their own methods of government. No two colonies were alike. But as the years went by there came to be in all of them an American way of life.

Talking Together

1. People living in the various colonies did some things alike and some things differently. On the blackboard, make a chart which will show the likenesses and differences between the groups of colonies. To do this, make three columns, headed New England Colonies, Middle Colonies, and Southern Colonies. At the side, list such topics as Homes, Food, Occupations, Government, Manners and Customs, and Schools. Then fill in the columns as the class discusses each topic.

2. Most of the Puritans of New England lived in towns, but most of the early settlers of Virginia lived on plantations. Can you tell why this happened?

3. How much did a colonial family have to depend on others for food, clothing, and shelter? How much does your family depend on others for these things?

4. Are there old houses, monuments or markers, a museum collection, or special names of streets and parks in your community connected with its early history? What can you tell your class about any of these?

Interesting Things to Try

1. The United States Post Office has often issued commemorative stamps on the anniversary of important historical events or to honor national heroes. Ask the stamp collectors in your class to bring in commemorative stamps from their collections and explain them.

2. Some of the girls may like to dress dolls to represent Puritans and Quakers.

3. Make a list of things that we have in our homes today that the colonists did not possess.

4. Choose a topic about which you would like to make a booklet. The following would make good subjects: (a) Shipbuilding; (b) Fur Trading; (c) A Colonial Home; (d) White Men and Indians. What might you do with the finished booklet?

5. Plan an assembly program, "Then and Now," for your school.

Learning How to Select Material for a Report

When you prepare a special topic, you usually look up your subject in reference books. Often you find a great deal more information than you can use. It is important to know how to select the best of that material and to pick out quickly what belongs to your particular topic.

Suppose you have been asked to report on one of these topics: (a) Colonial Homes; (b) Colonial Manners and Customs; (c) Colonial Occupations. In a good report you will not talk about "manners and customs" if your topic is "occupations."

A list of nine statements follows. Each might be the first sentence of a paragraph in some book. Your topic is "Homes of the Colonists." Ask yourself: "Judging from the first sentence, shall I find that this paragraph tells something about my topic?"

1. Lumbermen cut tall trees for masts.
2. Often the first shelter was of bark, or was a cave.
3. The Pennsylvania Germans were a thrifty people.
4. The Virginians were fond of horse racing and hunting.
5. When the house was done, rude furniture was built.
6. Quakers would not take off their hats even to the king.
7. Fire helped in clearing the land.
8. The minister sometimes preached for two hours.
9. The log houses had oiled paper for windows.

Let's Read

America My Home, Then and Now, by Harold B. Clifford. If you would like to know how a family lived in New York State about 1690, this story will tell you.

New Amsterdam Colonial Days, *New England Colonial Days*, and *Southern Colonial Days*, three books by Marcelle Laval Duffé. You will be glad to make the acquaintance of Peter Van Doorn of New Amsterdam, the Jeffries children of New England, and Richard Wakefield of Virginia.

Days of the Colonists, by Louise Lamprey. Here are surprising stories of Indians, pirates, pioneers, and traders.

The Colonial Twins of Virginia, by Lucy F. Perkins. Many exciting things happen to these twins on a plantation.

Those Who Dared, by Carrie Willis and Lucy Saunders. The chapter "A Friend to the Homeless" tells about the founding of Georgia, and "Penn's Woods" about early Pennsylvania.

Quiz Yourself

I. Number your paper from 1 to 5. Opposite each number put *A* if the event came *after* the settlement of the Massachusetts Bay Colony, or put *B* if the event came *before* that settlement.

1. Arrival of the first slaves in Virginia
2. Founding of Harvard College
3. First meeting of the House of Burgesses
4. Founding of Providence, Rhode Island
5. Change from New Netherland to New York

II. Number your paper from 1 to 3. After each number write the name of the colony (Massachusetts Bay, Pennsylvania, Maryland, Virginia, New Netherland) about which the statement is true.

1. It was founded by a Catholic to offer religious freedom.
2. It banished those who refused to obey the church officers.
3. The founder of this colony made a "Great Treaty" with the Indians.

III. Here are some statements about four of the following men: William Penn, Champlain, Lord Baltimore, Roger Williams, Thomas Hooker, Oglethorpe, Peter Stuyvesant, John Winthrop.

Number your paper from 1 to 4. After each number write the name of the man about whom the statement is true.

1. A Quaker founded Pennsylvania.
2. This Dutchman gave up his colony to the English.
3. He was the first governor of the Massachusetts Bay Colony.
4. He received the grant of Maryland from the king of England.

V AMERICANS MAKE A NEW NATION

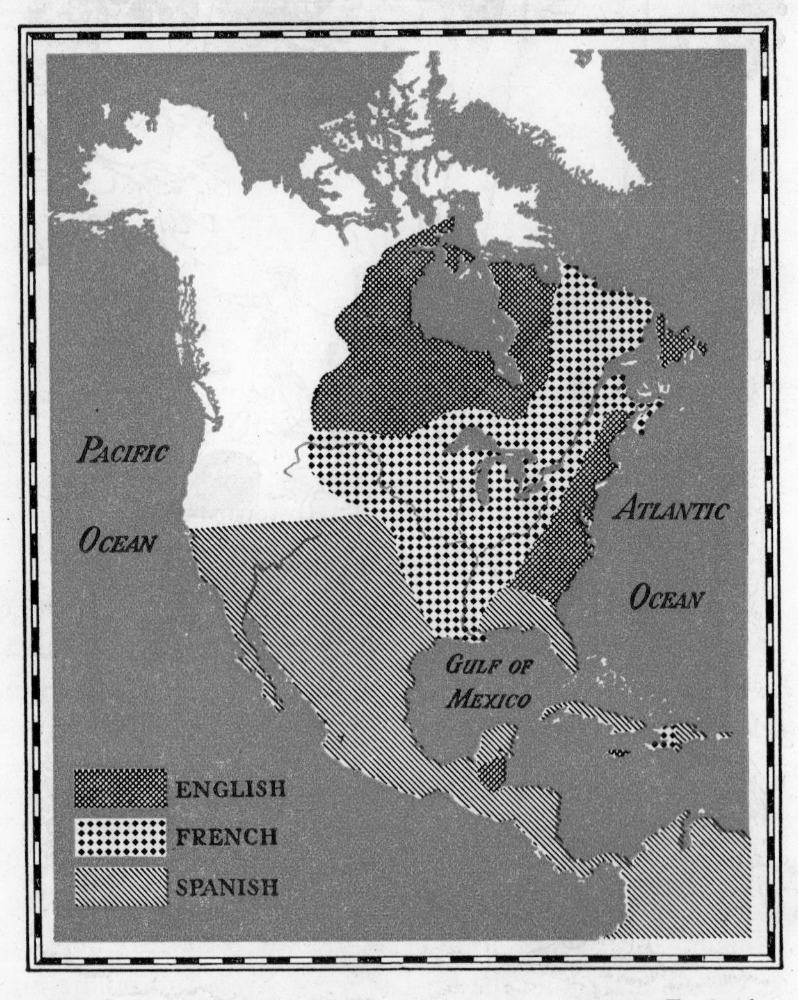

EUROPEAN CLAIMS IN NORTH AMERICA IN 1750. *England, France, and Spain claimed most of North America at this time.*

AMERICANS MAKE A NEW NATION

LA SALLE PLANS A FRENCH EMPIRE

While the English were building their colonies along the Atlantic coast, the French continued to go inland. At Quebec a French governor and a great explorer were planning to occupy the river valleys in the center of the American continent.

News of the expedition of Marquette and Jolliet came to a man in New France who had been planning to make a search for the "great river," of which he had heard from the Indians.

Robert Cavelier, better known as La Salle, was born in France in 1643, the son of a wealthy merchant. As a schoolboy he read of the new lands across the sea and longed to go to them. At last he could endure his student life no longer. In 1666 he journeyed to New France, where he took up land along the St. Lawrence River and built a big log house. Past his home came in the fall the canoes of fur traders, both white men and Indians, bringing their loads of precious skins from the wilderness. La Salle talked with them and with the Indians who used the trails across his lands. He set himself to learn the speech of different tribes of Indians and became familiar with no less than nine languages. He went on exploring expeditions to Lake Ontario and into the lands south of Lake Erie.

"The more I see of this country, the more I like it," La Salle wrote home.

In 1672 a new governor, Count Frontenac, came to New France. He was a man of action, eager to build up a great fur trade with the Indians.

La Salle shared with the governor his own dream of a French empire. To defend this empire he wanted forts established at important points on the Great Lakes and on all the rivers. Frontenac sent La Salle to France to tell his tale to the king and get money and support. When La Salle returned with the king's approval, he was given charge of a fort on Lake Ontario, which he rebuilt as a supply center for his explorations inland.

One of La Salle's first needs was for ships. In 1679 a small sailing vessel, the *Griffon,* was built at a point on Lake Erie above Niagara Falls. This vessel carried La Salle to Green Bay and, while he went on, it was sent back with a valuable load of furs. But the ship was never heard from again. It probably went to the bottom in a quick, fierce storm which swept Lake Michigan soon after it started.

This was the first of many misfortunes which happened to La Salle. Two years went by while he explored and planned. He never gave up, and at last the day came when he and a party of fifty men traveled down the Illinois River to the Mississippi. They floated on for hundreds of miles, marveling as the river grew wider. Plants and trees of the South began to appear along the banks. At last the water became salty, and La Salle knew that he was near the sea. Rounding a bend, he saw before him the waters of the Gulf of Mexico and knew that he was the first European to complete the long journey from the great inland lakes to the Gulf of Mexico.

The Frenchmen set up a column and put on it the name of the French king and the date, April 9, 1682. With the Indians looking on, they chanted a hymn of praise, fired their guns, raised their flag, and announced to the world that all lands and peoples of the entire Mississippi River valley belonged to King Louis the Fourteenth of France.

"I name thee Louisiana!" La Salle shouted, and the Frenchmen cheered for the new empire.

When La Salle got back to Canada, he found that Count Frontenac had returned to France. The men who were in power would give him no help. He went to France and persuaded the king to put him in command of an expedition to start colonies. It was decided that this time he should start at the mouth of the great Mississippi, at the Gulf of Mexico.

The expedition to that region met with disaster. One of La Salle's ships was captured by the Spaniards. The others missed the mouth of the Mississippi and went along the coast hunting for it until they landed four hundred miles too far west. In a section of what is now Texas, La Salle and his men nearly starved. For two years he searched up and down the coast and then decided to start by land for Canada. Many of his men had already deserted, and others had turned against him. One of his own party shot him, and so his life ended in those southern lands which he had claimed for France.

Several years passed before other Frenchmen awakened to the importance of La Salle's project. Then forts were built along the Mississippi, and a small colony was started which grew into the city of New Orleans. The line of French settlements—most of them hardly more than forts—now lay in a great curve across America from north to south, like a sickle with its handle in Canada, its slender blade reaching across the Great Lakes and down the Mississippi, and its point at New Orleans.

One of these settlements was at Detroit. It was founded in 1701 by a French fur trader, Antoine Cadillac. With him came fifty soldiers and fifty settlers. All the long way from Montreal these men had paddled, pushed, and carried their canoes, which were heavily loaded with provisions, tools, supplies for building, guns, and gunpowder. It was with rejoicing that they came ashore at this beautiful spot. The river was bordered by trees bending under the weight of their fruit. In the woods and on the prairies beyond, deer, turkeys, pheasants, and quail abounded. Here, at Detroit, Cadillac began to build the first permanent settlement in this lake country.

Cadillac marked out a space of a little less than an acre which the men enclosed by a high palisade. This was made of small tree trunks driven into the ground. At the four

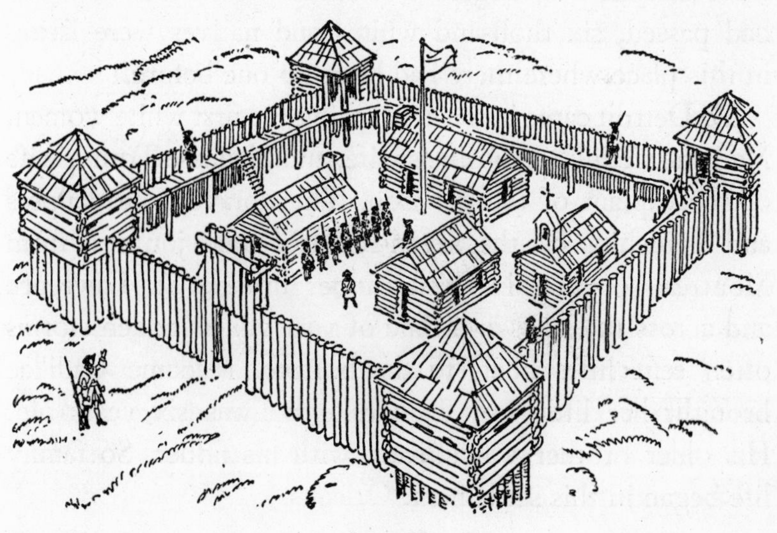

corners the walls were built out so that soldiers could stand and shoot along the outer sides of the fence. Inside, Cadillac laid out a street twelve feet wide with small lots marked out along it which the settlers could buy. Fifty hours after their landing the soldiers began a chapel which was finished within a month. Storehouses were put up, then log huts for homes. Before the end of August the settlement was well under way, and wheat had been sown for the next summer.

Cadillac was a rough, active soldier, just the man to start a frontier post and handle the Indians. From years of experience he had made his plan. The best way to protect the little settlement and encourage trade would be to have it surrounded by a ring of friendly Indians. He summoned nearby chiefs to a council and invited them to come and build villages under French protection. Within three months they began to arrive, and long before a year had passed, six thousand whites and natives were living in this place where there had been no one before.

To Detroit came in the next spring the first white women, Madame Cadillac, Antoine's wife, and Madame Tonty, wife of the captain of the garrison. They braved the dangers and hardships of the seven-hundred-mile journey from Montreal, coming in open canoes up the St. Lawrence and across the lakes at a time of year when sudden storms often sent little boats to the bottom. Madame Cadillac brought her little boy Jacques, who was six years old. His older brother was already with his father. So family life began in this settlement.

Fifty years after the founding of Detroit a notice was posted in all the villages along the St. Lawrence River. It showed the eagerness of the governor general of Canada to make the new colony a settlement instead of a frontier fort. This was his offer:

> Every man who will go to settle in Detroit shall receive one spade, one ax, one plow, one large and one small wagon. We will make an advance of two other tools to be paid for in two years only. He will be given a cow, also a sow. Seed will be advanced the first year, to be returned at the third harvest. The women and children will be supported for one year.

To that call one hundred persons responded at once. If the French could have persuaded more families to come to Detroit and other lonely frontier forts, they would have stood a better chance of holding their great inland empire. There were many forts and missions, but the settlements near them remained small.

Trouble came in America when the French and English met. The struggle was the more sharp because France and England were fighting a series of wars all over the world. The wars in North America were part of that great hundred-year struggle. There were raids by the French and Indians on the frontier settlements of New England, and battles in northern New York and in Nova Scotia. The final struggle began in the Ohio Valley. It was called the French and Indian War.

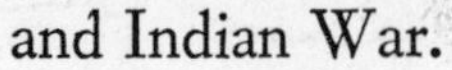

Two men came to the Ohio Valley in the years 1749 and 1750. One was a Frenchman; the other was from Virginia.

The Frenchman arrived first. Reports had reached Montreal that the English were crossing the Blue Ridge and the Allegheny Mountains and claiming lands along the Ohio River. The governor of New France sent Pierre Joseph Céloron, a military man nearly sixty years old, to reinforce the French claims.

Céloron started out from Montreal. He went down the Ohio River, warning the Indians to have nothing to do with the English. According to the French custom he stopped at each important point and laid claim to the land. He had with him a number of leaden plates on which the French king's claim was written. These he buried, one by one, and over each one he nailed to a tree the emblem of France. Then he returned to Montreal to report.

In the next year Christopher Gist, a frontiersman from the Virginia colony, came to the valley of the Ohio. Gist was looking over the country for a group of Virginia gentlemen who had obtained from the king of England a huge grant of land.

Gist was a surveyor. He went up and down the rivers and streams making maps, and into the Indian villages making friends. When he returned to Virginia, he reported:

> It is fine, rich, level land, well timbered with large walnut, ash, sugar maple, and cherry trees, well watered with a great number of little streams and rivulets; full of beautiful natural meadows with wild rye, bluegrass, and clover, and abounding with turkey, deer, elks, and particularly buffaloes—thirty or forty of which are frequently seen in one meadow.

YOUNG GEORGE WASHINGTON

Two years went by, and reports were brought to the governor of Virginia that the French had begun building forts in the Ohio country, driving out Englishmen, and winning the Indians over to their side. The governor decided to send a protest. To carry it, he chose the best Virginian he could find, George Washington. Young Washington was then twenty-one years old. He had had some military experience, and he was a surveyor.

Washington started in the middle of November, 1753, taking with him Christopher Gist and several others. They had a hard journey over two mountain ranges to a French fort on the upper Ohio River. There Washington was courteously received by the commander. But as he sat at supper with the French officers, he heard them say, "We mean to take possession of the Ohio."

The journey back in midwinter was through deep snow. Finding it impossible to get the horses through, Washington left them with his men while he and Gist pushed on afoot with their packs on their backs.

They had to walk in the beds of frozen streams and sleep in the woods with no tent to protect them. Washington nearly lost his life when his raft overturned in a rushing stream packed with pieces of moving ice.

When they did get back to Virginia, Washington gave the governor the letter which he had brought from the French commander and also his own journal of the trip. In it were careful drawings of the enemy forts and also an account of the western country. This report, which was published, made young Washington known through the colonies and in England.

The same year he returned to the Ohio River, where the French were occupying two forts. He fought his first battle in a night attack on a company of French soldiers. Moving up the river, he and his men camped at a place near the Forks of the Ohio. Here they built a small fort, which they named Fort Necessity. A month later it was attacked by a large army of French and Indians, and Washington was forced to surrender it. He returned to Virginia. But a few months later he came back with General Braddock, who was leading a British army against the French.

This expedition was defeated. The general was killed. Washington had his horse shot under him, and his coat and hat were cut by bullets. But he came through safely and led the survivors back to Virginia.

The memory of Washington's bravery and military skill in this Ohio warfare lasted long. It helped to make him the leading soldier of the colonies.

At the close of the French and Indian War, he was elected to the Virginia House of Burgesses. As he took his seat, the speaker of the house, a courtly older man by the name of John Robinson, welcomed him and thanked him, on behalf of the Virginia colony, for his recent military service. Washington rose, blushed, tried to speak, stammered, swallowed, and could not manage to utter a sound.

Mr. Robinson came to his rescue, saying with a smile: "Sit down, Mr. Washington. Your modesty is equal to your valor; and that surpasses the power of any language I possess."

The defeat of Braddock had left the whole western frontier open to savage attacks by the Indians. There followed other British defeats on northern and western battlefields. At last England became roused as the war with France went against her not only in North America but in India and elsewhere. A wise Englishman, William Pitt, was put in charge of the war.

Pitt sent an army of twenty-two thousand British soldiers overseas to defend

the English colonies in America, and chose able young generals to lead them. One of these men, General James Wolfe, captured Quebec in 1759 from its brave French defender, the Marquis de Montcalm.

Both generals lost their lives in the battle on the Plains of Abraham outside the city of Quebec. Canada gives to both equal honor. In the governor's garden at Quebec there stands a monument to the two. Under their names is this inscription: "Valor gave them a common death; history, a common fame."

This monument is a symbol of the union of French and British in Canada which has continued to the present. When peace was signed between England and France in 1763, France gave to England all of Canada and all her lands east of the Mississippi River. To Spain, because of help in the war, France gave as much of Louisiana as lay west of the Mississippi River, and also New Orleans.

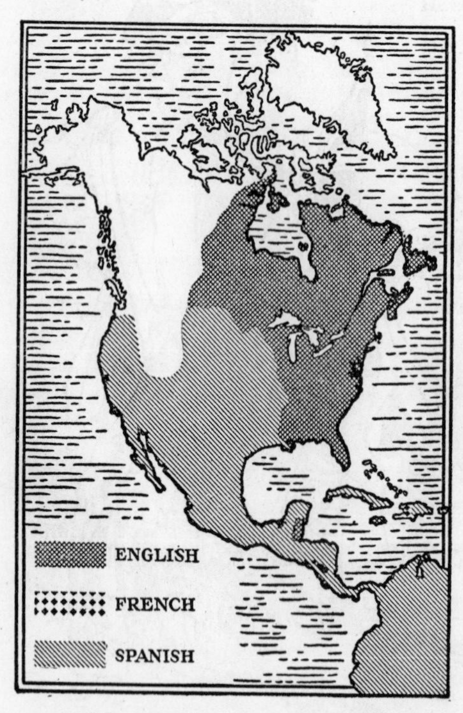

North America in 1763

The French flag was pulled down in North America but the French people stayed on. It was part of the treaty of peace that the long-time French settlers should be protected by law. Since that time the two peoples, the French and the English, have lived side by side. Canada is remarkable as a nation with two languages, both used for every official paper. Each people has kept its own speech and its own customs. Yet they sit together in their national assemblies, making up a united nation.

FRANKLIN URGES UNION FOR THE COLONIES

A traveler who visited America in 1748 noticed that each colony went its own way independently of the others. "Each may be looked upon as a state by itself," he wrote. Lack of union among the colonies was bothering many of the wiser leaders. Among these was Benjamin Franklin of Pennsylvania.

Benjamin Franklin has been called the first true American. Certainly he was wholly American. He saw everything from the American point of view and belonged to all America, not simply to one colony or group of colonies.

He was born in Boston, Massachusetts, in 1706, the fifteenth of seventeen children of a candlemaker. When he was seventeen years old he ran away from home and got a job in a printing office in Philadelphia. Before he was twenty he went to London to buy type and other printers' supplies. There he worked at his trade to get money to come home. When he returned to Philadelphia, he set up his own printing shop.

Soon he bought a newspaper which was failing, named it the *Pennsylvania Gazette,* and made it the most successful paper in the colonies. Newspaper men say that he was the first to have a cartoon in his paper, that he published the first weather report and put in the first bits of humor, and that he started the custom of having an editorial column. He also published comments on government and freedom which the people of Pennsylvania and other colonies liked to read.

Franklin was not the first to urge union of the colonies. There had been such plans since the early days of settlement. Groups of colonies had united for defense of the frontiers against the Indians. But such unions lasted only as long as the colonists needed protection for themselves and their homes.

Franklin saw other reasons why the colonies should unite. He took a carefully worked-out plan for union to Albany in 1754. A meeting had been called there to plan defense against the French. He also took the first American cartoon, a little picture showing the colonies as parts of a snake, with the words "Join or Die" printed below.

Another delegate to that meeting told how far apart the colonists were in their ways and ideas. It was as if the delegates were ambassadors from different countries. Copies of the Albany plan were taken back to each colony, but not a single assembly approved of it.

"Why should we look beyond our own borders for trouble?" the men said. "We have enough to do looking after our own affairs."

Franklin was already helping toward union in another way, a way which everyone liked. He had been postmaster of Philadelphia. In 1753 he was made deputy postmaster general for the colonies under the British postal system. He went at once up and down the country to visit the little post offices, and began to speed up the service.

There must be post roads, he said, along which riders could carry the mail more swiftly. Roads brought the people of the colonies closer together. For many years they had depended only on the ships that went from one Atlantic port to another. Swifter mail meant news not only in letters but in newspapers, which reported what was happening in other colonies. All this was very important when the colonies came to unite for independence.

Each colony was in many ways a state by itself, though all were under English rule. No two colonies were ruled in exactly the same way. The differences came from the way the colonies were started, some by proprietors, some by companies with trading charters, and others more independently.

Maryland, Pennsylvania, and the newer little colony of Delaware, which had been set up under the Penns, were managed by their proprietors. Seven colonies were royal provinces, among them Virginia and New York as well as the newer colonies of North and South Carolina, Georgia, New Jersey, and New Hampshire. Connecticut and Rhode Island, which had begun as self-governing colonies, had managed to stay so, with precious charters of their own. Massachusetts was a royal province but had its own charter. It had governors appointed by the king, with whom it often quarreled, but it had also a General Court which controlled its local affairs. Massachusetts men had become accustomed to working together, in their town meetings and assemblies, for good government. It was no secret that the king and his Parliament found Massachusetts the most difficult of the colonies to manage.

TROUBLE OVER TAXES

Troubles began over taxes, though there was much more to the matter than money. England needed money. The war with France had cost a great deal. British armies had been sent to America to protect the colonists and drive back the French and Indians. Britain was still having to keep a large army of soldiers in America to guard the new frontiers and police the northern boundaries. King George III and his ministers began to look for ways to get the money that was needed.

One way was to tax American trade. This was done, and then Parliament passed a Stamp Act. Every official paper, such as a deed to land bought, every newspaper, and all almanacs must have stamps placed on them. Money from the sale of these stamps would help to pay the expenses of the English army which was protecting the colonies. The money, raised in America, was to be spent for Americans. No one in England expected any trouble to come from this tax, except the usual protest against any new tax. But Americans thought differently. Patrick Henry expressed their ideas when he spoke in the Virginia House of Burgesses in 1765.

Patrick Henry was a young Virginia lawyer who had been elected to the assembly after winning a case in court as champion of people's rights. The newcomer, a tall,

plainly dressed, awkward fellow, rose in that assembly of distinguished men and began to address them. Englishmen, he declared, could not be taxed without their consent. From the time when the first adventurers and settlers came to the shores of America, they had been granted by the king all the liberties which would be theirs if they were living in England. Now these liberties were being taken away from them by the Stamp Act.

"The taxation of people by themselves, or by persons chosen by themselves to represent them, is the distinguishing characteristic of British freedom," declared Patrick Henry.

Virginia protested the Stamp Act. Other colonies followed her example. Protests were sent to England, and the Stamp Act was finally repealed by Parliament. The colonies had begun, however, to watch their rights. When new taxes were placed on paper, glass, tea, and other articles imported from England, the colonists grew angry. When officers began to search their homes, the excitement became intense.

A leading patriot of New England was Samuel Adams of Boston. He set himself to rouse the people. He wrote many pamphlets, arranged meetings of protest, and even started street riots. Most important of all, he got committees organized all through the colonies, and arranged that they should write to one another news of happenings in their regions. At a time when news was carried slowly and newspapers were few, these committees did much to unite the colonies and rouse public feeling.

King George III was a stupid and obstinate person. While Parliament wisely held back and did not press the acts which so disturbed the colonists, the king said: "We must still keep a tax on something, to show that we have the right to tax the colonies."

THE BOSTON TEA PARTY

One of the king's ministers worked out a clever scheme. He hoped to tempt the colonists into paying a tax, and also to help out the East India Company, which needed money and had a very large supply of tea in its English storehouses. It was arranged that the company should send a large amount of its tea to American ports. The price for this tea, with a small tax included, would be less than the regular price in Boston and other colonial markets. The American buyers would save money, but they would also pay the tax. Ships bringing the tea arrived in several American ports.

Samuel Adams and the other Boston patriots protested to the royal governor of Massachusetts that the tea must not be unloaded. The ships must be sent back with the tea untouched. The governor refused to give the order.

"Boston harbor will be a teapot tonight," said one of the patriots. He knew what plans had been made.

A group of the patriots, disguised as Indians so that they would not be recognized, dashed to the wharf where the tea ships lay. They rushed aboard, broke open with their hatchets more than three hundred chests of tea, and threw the sweet-smelling stuff into the water. Great crowds of people stood on the shore watching and sniffing the air while twenty thousand dollars' worth of British property went into the harbor.

Paul Revere, a skillful silversmith well known in Boston, was probably one of the "Indians." He was a most active and useful patriot. Two weeks before the "tea party" he had ridden to Philadelphia, taking the news that the tea was coming. Other colonies were also warned. They too refused to allow ships, when they arrived, to land their tea. After the "tea party" Revere rode south again, to take the news to the Southern colonies.

British officials were thoroughly roused by this American defiance. Indeed, the more cool-headed of the American leaders disapproved. A new governor, General Gage, who had been with the British armies on the western frontier, was sent to Massachusetts. His orders were to close the port of Boston to all shipping and to keep it closed until the people paid for the tea destroyed and showed themselves willing to be good subjects of the king.

General Gage, a calm, efficient person, carried out his orders thoroughly. The port was closed. Not a sail was raised on the water front. To keep it closed and maintain order, General Gage brought five thousand red-coated British soldiers to Boston.

This punishment of Massachusetts angered many colonists who had accepted the taxes calmly. It aroused the patriots in other colonies. They sent wagonloads of food and other supplies to blockaded Boston. They also called a meeting at Philadelphia to discuss what should be done.

THE FIRST CONTINENTAL CONGRESS

To this meeting, which was held on September 5, 1774, came delegates from every colony except Georgia. Among them were Samuel Adams, Patrick Henry, John Adams, George Washington, Benjamin Franklin, and other wise leaders. After much discussion for over a month, these men drew up a statement of their rights and their complaints and sent it to England. They also agreed that colonists should neither buy English goods nor sell anything to

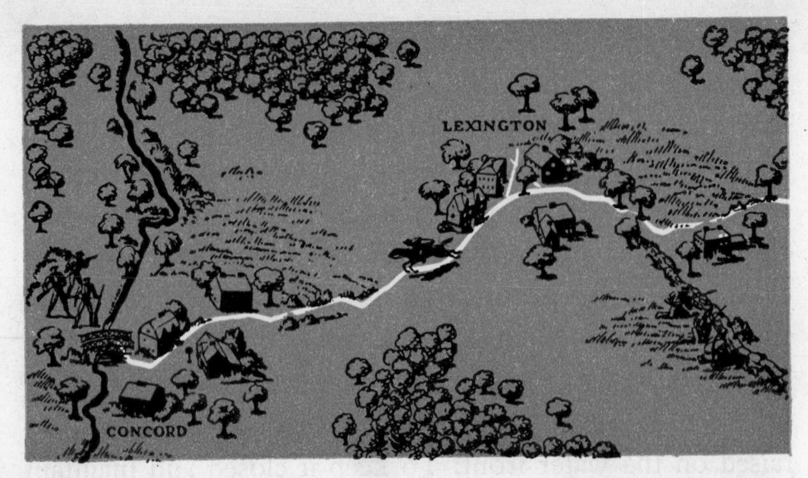

PAUL REVERE'S RIDE. *Revere was captured after leaving Lexington.*

England. The meetings of the First Continental Congress showed for the first time that the colonies could act together. The delegates set May 10, 1775, as the date for the meeting of the Second Continental Congress.

LEXINGTON, CONCORD, AND BUNKER HILL

The patriots of Massachusetts organized groups of "minutemen," who would be ready to fight, if necessary, at a minute's notice.

General Gage knew that the patriots had supplies of ammunition stored at the little village of Concord, Massachusetts, twenty miles or so outside Boston. These it was his duty to destroy. He prepared to send a thousand of his men to take them, and the patriots learned of the plan. On the night when the British were to start, Paul Revere mounted his horse and sped toward Lexington and Concord

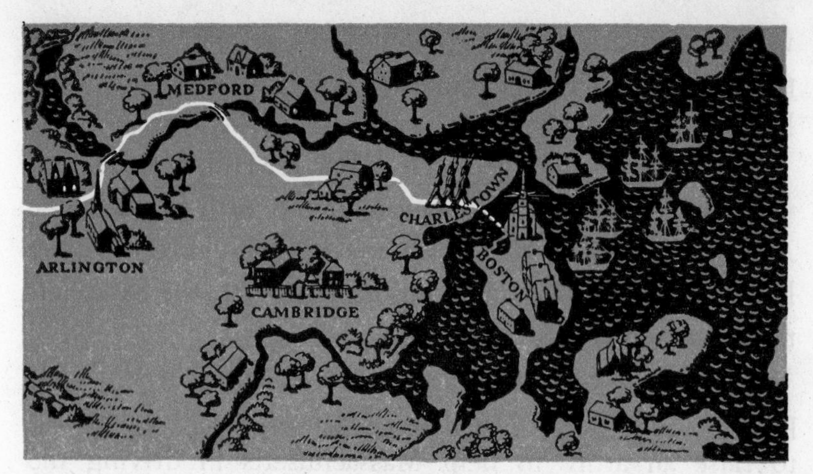

Dawes escaped. A third man carried the warning on to Concord.

with the news that the British were coming. Another rider, William Dawes, took a different route.

At dawn on April 19, fifty minutemen were waiting for the marching British redcoats when they arrived at Lexington Green. The leader of the patriots had given to his men the command: "Don't fire unless fired upon; but if they mean to have war, let it begin here!"

There was firing. Eight of the patriots were killed, and ten wounded. The redcoats marched on to Concord, where more patriots had gathered hastily at a wooden bridge. More shots were fired and men on both sides were killed. The American poet Emerson later wrote that these opening shots of the Revolution were "heard round the world."

The British destroyed the guns and ammunition which they had come to find. As they marched back along the road to Boston, they found the countryside had been warned. Farmers shot at them from behind every stone wall. The march turned into a hasty retreat, and before the troops reached Boston, nearly a fourth of the men who had started that morning had been killed or wounded.

On June 17, 1775, the battle of Bunker Hill, near Boston, was fought with heavy losses on the British side. The Americans were driven from the hill only because they had used up all their ammunition. However, the battle left the British in control of Boston.

The Continental Congress, then meeting in Philadelphia, still hoped for peace with England. But it voted also to raise an army to help Massachusetts in driving the British out of Boston. George Washington was appointed commander in chief of that army. He could not act until the following year, for he had neither trained men nor supplies. Meanwhile a strong feeling in favor of separation from England spread through the colonies.

THE DECLARATION OF INDEPENDENCE

Thomas Paine, who had lately come from England, was helping to prepare the people of the colonies for independence. In a pamphlet called *Common Sense* he declared, "A new method of thinking has arisen. Every spot in the Old World is overrun with oppression. The birthday of a New World is at hand."

He said that America was the child not only of England, but of America. It was absurd for a continent to be governed by an island. A hundred and twenty thousand copies of this pamphlet were distributed in the colonies during the early months of 1776. Everywhere patriots quoted it and agreed with Paine.

In June, in the Continental Congress at Philadelphia, Richard Henry Lee of Virginia moved that "These united colonies are and ought to be free and independent states." John Adams of Massachusetts seconded the motion. A committee, of which Thomas Jefferson was a member, was appointed to write a Declaration of Independence. Jefferson wrote it—out of his heart and head, as he said, without turning to book or pamphlet. John Adams and Franklin, also on the committee, made slight changes in it. On July 4, 1776, the document was adopted by the Congress. The signing came later. The bell ringer of Independence Hall, where the Congress was meeting, rang out the news. A new nation had been born.

The War of Independence, which is also called the American Revolution, was fought to win the independence which had been so boldly declared.

Washington had taken command of the troops at Cambridge, Massachusetts, in July, 1775. In March, 1776, he forced the British to leave Boston. They attacked New York, and Washington's army was too small to defend it successfully. He had to retreat across New Jersey and the Delaware River, but he returned at the very end of the year 1776 and won battles at Trenton and Princeton, both in New Jersey. Washington's army became small. Little by little, so many men left and returned to their homes that he had hardly more than three thousand men during this winter in New Jersey. The colonies were not united in their support of the Continental Congress. Their new state governments had little power. Neither these governments nor Congress supplied the necessary money for carrying on the war.

The British held New York and wished to take Philadelphia, which was the largest city in the colonies. Washington delayed them for a time, but was defeated at Germantown. He and his little army spent a hard winter at Valley Forge, twenty miles north of Philadelphia.

Meanwhile, in the north, a British army under General Burgoyne started southward from Canada in the summer of 1777. It was his purpose to take the upper Hudson River and cut the colonies in two by separating New England

THE REVOLUTION IN THE NORTHWEST AND SOUTHEAST

from the other states. He was defeated at Saratoga, New York, in October, 1777, in one of the most important battles of the war. News of this victory came to Washington at Valley Forge. At this time, too, France decided to come to the aid of the United States. She promised to send supplies, money, soldiers, and ships.

The British attacked also in the Ohio Valley, but were outwitted by George Rogers Clark, who made long, daring marches and captured strong forts on the western frontier as far as the Mississippi.

Other British forces moved into the South, capturing Savannah, Georgia, and Charleston, South Carolina. For two years bitter fighting went on in this region. In 1781, Lord Cornwallis, the British commander, moved his army into Virginia. Lafayette, a young Frenchman, who was in command of a small American army, was sent there. At this time a French fleet came up from the West Indies to help the Americans. General Washington saw his chance. He brought a strong army from New Jersey to join Lafayette's army. Troops came ashore from the French ships to fight. Cornwallis and his army were surrounded at Yorktown. In October, 1781, he surrendered. This brought the war practically to an end. It had been fought from Canada to Georgia and from the Atlantic to the Mississippi.

When a war is over, the record of individual men and their bravery is recalled more often than the details of battles and the way they were won. Many men showed high courage in the American Revolution. Here are stories of some of them.

ETHAN ALLEN AT TICONDEROGA

In the early hours of a May morning in 1775, three weeks to a day after the fighting at Lexington and Concord, a small company of Vermont men crossed the southern end of Lake Champlain to surprise the British at their Fort Ticonderoga. Leading them was Ethan Allen, so tall and broad-shouldered that he towered like a giant above his "Green Mountain Boys," who were themselves of more than average height.

They had been hastily gathered when word came from Connecticut and Massachusetts that the patriots wanted this fort taken. Along the backwoods trails Ethan Allen had gone afoot, sounding the call which was like the "deep boom of a war drum." Another man who had gone out to give the call had run sixty miles through the wilderness in less than twenty-four hours, a record which an Indian could hardly match. At the call hunters, trappers, and back-country farmers dropped whatever they were doing and hurried to the meeting place on the lake.

At Fort Ticonderoga the British officer in command had not even heard of the clashes at Lexington and Concord. He was wakened by the sounds of the arriving men, who had surprised and captured his sentry. Half-dressed, he came hurrying out of his room. On the stairs he was met by Ethan Allen with a sword in his hand. The British officer demanded, "By what authority have you entered His Majesty's fort?"

In his booming voice Ethan Allen replied, "In the name of the Great Jehovah and the Continental Congress."

The fort was taken without fighting. With less than fifty men the officer had no choice but to surrender it.

General Washington needed desperately the cannon and other military supplies which were captured at Ticonderoga, but he had to wait until there was snow on the ground. In December a young American colonel, Henry Knox, went to get the fifty-nine cannon, the cannon balls, and other valuable ammunition.

He had these heavy pieces brought across the lake on flat-bottomed boats. Then his men cut trees and put together forty-two sleds, for which Colonel Knox somehow got hold of eighty-one yoke of oxen. The procession of guns moved past Saratoga and Albany, east through the mountains to Springfield, and on to

Cambridge, with the people all along the way coming out to look at them. It was a big task to bring those cannon two hundred miles through forest country covered with deep snow.

When the guns arrived in January, 1776, General Washington had them set up on some hills overlooking Boston, where the British troops were quartered. On March 17 the English took to their ships in the harbor and departed from Boston.

NATHAN HALE

Nathan Hale of Connecticut was a young man of good family who had graduated from Yale College and was teaching school when the call for volunteers came after the battle of Lexington. He joined Washington's army, spent four months with it near Boston, and then went to New York, which the British were trying to take. If they could do this, they could move with their fleet up the Hudson and cut New England off from the Southern colonies. General Washington needed to know what the British were planning to do next.

If only someone could go inside the enemy lines and get the information and bring it safely back, the British plans might be successfully opposed. Young Nathan Hale volunteered for this mission. He disguised himself by changing his officer's uniform for a plain suit of citizen's brown with a round, broad-brimmed hat. He was going to pass himself off as a Dutch schoolmaster. He went inside the British lines and got his information, but was caught with drawings of the New York forts and other papers as he was leaving four days later.

Some say he was betrayed by a man whom the patriots had trusted. At once he declared his name and rank, giving, as the British report said, "his own full confession." That was like him. If he must die, he would not deny that he was on this mission for his country's good. The next day he was put to death as a spy. His last words everyone should know: "I only regret that I have but one life to lose for my country."

MEN AND LEADERS AT VALLEY FORGE

The name Valley Forge will always stand to Americans for the bitter suffering of the men who spent the winter of 1777–1778 at that place. It is about twenty miles from Philadelphia. In that city the British were comfortably encamped, well housed, and well fed. At Valley Forge the American army was starving in the midst of plenty. General Washington had only paper money, put out by the Continental Congress, to offer the prosperous farmers of the valley for their products. The British had gold with which to bid for and get all the food there was. Even the horses were dying for lack of forage, and soldiers were harnessing themselves with grapevines to drag little wagons which they had built.

As bad as the shortage of food was the lack of clothing and shoes. In the bitter cold, few of the men had shoes. The lines of their marches and drills could be traced by bloodstains on the frozen ground. They had no uniforms; indeed, there was no regular American uniform until the fourth year of the war. Most of the soldiers did not have enough clothing of any kind to cover them. Blankets and anything else that could be cut into some kind of shape were used as garments. Yet they had their leader, their beloved General Washington. While many of the men gave up and went home, unable to endure the misery, those who stayed developed a tremendous loyalty to their chief.

General Washington shared their misfortunes. Even on his Christmas dinner table he had no bread, sugar, coffee, tea, or milk.

While the British soldiers were living idly in the city, the Americans were drilling for battle. In the poorly equipped camp at Valley Forge were some officers from Europe who had crossed the ocean to help in the fight for freedom. Baron von Steuben, a German military man, raged at the lack of food and arms and clothing. He scolded, too, about the great independence of the American soldiers, who did not take kindly to being drilled. But the baron was admiring these ragged heroes even while he scolded them. The young French Marquis de Lafayette was

also there, giving cheer to General Washington and sharing his misfortunes.

Early in August of 1777 the general had received a letter from Franklin, then representing the new nation in France. It said:

> The Marquis de Lafayette, a young nobleman of great family connections here and great wealth, is gone to America in a ship of his own, accompanied by some officers of distinction, in order to serve in our armies. He is exceedingly beloved, and everybody's good wishes attend him.

The Frenchman was not yet twenty years old when he arrived. He was a slender, good-looking youth, with large eyes and a quiet, aristocratic manner. There were several reasons for his coming. He was an adventurer, eager for fighting. Frenchmen still remembered their defeat and the loss of their American colonies. If England could now be made to lose those same colonies, they would be well pleased. In addition, Lafayette had a real interest in the cause of freedom.

Congress accepted Lafayette's offer of service and made him an officer. He and General Washington became close friends. The friendship began in that winter at Valley Forge. Washington was embarrassed to show to this young nobleman his little army of ragged, ill-fed men. He said so, and was touched by Lafayette's instant reply, "I am here, sir, to learn and not to teach."

When the young officer was wounded in a battle, General Washington said to the doctor, "Treat him as if he were my son, for I love him as if he were."

It was important in those days of hardship and discouragement that Washington had such a friend. Lafayette's influence was also helpful in bringing French troops across the seas to fight on the American side.

JOHN PAUL JONES

In a letter written in England early in the war there was this report:

> A strange flag lately appeared in our seas bearing a pine tree with a rattlesnake coiled at its root, with the daring words, "Don't tread on me." We learned that the vessels bearing this flag have a sort of commission from a society of people in Philadelphia calling themselves the "Continental Congress."

A rattlesnake flag much like this was one of the flags carried into English waters by a sturdy American captain named John Paul Jones. He was only five feet six inches

tall, with a broad chest and unusually long arms, sandy hair, and keen blue-gray eyes. Born in Scotland, he had come to America in 1773. After the battle of Lexington he wrote to Congress, offering his services.

At that time there was no American navy, and the English fleet was moving from place to place along our coast, making much trouble for General Washington. The colonists had only merchant ships which they had fitted with guns. These ships were called privateers and were given authority to fight. They destroyed or captured many English trading vessels.

At the end of the year 1775, the Continental Congress created a navy. John Paul Jones was appointed senior lieutenant, and did fine service along our coasts. Then, in command of the *Ranger*, he was sent to France with dispatches. Congress, meanwhile, had adopted the Stars and Stripes as the American flag on June 14, 1777. Jones was the first to carry this flag into foreign waters and to receive an official salute from a foreign government.

When France came to the aid of America, she gave five vessels to the new American navy. Jones took these ships into British waters and won several victories. The most famous was that of the *Bonhomme Richard* over the English *Serapis*. After a bitter fight, the English commander saw that the American ship was badly damaged and afire. Sure that she must be ready to surrender, he shouted, "Have you struck your colors?"

"I have not yet begun to fight," John Paul Jones roared back, and he proceeded to prove it.

The English captain was forced at last to surrender to the victorious Americans, but by that time the *Bonhomme Richard* was sinking. The men sadly left her and reached port in the crippled *Serapis*.

The amazing victories of John Paul Jones were a challenge to England's claim that she was mistress of the seas.

GEORGE ROGERS CLARK

Most of the fighting of the Revolution was done along the seacoast, but a Virginian, George Rogers Clark, was out in the western settlements doing his part.

For some years settlers had been following the line of the Ohio River, making clearings along the banks, and building cabins and starting villages. When war came, the British officials in the Ohio country gave orders which let loose the Indians against these settlers. One raid followed another until the men were desperate. They must have help from the government back home in Virginia. They met in convention and sent young Clark to ask for help. He came to the capital, Williamsburg, where Patrick Henry was the new governor. Henry listened with sympathy and sent Clark back with five hundred pounds of powder for the settlers to use in their fighting.

It would have been hard for anyone to refuse Clark anything. A tall man, with broad forehead, keen blue eyes, and a dash of red in his hair, he had a way of making people see things as he did and convincing them that he could do whatever he set out to do.

The next year Clark and his frontiersmen captured several forts along the Ohio and the Mississippi. The British were unprepared to have any colonial soldiers appear out there, so many hundreds of miles from the scene of the main fighting.

In the winter of 1778 Clark set out with one hundred fifty men to capture the fort of Vincennes, on the Wabash River. General Hamilton, the British commander, was reported to be there. Clark and his men had to cross two hundred miles of "drowned lands." The snow was melting in February thaws. The icy rivers were overflowing. At night, after a day's march through water that was often up to the men's waists, they would come to a place where the wood was so wet that no fire could be started, and there was no shelter of any kind.

On the march Clark went from one end of the line to the other, encouraging the men. He had a little drummer boy, a French lad, whose gay cheerfulness helped everyone. When the rains swelled the streams until tall men were up to their shoulders in water, the drummer boy, who could not keep his footing, was seen floating along on his drum. A young giant picked up the lad and carried him on his shoulders. Sitting there, the lad drummed gaily away. Once more the men pushed on.

They came across the last waters to Vincennes. Though they had lost their baggage long since, the men had kept the flags with which each little company had started. These were on tall poles, and the men marched back and forth with them, behind and around low slopes and heights. The people looking out from the settlement counted the same dozen pairs of flags again and again and were deceived. They were sure that the few men they saw were part of a large army. The fort was taken, and General Hamilton surrendered. The French folk who still lived at Vincennes were glad to see Americans in command in place of the English.

When the terms of the treaty of peace were fixed at the end of the Revolution, men saw the importance of Clark's victory. If it had not been for his conquest of this region, the territory out of which were made the five states of Ohio, Indiana, Illinois, Michigan, and Wisconsin might have belonged to the British instead of the United States.

WASHINGTON, COMMANDER IN CHIEF

Other men played important parts in the War for Independence, but George Washington led them all. The command of the American armies which Congress entrusted to him, he held through the seven years of war. To him the Americans owed their victory. He kept the armies together through dark years and made the plans by which they won in the end.

Washington was forty-three years old when he took the position of commander in chief. It was twenty years since he had served as an officer in the war with the French and the Indians on the Ohio River, but his brilliant service there had been remembered. In the years between, he had been a Virginia planter, making his home on his estate at Mount Vernon. He had traveled much in the newly acquired West and in the South, and therefore knew the country as few men knew it. He had served in the assemblies which governed Virginia. But he had never done anything like that which was needed in this war.

He had no regular army. Volunteers served for a time, and then went home when cold weather came or farm crops

were ready for harvesting. There were only a few trained officers to drill the men. There was never enough money to buy supplies or pay the troops properly. Yet Washington inspired the men with his own spirit. He shared their hardships. Everyone knew that he accepted nothing for his services except his expenses. In the darkest hours of the war he kept his courage and encouraged others.

Washington saw his armies defeated again and again. There were times when all seemed lost. But he made new plans and waited patiently for the chance to strike new blows. The war was fought in campaigns in many sections of the country. Yet all the plans worked out together. The British never knew where the next attack would come.

Washington's own men honored him and trusted him. They were ready to follow where he led. Sometimes he had to wait for months or even years for his opportunities. But when they came, he moved quickly. The British generals came to respect him as a dangerous enemy.

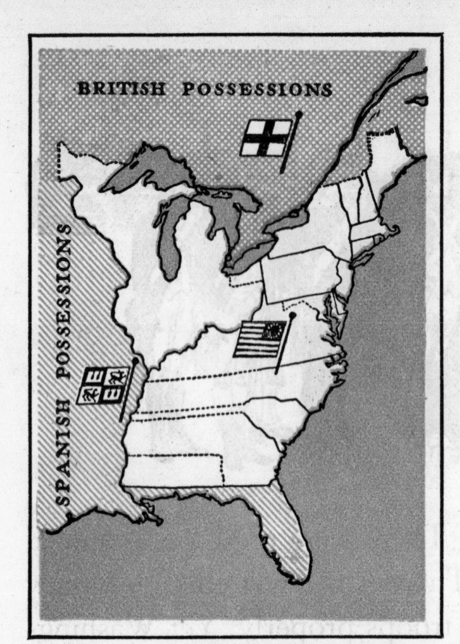

THE UNITED STATES, 1783

When the war was over, Washington said good-by to his officers and went home to Mount Vernon. He was weary of military life and was anxious to return to his farm.

A NEW NATION AND A NEW FLAG

By the treaty of peace of 1783, England agreed that the United States was a "free and independent nation." Its lands were to extend westward to the Mississippi River. England kept Canada. Spain was in possession of Florida and the lands on the Gulf of Mexico as well as those west of the Mississippi.

In 1750, three flags had floated over North America—the English flag over England's colonies, the Spanish flag over Spain's territory, and the French flag over New France. At the end of the century flags still floated over North America, but the picture had changed. The French flag was gone. The English flag had taken its place in Canada. The Spanish flag still floated in regions to the south. Between these two, over lands which had been either English or French, there floated a new flag. The stars and stripes of this American flag stood for thirteen colonies which had come together to make a new nation. Of that flag, which was adopted by Congress on June 14, 1777, Washington said:

> We take the star from Heaven, the red from our mother country, separating it by white stripes, thus showing that we have separated from her, and the white stripes shall go down to posterity representing liberty.

Although the flag had changed, the same people remained. Except for groups who had moved to Canada in order to stay under British rule, there were the same people living on the farms, in the towns and cities, and in the settlements on the frontier. But there had come to them a new loyalty to a new nation, their own United States. They did not forget the lands across the ocean from which they or their fathers or their grandfathers had come. They kept many of the customs of those homelands. They lived under forms of government which had come from England, but they were citizens of their own republic.

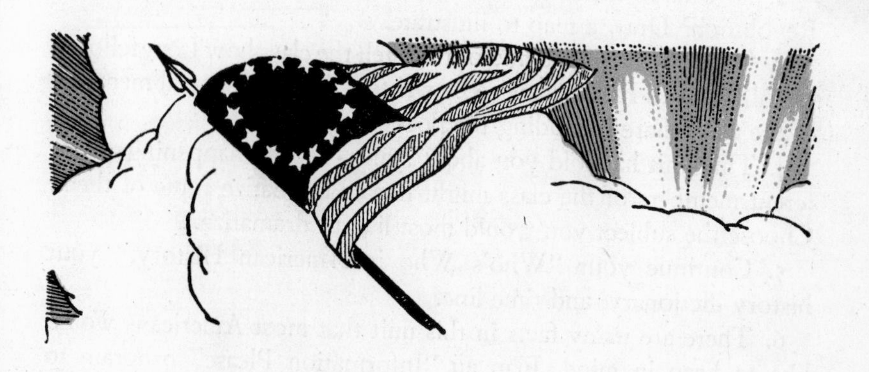

Talking Together

1. Making a Declaration of Independence and winning the American Revolution did not settle the difficulties of the colonists. What problems did they have to face next?

2. Until the American Revolution the people living in the United States were thought of as Englishmen, Frenchmen, Dutchmen, and so on. How had they lived and what had they done that was making them all into Americans?

3. When British soldiers sang "Yankee Doodle," they were making fun of the Yankees. Can you tell how? Find a copy of the song with all the verses and then sing them.

4. How was George Rogers Clark able to do so much with so few men?

Interesting Things to Try

1. Make a booklet called "Benjamin Franklin, American Patriot." Plan it carefully so as to include the many different kinds of activities in which he took part during his life. The booklet will make a fine gift for your classroom library. Different groups might make booklets about different men.

2. How large was the United States at the close of the American Revolution? Draw a map to illustrate.

3. Choose someone to find out and tell the class how Longfellow's "Paul Revere's Ride" came to be written. Then let several members of the class share in reading the poem aloud.

4. This unit has told you about many exciting happenings. Different members of the class might like to dramatize some of them. Choose the subject you would most like to dramatize.

5. Continue your "Who's Who in American History," your history dictionary, and time line.

6. There are many facts in this unit that most Americans would like to keep in mind. Plan an "Information Please" program to test your memory.

Learning How to Outline

An *outline* is a plan. A book like this one has to have a plan, or outline, before it can be written. This is necessary to make sure that all important points are included, and that they are arranged in the best order.

The title of this unit is "Americans Make a New Nation." The subject is taken up under three main divisions, which are not named in the text, but which would appear in an outline as A, B, and C.

Americans Make a New Nation

A. The French empire in America
B. The American Revolution
C. A new nation and a new flag

Each of these main divisions of the subject has many parts, or *major ideas*. These major ideas are often shown in the headings, or titles, of the different sections of the text. On a separate sheet of paper copy the following beginning of an outline of this unit:

Americans Make a New Nation

A. The French empire in America
   1. La Salle plans a French empire
   2. A French settlement at Detroit

Now find in your text the other section headings, or major ideas, which have something to do with "The French empire in America," and add them under A. Do the same for B. You will find only one heading for C, which is the summary, or conclusion, of the unit.

Major ideas are also made up of many *minor ideas*. Topic 1 under A has eleven paragraphs, and an outline of it would start like this:

1. La Salle plans a French empire
   a. Where the French hoped to settle
   b. Coming of La Salle to America

Find the other minor ideas under this topic in your text and add them to your outline.

Let's Read

A Book of Americans, by Rosemary and Stephen Vincent Benét. Poems about famous Americans.

George Washington's World, by Genevieve S. Foster. This book gives a clear idea of what was happening in Washington's time, not only in this country but in other parts of the world.

Watchwords of Liberty, by Robert Lawson. A beautifully illustrated book about quotations famous in American history.

Tonty of the Iron Hand, by Everett McNeil. An exciting story of a boy's adventures with La Salle and Tonty when they explored the Mississippi River.

Quiz Yourself

Number your paper from 1 to 5. After each number write down the letter of the choice that best completes the sentence.

1. The flags of three of these nations were flying in North America in 1750: (a) England, (b) Holland, (c) Spain, (d) France. Which nation had no flag there?
2. The first man who tried to work out a careful plan of union for the colonies was (a) Washington, (b) Samuel Adams, (c) Paul Revere, (d) Benjamin Franklin.
3. The wars between the French and English (a) drove the French out of North America; (b) left the French with only New Orleans; (c) left the English with less territory than before; (d) destroyed the settlements around the Great Lakes.
4. The United States became a separate nation when (a) the battle of Lexington and Concord was fought; (b) the Declaration of Independence was signed; (c) the treaty of peace was signed; (d) the people refused to pay the taxes England demanded.
5. When the war began, the colonies were fighting because (a) they hated England; (b) they wanted to be an independent nation; (c) they objected to the soldiers England had sent; (d) they wanted the rights of Englishmen.

VI NEW FRONTIERS IN A NEW NATION

WESTWARD TO THE MISSISSIPPI. *By the year 1800 the westward movement was in full swing. Settlers were pouring across the mountains into the Ohio and Mississippi valleys, forming territories which grew into states.*

NEW FRONTIERS IN A NEW NATION

During the war men from the different states had learned to know and respect one another. In 1787 a convention of delegates from the states met to form a new government. The Confederation which the states had formed during the war was not working well. There were bitter quarrels between the states. The Congress had been given little power to decide or to act.

FRAMING THE CONSTITUTION

Nearly all the real leaders then living in the United States sat down together in Independence Hall in Philadelphia to plan the new government. The delegates had been elected by their state legislatures. They were thus a truly representative company. Only Rhode Island failed to send delegates. Washington was made president of the Constitutional Convention.

The members worked together from May until September. Often they disagreed bitterly. Some delegates became so angry during the discussions that they went home.

The questions on which the members of the Convention disagreed were often very important. There were large states and small among the thirteen states. How should they be represented in the new Congress? The small states were afraid that the large ones would get all the power. The large states said that they had more people, and that those people had a right to be represented. How could both sides be suited? It was finally agreed that there should be two branches of Congress, a Senate and a House of Representatives. Each state, whether large or small, was to have two Senators. In the House of Representatives the number of members from each state was to depend on the population of that state. This is an example of the difficult matters which had to be decided.

James Madison, a young Virginian, took such an important part in the Constitutional Convention that he has been known ever since as the "Father of the Constitution." When the delegates had signed the Constitution, it was sent to the states. After much discussion all the thirteen states adopted it. The Constitution became the law of the land in 1789.

WASHINGTON AS THE FIRST PRESIDENT

New York City was chosen as the first capital of the nation. George Washington was elected the first President. He did not want the office, but he was told that he was the one man whom all the people would trust to start the new government.

He came from his home at Mount Vernon through Pennsylvania and New Jersey along the route where he had led armies. Everywhere the people came out to honor him. In New York, on April 30, 1789, he took the oath of office and became President of the United States. This office he held for eight years.

MACHINES AND A NEW KIND OF FREEDOM

During the same years in which Americans were set free by the Declaration of Independence, the Constitution, and their new government, men were set free in another way. The first machines began to do the work that hands and fingers and muscles had been doing for thousands of years.

In England James Watt was inventing a practical steam engine, and men were finding ways to spin and weave by machinery. James Hargreaves patented his spinning jenny, a machine in which a single wheel turned many spindles at the same time. This spinning jenny was run by hand and foot power. Richard Arkwright invented a spinning machine which used the running water of streams and waterfalls to supply power. In 1789, Edmund Cartwright set up his big loom for weaving by steam power.

In 1789, the year when Washington became President, a fresh-faced young Englishman landed in New York. England had made laws that no pattern or model of the new spinning machines was to go out of the country, and no mechanic who knew how to run them was to be allowed to take ship. Samuel Slater had somehow managed to get out of England although he had worked for seven years as a mechanic in the Arkwright shops.

From New York the young Englishman went to Rhode Island, where Moses Brown, a Quaker merchant, was interested in building spinning machines. After months of effort Slater succeeded in building machines which were run by water wheels, on the Arkwright plan. The old mill at Pawtucket, Rhode Island, where cotton spinning was first done in America by water-driven machinery, still stands. It was built in 1793.

From spinning thread to making cloth was only a short step. By 1800 the great cotton textile industry was well started in New England and New York.

At the close of the American Revolution farming was

the chief occupation of Americans. In the South one of the crops was cotton. Raising cotton was not, however, a profitable business because it took so long to prepare the plant for the market. The seeds were closely caught in the fibers, and could be separated only by hand. This was a slow process.

In 1793 Eli Whitney invented the cotton gin. He had gone South to teach, and meantime turned his mechanical skill to use by inventing a simple machine for cleaning cotton. His cotton gin, which was run by hand, would do the work of ten persons. If it could be connected to water power, such a machine would do the work of fifty persons.

The cotton gin changed the whole history of the South. It came at the time when the new spinning and weaving machines of England and America were ready to use all the cotton that could be produced. In 1808 seventy-five million pounds of cotton were produced, where there had been only a million and a half pounds in 1790.

Whitney soon turned his inventive skill to a new problem. The government needed guns, and needed them badly. Americans were buying many of their guns abroad. In case of war they would not be able to get them. The rest of the supply came from gunsmiths who made them slowly, one by one, by hand.

Whitney got a government contract to furnish a large number of guns at a very low price, and then retired to New Haven, Connecticut, to make them. He sent in a first small lot, and then for a couple of years no guns appeared. Government officials wrote letters insisting that they must have them.

In December, 1800, Whitney came to the new capital at Washington, D.C., and showed what he had been doing. He had brought with him the parts of a number of guns. These he laid out in piles on a table, and then he proceeded to put together muskets from the piles. Out of all the piles he made ten muskets, while the officials looked on in wonder.

Eli Whitney had seen that the only way to make guns quickly was to make up a quantity of every part of a gun separately. When these were made, the parts could be put together quickly. The trick to that plan was that all of a certain part had to be exactly alike. Then any piece would fit into its place with the other pieces. Whitney had spent his two years building machines for the making of the parts.

That way of doing things is taken for granted now. Modern automobiles, radios, clocks, and watches are all put together from separate pieces made by machines. In Whitney's time the idea was new. Every workman had been making all his own parts and fitting them carefully together to make one clock or one gun or one lock at a time.

The government got its guns at Whitney's low price and got them by the time they were needed, but more than that had happened. A new and quick American way of making things had been started.

DANIEL BOONE AND THE WILDERNESS ROAD

In the days when Washington and Patrick Henry and Samuel Adams and Paul Revere were working for freedom, other men were making their fight to settle in new lands which only the Indians and the buffaloes had held.

One of the most famous of these pioneers was Daniel Boone. He was born in Pennsylvania and spent his boyhood on its frontier, getting his education in the woods. When he was sixteen years old, his father went southward with his family to North Carolina to a frontier region of blue grass, large trees, and plenty of fish, fowl, and venison. Daniel liked to go on long hunting trips by himself. He left the misspelled record of one such trip carved on a tree: "D. Boon cilled a Bar on this tree 1760." Boone was with Braddock's army in 1755 and met Major Washington at that time.

As the years went by, Boone was always hearing of the wonderful land beyond the mountains which had "deer at every lick, birds in every bush, and herds of buffalo." On its meadows grew the rich bluegrass which was to give pasturage in later years to the fine horses of Kentucky. There were Indians ready to kill any settler who tried to make a home in their country. Cumberland Gap was the pass through which hunters entered *Kan-tuck-hee,* the "dark and bloody land" of the Indians. Boone led a party of six men into this wilderness, blazing the way which was to become the Wilderness Road, along which thousands of settlers traveled a few years later.

During two years of exploring, Boone's little party saw many thousands of buffaloes. When the rest of the party went back across the mountains, Boone stayed on alone, "without bread, salt or sugar, without company of fellow creatures or even a horse or a dog." Then he went back home, got his family, and persuaded other settlers to come to start a little settlement called Boonesborough. It was begun on April 2, 1775.

A fort was built on a new plan, which became the model for Kentucky pioneer settlements. The log dwelling houses were built into the wall of a big fort, with block houses for defense at the corners, and a strong gate for entrance.

Such a settlement could hold out for some time against Indian attack. Here young George Rogers Clark came with his father and mother to be neighbors of the Boones.

Until after the War of Independence, this western country was a part of Virginia. In 1792 it became the new state of Kentucky.

So long as there was need to fight the Indians and clear the wilderness, Boone stayed in Kentucky. When the settlers became too many, he moved on, seeking and finding another wilderness in Missouri. There he lived to be an old man and saw the frontier moving ever westward.

To the people of his own time, as to us of today, Boone was always the scout, the pathfinder, the man who mastered the wilderness. He is remembered as he stood, tall and straight in his deerskin shirt and trousers, with moccasins on his feet and a coonskin cap on his head. As such he stands for all the men who won the wilderness from the Indians and wild beasts and prepared the way for the settlements which were to grow into cities.

THE NORTHWEST TERRITORY

Soon after the close of the War of Independence, Congress made plans for opening up the great unsettled region between the Ohio River and the Great Lakes known as the Northwest Territory. The government sold land to groups of men who had formed land companies. They were to handle the sale of small portions of land to settlers who came into the country from the East.

Congress also passed a wise law called the Northwest Ordinance of 1787, which set up a form of government for this territory. When there came to be settlements, the people were to elect their own officers and make their own laws. There were to be churches and schools. Each section of land was to be so divided that one part was public land

THE NORTHWEST TERRITORY

on which a school was to be built. When there were enough people in this region, states should be formed. These states were to have the same rights and powers as the thirteen states along the Atlantic coast. Citizens of these new states were forbidden to own slaves.

By this Northwest Ordinance, Congress set up a plan which could be followed for all western lands. As settlers occupied them, they could make their own governments and work toward the time when new states would be admitted to the Union.

Pioneers moved into the Northwest Territory at once. In 1788 Rufus Putnam took a group of emigrants west to found Marietta on the Ohio River. This opened one great region. Cincinnati was founded in that same year. For several years these pioneer settlements were often attacked by the Indians, but more and more people continued to pour into this rich country.

The only roads which the explorers and pioneers found when they came to new country were Indian trails and buffalo "traces." Traces were ditches two to four feet wide and from six inches to two feet deep, trodden by thousands of hoofs as herds of buffaloes stamped along in single file behind their leaders. When the first path became too deep for comfort, the buffaloes would leave it and begin a second path beside the first. Thus the traces would be widened. Sometimes an immense herd of these heavy animals would crash through the forest, breaking a broad road from one feeding ground to another. As this route was followed again and again, it would become level and hard as a rock.

Weary road builders, struggling through forests or swampy regions, were glad when they came upon a firm, solid buffalo trace. Nor was this an uncommon experience.

The line of these roads is followed today by our railroads and highways, as it was followed earlier by the first roads and canals. The buffalo was a good surveyor.

Indian trails were narrow footpaths, from twelve to eighteen inches wide, along which the Indians traveled in single file. Like the buffalo roads, they were often worn deep. The French explorers called the Iroquois trail westward from the Hudson River the "Beaten Road." It was unusual because it was a peace-path. The Iroquois rarely quarreled among themselves, but kept up an exchange of goods and messages that was remarkable among savages. Runners were trained to carry the summons to a council and to spread news. It was said that it took only three days and three runners to send a message from Albany to Niagara. Each Indian was expected to cover one hundred miles of the trail in a day.

Along the line of this Iroquois trail the American pioneer built his log roads. They were rough affairs, and the travelers who jolted over them in carts and wagons without springs were far from comfortable.

Here, as in all the colonies, the town and county governments made the first roads. Next, companies of persons were given permission to build roads and charge tolls for their use. The name of "turnpike" was given to such a highway because, at the place where toll was collected, a long pole, or pike, was swung across the road to stop people till the money was paid. Along this western route went hundreds of families, pouring into the new lands of the Northwest Territory, as they were opened up by the government in 1787.

The peace treaty with England in 1783 turned over to the United States all the territory, except Florida, east of the Mississippi River and south of the Great Lakes. There was doubt in the minds of many people as to whether so big a territory could be held together under government by the people. A free nation of such a size had never been dreamed of until those days.

There was reason for these fears in a time when it was so hard for people to get from one place to another. It took Washington nearly two weeks to get from Mount Vernon to New York to be inaugurated as the first President of the United States in the spring of 1789, and the ceremony had to be put off from the first of March to the end of April because so many of the senators and congressmen arrived late.

When Washington took that office, he was one of the most traveled men in the country. Not even Benjamin Franklin, who had been going up and down the colonies to get the postal service organized, had covered so much ground as Washington. He had been almost everywhere along the Atlantic coast, and had gone beyond the mountains as far as he could into the West.

Five years before George Washington was called back into the service of his country as the first President, he had left his comfortable Virginia plantation and set out alone on horseback to see this West in which he was so much interested. While he was on that trip he wrote home to the governor of Virginia that every effort must be made to connect this new West with the settlements back east.

"The more communications are opened to the Western country," he wrote, "the closer we bind that rising world to our interests, and the greater strength we shall acquire by it."

Washington saw Detroit as the future center of the new "empire." There were few Americans in those days who saw so far beyond the center of government on the Atlantic seacoast. Washington, with his wise foresight and varied experience, was the right man to head the government at its beginning.

In the year 1789, when he took office, the United States had a population of nearly four million people. The five leading cities were Philadelphia, New York, Boston, Charleston, and Baltimore. The largest city had only forty-two thousand people. By far the greater number of people lived outside the cities in villages or on farms and along the frontier.

The history of the United States for eighty and more years after the adoption of the Constitution was a tale of a steady stream of people moving west. A family would start in the spring in a wagon with a canvas cover stretched over it, the wagon drawn by horses or oxen. Tied to it would be a cow or two. The start was made in the spring, in the hope that by fall they would reach a place to stop and settle. Anyone living on the New York State turnpike and the National Road of Virginia in the 1820's and 1830's saw long lines of these wagons passing. Sometimes there would be forty wagons, one after the other. A wagon might have ten horses to pull it over the rough roads.

The speed with which the Ohio and Mississippi valleys were settled by these people is shown by the dates when new states were formed there. A territory must have a population of at least sixty thousand before it could become a state. Kentucky and Tennessee came into the Union in 1792 and 1796, before the new century began. Then came Ohio in 1803, Louisiana in 1812, Mississippi in 1817, Illinois in 1818, Alabama in 1819, and Missouri in 1821. Then the frontier moved farther west. Settlers began to follow trails beyond the Mississippi which western explorers had marked out.

During these years Americans invented new machines to help in transportation.

ROBERT FULTON'S STEAMBOAT

One of the first inventions was the steamboat. In August, 1807, a steamboat named the *Clermont* went upstream from

New York to Albany. The inventor, Robert Fulton, told the story of that trip in a letter to a friend:

> My steamboat voyage to Albany and back has turned out rather more favorable than I had calculated. The distance from New York to Albany is 150 miles. I ran it up in thirty-two hours, and down in thirty; the latter is just five miles an hour. I had a light breeze against me the whole way coming and going, so that no use was made of my sails, and the voyage has been performed wholly by the power of the steam engine. I overtook many sloops and schooners beating to windward, and passed them as if they had been at anchor.

An important change in transportation had begun. Fulton's was not the first steamboat on American waters. Experiments had been made before, and had come near to success. Practical use of the steamboat, however, began with Fulton's historic trip up the Hudson.

On the Mississippi and Ohio rivers flatboats were then in use. These were big flat-bottomed boats with square ends, sometimes roofed over so that they looked like moving vans. On such boats the settlers going west often loaded their animals and possessions. Farmers along the Ohio and Mississippi used flatboats to take their products downstream to the busy Spanish port of New Orleans. Another boat much in use was the narrow, pointed keelboat, which was pushed along with poles by a crew of men. It had the advantage of being able to move both upstream and down.

The first Mississippi steamboat was the *New Orleans*. She was built in 1811 through the efforts of a New Yorker, one of the earlier members of the famous Roosevelt family.

When she was launched at Pittsburgh, she ran downstream a short way to the dock from which she was to start her real voyage. There a great crowd had gathered.

"Even a raft can float downstream," people were saying as they watched the smoke coming from her engine. "Just wait till the old teakettle tries to go upstream."

When she left the dock and turned into the current, she did go upstream. Her paddle wheels threw out waves of foaming water as she pushed noisily along. The watching crowd cheered. Steam had proved its power on the great rivers of the West.

The American settlers were used to traveling by water. That had always been the easiest way for them. Explorers had noticed how short were the distances between one river and another, or between a river and a lake. Indians and white men had carried canoes over such places, which were called portages. Back in 1760 Franklin wrote that the western country could be reached mostly by water, and that it was possible to go from New York City to Lake Ontario with only twenty-seven miles of portage. Soon men became eager to dig canals which would connect bodies of water. Then travel would be easy and trade would move faster.

Washington, who had been trained as a surveyor, studied the whole country to see where the Atlantic Ocean could be connected with the great central rivers of the continent by the digging of short canals. That was the chief reason for his long western trip. He did not live to see his favorite project completed, the joining of Chesapeake Bay with the

Ohio River by a canal. But he did see work begun on it near the present city of Washington.

Canal digging was a hard business in those days when there was no machinery run by power. Forests had to be cut down, huge roots of trees pulled up by men's labor, and tons upon tons of earth dug out with only hand shovels. The story of the many canals which were built in this period of our national life is an amazing tale.

THE ERIE CANAL

In 1817 the legislature of New York voted to build a canal that would connect the Hudson River with Lake Erie. Surveyors went along the chosen route driving lines of stakes. Farmers watching the surveyors thought them crazy to plant their little pieces of wood in swamps and forests,

on rocky ledges and in the middle of streams. Yet the canal was soon built along that route. In spite of swamp fever, which laid low a thousand men in a single week, the three hundred and sixty-three miles were completed in eight years and four months.

On October 26, 1825, Governor DeWitt Clinton of New York started on the first canal trip east from Buffalo. More than any other man or group of men, he was responsible for the building of this waterway, which was called "Clinton's big ditch." On a new canalboat, the *Seneca Chief*, had been placed two kegs containing Lake Erie water, which was to be mingled at New York with that of the ocean. The *Seneca Chief* was followed by other canalboats carrying the "products of the West"—a bear, two eagles, two fawns, several fish, and two Indian boys.

As a signal gun was fired, four fine gray horses pulled at the towrope, and the *Seneca Chief* began to move. At almost every town and village the boat was welcomed with special exercises, dinners, addresses, and fireworks. The governor's party had to stop so often to be welcomed that it took them six days to make the journey to Albany.

On the afternoon of November 2 the boats entered the last lock at Albany. From there they were towed down the Hudson to New York, where a great celebration had been prepared. Governor Clinton poured the Lake Erie water into the ocean, and the waters of the Atlantic and the Great Lakes were "wedded."

From this time on, travel and trade went along the new waterway. The Erie Canal was one of the chief gateways

to the West. It also did much to make New York City the great port which it soon became.

THE FIRST RAILROADS

Men had been experimenting with the use of the steam engine on railway tracks for travel on land. Within a few years the first steam locomotives were being used to pull passenger cars over iron tracks.

A railroad was built following the line of the old Iroquois trail across New York. An important trip on this Mohawk and Hudson Railroad was the one on August 9, 1831. Short sections of railroad had already been used for hauling goods in other parts of the country. On this trip passengers for the first time paid fares. The cars were pulled by an engine named the *DeWitt Clinton.* They went from Albany to Schenectady, a distance of seventeen miles. This important event attracted attention all over the country.

With the coming of the railroad the different parts of the country were joined together as they could not have been in any other way. Railroads began to help in carrying thousands of settlers into the Mississippi Valley. Within twenty years, Chicago on Lake Michigan became a busy railroad center.

EDUCATION FOR DEMOCRACY

As settlers moved west, they left behind the schools of the eastern cities and towns. One of their cares was to see that their children were properly taught, but this was not easy. Teachers were few, and distances between farms and settlements were great. A book which did much for education and democracy was Noah Webster's spelling book.

No American has ever been schoolmaster to so many children as was Noah Webster. During the many years of colonial life the books used in the schools had been chiefly English. Many of them were printed in Great Britain. But

there had grown up an American way of speaking English. Some words were spelled differently from the way they were spelled in England. There were differences, too, in the speech and spelling in different colonies. Webster, a New Englander, felt that the people of the new republic must be united. It would help if the children in all the states were taught the same spelling for all common words and the same pronunciation.

No one knows how many American children learned their words from Webster's spelling book. It was called by the children the "blue-backed speller," because it was bound in blue paper covers. It went west in the covered wagons of the pioneers. It was used in one-room schoolhouses in the forests and on the prairies. Nearly one hundred million copies of it were sold during the eighty years it was used. Democracy owes much to the patriotic schoolmaster who taught children everywhere in the states to speak and spell correctly.

Another man who prepared schoolbooks at a time when they were much needed was William Holmes McGuffey. He was one of a pioneer family which migrated to Ohio soon after it became a state. The people of the great farming regions of Ohio and other western lands had few books. Many of them came from the old middle colonies, where they had lived in settlements made by Germans or Swiss or other European peoples. They wanted their children to learn to speak and read English better than they did themselves. For them McGuffey made a set of readers which were used far and wide. The first of these books was published in 1836. On a frontier where many kinds of people were coming together to form a new America these books helped to teach American ideas and patriotism.

The leaders of the new states believed that education should be free to all children. They began early to plan for it. By the Northwest Ordinance, land in every region was set apart for schoolhouses. Soon the states began to make plans for education from the primary school to the university. Michigan led the way in 1817. Other states did much for their schools.

In Massachusetts, Horace Mann worked to give children better schools. As a country boy, he had found it hard to get an education. His father died when he was thirteen years old, and he and his mother tried to carry on the farm. Winter was the only time when he could go to school. Often school was only one short term of eight or ten weeks in a one-room schoolhouse for children of all ages. But Horace had books to read. Benjamin Franklin had given the town a public library, and young Horace read every one of its hundred books. In later years he said: "Had I the power, I would scatter libraries over the whole land, as the sower sows his wheat field."

He worked his way through college and was chosen in 1837 Secretary of the Massachusetts Board of Education. He helped to start a school for teachers, the first in the United States. He was always eager for new ideas, and went abroad to study the schools of other countries. Many of the new methods which he brought home were adopted in all parts of the nation. He was greatly interested in the growing West and went in 1852 to Ohio to be president of a new college. Horace Mann was pleased when he was called the "Friend of Children." He once said: "The children of the country are in my mind every day. I want them to have the best."

The schoolhouse became the center of every American community. To it came children from all the homes. Here boys and girls learned to be democratic American citizens.

Talking Together

1. How many things can you name that you have and use every day that were not made by machines?

2. Some frontier families would settle down for a time and then sell their home and land in order to move farther westward. Why did they do this five or six times in some cases?

3. The frontiersman was usually sure to take with him an ax, a spade, and a rifle. Why were these necessary tools?

4. How did the new inventions mentioned in this unit change the ways in which people lived?

Interesting Things to Try

1. Compare the map of the Northwest Territory on page 223 with a geography map of the same region to find out the names of the five states that were made from the Northwest Territory.

2. Imagine that you have traveled from the East to a new home in the Northwest Territory. Write a letter to a friend about your new home or some dangerous experience that you had in traveling west. What date will you put on your letter?

3. On an outline map of the United States draw in heavy black the Mississippi River and all its branches toward the east. In the same way draw in other important rivers between the Mississippi and the Atlantic coast. Put in the Appalachian Mountains. This will show you the importance of rivers for travel.

4. The pioneers were fond of singing. They sang songs like "Quilting Party," "Old Zip Coon," and "Pop Goes the Weasel." Find a collection of these and other early songs and sing them.

5. Choose committees or individuals to make oral reports to the class on topics suggested by this unit. Try topics like these, looking for additional material in books and encyclopedias:

Making the Constitution	Railroads Then and Now
Pioneers and Unfriendly Indians	Canals: Roads Made of Water
Mississippi River Boats	The First Factories

Learning to Illustrate Oral Reports

You have been learning how to use a table of contents and an index, how to hunt for information, how to select and reject material for a report, and how to outline material. All these things will help you in making an oral report. To make a report in which all of the class will be interested, do something more than talk. Have something special to show them.

Use a cartoon, poster, graph, chart, or map to illustrate your talk, choosing the one that best fits your subject. Your teacher will explain what each of these is.

Here are some suggestions for illustrations for reports on topics connected with this unit:

1. A cartoon about Whitney's cotton gin
2. A poster of an early settler's cabin in Kentucky
3. A graph of the population of New York each ten years from 1790 through 1830. It could be continued to the present.
4. A chart of the various early inventions, showing the machine, the date, and the inventor
5. A map showing the size of the United States when Washington became President

Can you think of other cartoons, posters, graphs, charts, and maps to make?

Let's Read

Our Nation Begins, by Eugene C. Barker, William E. Dodd, and Walter P. Webb. In the section "The Pioneers Move Westward," there are more stories about Kentucky and Tennessee.

Hello, the Boat! by Phyllis Crawford. Here are the adventures of a family traveling by boat from Pittsburgh down the Ohio River in 1817.

The Iron Horse, by Adele G. Nathan and Margaret S. Ernst. A story of railroads, from the first one that carried passengers down to the railroads of the present time.

Singing Wheels, by Mabel O'Donnell. Isn't that an interesting title for a story about a pioneer family?

Wagons Away, by Josephine E. Phillips and Howard E. Wilson. Wagons were very important in helping people move westward. You will want to read this if you are at all interested in pioneers.

Frontiers New and Old, by Nila B. Smith and Stephen F. Bayne. On page 310 begins the story of "Eli Whitney's Jigs" and the changes they brought about in American manufacturing.

Quiz Yourself

I. On a separate piece of paper, arrange these events in order of time. Put 1 in front of the event that happened first, put 2 in front of the event that happened next, and so on. *Do not write in this book.*

____ The first passenger railroad is built.
____ Washington becomes first President of the U.S.
____ Robert Fulton builds a steamboat.
____ Eli Whitney invents the cotton gin.

II. Number your paper from 1 to 3. After each number write down the letter of the choice that best completes the sentence.

1. Trappers and hunters were the first to move westward because (a) they wanted to discover new lands; (b) they were interested in fur trading; (c) they were braver than their neighbors; (d) they wanted to fight Indians.
2. People went west in groups because (a) they could carry their needed food more easily; (b) they wanted their neighbors to go with them; (c) they could protect themselves better; (d) they wanted help in clearing new land.
3. Pioneer people had to provide their own food and clothing because (a) they preferred not to buy things; (b) they did not like the kind of things they could buy; (c) they wanted to keep busy cooking and sewing; (d) they could not buy things in the wilderness.

VII AMERICANS ON THE MOVE

WESTWARD TO THE PACIFIC. *The Louisiana Purchase of 1803 stretched from the Mississippi River to the Rocky Mountains. Explorers charted new trails across the territory and on to the Pacific.*

AMERICANS ON THE MOVE

It has often been said of Americans that they are a restless people, always on the move. If they are, they are only following in the ways of their ancestors. They began to move by coming to this country, and they continued to move. In the century that followed the winning of independence, the boundaries of the United States were greatly extended, and Americans moved west into the vast unoccupied regions which came into their possession.

JEFFERSON, A MAN OF VISION

In 1801 Thomas Jefferson became President of the United States. He had long been active in the government. It was he who wrote the Declaration of Independence. He was active in planning for education and in establishing the University of Virginia. He helped to plan the system of American coins and advised the use of the dollar as our money unit. He encouraged Eli Whitney and was interested in every new invention. He was eager to have the West explored, for he had dreams of a growing nation.

THE PURCHASE OF LOUISIANA

In 1800 nearly half the commerce of the United States was passing through the port of New Orleans. So long as there had been little trading on the Mississippi and Ohio rivers, it had not mattered much that this port at the mouth of the Mississippi was in the hands of Spain. But with the coming of hundreds of American settlers into those river valleys the picture changed. The Americans did not like it at all that they had to do their trading through a port where everything they bought or sold was handled by Spanish officials. They were becoming so angry that they threatened to seize New Orleans by force and make it American.

This they did not have to do, for things took a new turn. In France the new ideas of freedom had brought on the French Revolution, during which the French people sentenced their king to death and tried to start a republic like that in America. Their attempt ended for a time when a military leader, Napoleon, became dictator of France and tried to be ruler of all Europe. His ambition to rule did not stop with Europe. As master of France he decided to put the French flag back in North America. It was the old

dream of the French explorers. As his first move he got Spain to turn over to him all that region which La Salle had named Louisiana. About this time New Orleans put a stop to American shipments through that port.

Americans might well be worried. Thomas Jefferson, newly elected President, wrote to Robert Livingston, our representative in Paris, "Every eye in the United States is now turned to Louisiana."

It had come to Jefferson's knowledge that Napoleon needed money. The President sent James Monroe to Paris to see if we could buy the port of New Orleans. At first Napoleon refused to consider selling. Then he changed his mind. For some reason he had decided that he must use all his forces in Europe and could not carry out his dream of an overseas empire. He told the astonished American delegates that he would sell not only New Orleans but all Louisiana to the United States. The price would be fifteen million dollars.

The Americans had no authority from Congress to make the purchase, but they decided that the chance must not be lost. They agreed to buy, and a huge tract of land reaching as far as the Rocky Mountains came into our possession. It was great good fortune that this territory could be gained by buying it instead of by fighting for it. The Louisiana Purchase, as it was called, was made in 1803. It changed the whole future of the United States, for it doubled the territory of the young nation. Within this territory there grew up thirteen new states.

Jefferson immediately persuaded Congress to send an expedition to explore the new lands. Two young men, Meriwether Lewis and William Clark, were to lead it.

THE LEWIS AND CLARK EXPEDITION

They started from St. Louis in May, 1804, in three boats, and went slowly up the Missouri, traveling sixteen hundred miles before winter came upon them. Then they made camp with the Mandan Indians in what is now North Dakota. President Jefferson had given them orders to make friends with the Indians all along their route. He knew that such friendship was important if these far lands were to be occupied. No one guessed, however, what a friend and helper the explorers were to find in an Indian woman.

At the Mandan camp were a Frenchman named Charbonneau and his Indian wife, Sacajawea. She was a member of the royal family of the Shoshones, a tribe which lived on the western slope of the Rocky Mountains. At twelve years of age she had been kidnapped by a warlike tribe which attacked the Shoshone camp. She had been brought east to the Missouri River, where Charbonneau saw her. He bought her as a slave, and when she grew older, made her his wife. Her name Sacajawea meant "Bird Woman."

Lewis and Clark asked Charbonneau to go west with them in the spring as guide, and to take his wife and baby son. The Americans knew that the Indian girl was young and the journey would be hard. But they hoped she would be a help to them when they reached her native country of the Shoshones. The party had been out only a few days when Sacajawea began to show herself a valuable member. When the boat in which she was traveling with several men nearly overturned in a gale, it was she who caught and saved many of the valuable supplies and surveying instruments as they were being washed overboard.

As the expedition moved on, Sacajawea began to notice places which were familiar. This was remarkable, for she had been over the route only once, and then she had been a child. As the months of weary travel went by, she became the guide.

When the explorers came to the source of the Missouri River, they left the boats behind and then turned west into the mountain wilderness. With her baby in a basket on her back, the Indian woman pushed on along the trail with the men. At last they crossed the mountains to the western side, where the camp of the Shoshones was. Lewis and Clark went ahead to talk with the chief, and sent shortly for Sacajawea to come to act as their interpreter. She came into the tent, sat down in the circle, and saw that the chief was her own brother. Jumping up, she made herself known and was welcomed as one returned from the dead.

The help given by this chief became all-important to the explorers. He furnished them with ponies, without which they might not have been able to cross the range of mountains. Sacajawea, now known as an Indian princess, rode one of these ponies as the party went on.

Before they came to the Columbia River, the travelers nearly starved for lack of food in the wilderness. When they had crossed the mountains, they still had to push wearily on, day after day, following the river westward. Fog lay often over the river, shutting them in. Then, on November 7, 1805, the clouds lifted and they saw before them in the distance the waters of the great ocean. They had reached their goal.

The party stayed on the Pacific coast all that winter, then started back, planning to make further explorations.

They came upon snow in some sections of the Rockies and suffered great hardships crossing over to the eastern side. Here the expedition was divided. Captain Lewis went eastward to explore, and Captain Clark, with Charbonneau and Sacajawea in his party, went down the Yellowstone River. One of the explorers told of waiting for an hour while a buffalo herd crossed the river. There were so many animals that they stretched from shore to shore, "as thickly as they could swim," though the river was a mile wide.

The two parties came together again on the Missouri. Sacajawea and her husband, with their baby, stopped at the Mandan village. The others went down the river to St. Louis, arriving in September, 1806, two years and four months after they had set forth. There was great rejoicing all over the United States at their success. Vast unknown regions had been explored and roughly mapped. Captain Lewis and Captain Clark both were scientific men who knew how to observe. In their careful journals was written down an immense amount of information about the country, the fur-bearing animals, and the Indians.

The path to the Northwest had been found, thanks to an Indian woman who had often pointed out the way. In Portland, Oregon, there is a statue of Sacajawea, erected by the women of the United States. She stands with her baby on her back, young and beautiful, with her arm uplifted, pointing west.

ZEBULON PIKE IN THE SOUTHWEST

While Lewis and Clark were on their way home, another young United States army officer, Zebulon Pike, was sent out to explore the Southwest. Those lands were still held by Spain in 1806.

Pike and his men started at St. Louis and went on across the plains. They discovered the great mountain in Colorado which has since been called Pike's Peak. Coming in the winter of 1807 to a large river, Pike followed it, thinking that it might bring him to the Mississippi. Instead, the river, which was the Rio Grande, led him into Spanish territory in what is now New Mexico. There he was arrested for trying to spy out Spanish lands, and was taken to Mexico. He was able to make the Spaniards believe that he had entered their territory by mistake and so was soon set free.

Pike had found out that there could be a trade route between Santa Fe and St. Louis. As soon as Mexico declared its independence of Spain in 1821, the news went out that American traders would be welcome in its territory. William Becknell, a Missouri merchant, made a trip

to Santa Fe on horseback in that very year. He did a good business there and came home to St. Louis to tell about it. The next year he set out with two wagons and took them safely through to Santa Fe. Since the route which he followed was across the plains, it could be used by wagons. An endless procession of them followed that trail in the next sixty years.

Thus two great parts of the West were opened up by early explorers: the Northwest and the Southwest.

While some Americans were looking west to new lands, others were looking east. Many on the Atlantic coast were seeking to expand their trade. Trouble came because of wars abroad. Napoleon was keeping all Europe and England at war, and Americans were affected when that war was carried to the seas. England and France each tried to shut off the other's trade. Americans had been carrying on a great part of that trade, with ships going into both English and French ports. Now their commerce was badly interrupted by the war.

Americans were also angered by something else. English warships began to stop American ships on the seas and search them to see if

there were any English sailors aboard who had escaped from their own ships. Then, if the officers did not find enough English sailors to fill up their crews, they would take American sailors and carry them off by force.

There were other troubles, too, left over from the time of the American Revolution. Settlers in the Ohio Valley and the region around the Great Lakes were having serious difficulties with the Indians. They were sure that the British in Canada were giving the Indians help in this constant warfare.

In 1812 Congress declared war against England. The United States was not prepared and her forces met many defeats. But there were also important victories on the sea and on Lake Champlain and Lake Erie. It was a widespread war. There was fighting at Detroit, at Niagara, and in the south in Florida. A British army was landed at Chesapeake Bay and burned the city of Washington.

The British fleet one night bombarded Fort McHenry outside Baltimore. A young American, Francis Scott Key, waited the night through, fearing that the attack would be successful. In the morning, when he saw the flag still flying over the fort, he expressed his anxiety and relief by writing the "Star-Spangled Banner," which has become our national anthem.

When Napoleon was defeated in 1814, and war on the seas stopped, delegates from the United States and England met and made a treaty of peace. The war had done much for Americans at home and abroad. The United States had won the respect of the world as a nation. The states had come together and forgotten their differences. When their commerce was interrupted, they had started many new industries. They were ready to forget the fighting in Europe and to move out and settle the vast western country which had been added to the nation by the Louisiana Purchase.

PLAINS INDIANS AND MOUNTAIN MEN

On the prairies and plains beyond the Mississippi lived the Plains Indians. They were warlike people who got their living by the hunt, and wandered back and forth over immense territory with the buffalo herds. On these animals depended their existence. They ate buffalo meat, drying it so that it would last through the long months between the great hunts. Sometimes they mixed the dried meat with hot fat and berries, making a food which they called pemmican. This would keep for a long time and serve them as a food on their journeys. The skin of the buffalo was used for their tepees and for their clothing. These Indians also hunted the goat, the elk, the bear, the antelope, and other mountain animals.

The Plains Indians resisted the advance of the white men. They knew that settlements would mean the end of their hunting grounds, and so of their way of life. Settlers going into this country had always to be on the watch for attacks by unfriendly Indians.

The only white men who knew the region well were the fur trappers. They were called "Mountain Men" because most of their work was done in the Rocky Mountains.

Many French trappers had explored the West in search of beaver. Following the return of Lewis and Clark from the northern country, Americans began to take on this trade. An interesting advertisement appeared in a newspaper published in St. Louis in 1822:

> To enterprising young men: The subscriber wishes to engage one hundred young men to ascend the Missouri River to its source, there to be employed for one, two, or three years.

The restless and daring young men who answered that advertisement lived as the Indians did. They learned from them how to trap beaver and other fur-bearing animals, and how to make themselves comfortable in the wilderness. They dressed like the Indians, wearing moccasins and leather leggings and fringed deerskin shirts, often trimming these, as the Indians did, with dyed porcupine quills or bright-colored beads.

Mountain Men had an important place in the development of the Middle and Far West because they were able to serve as guides to pathfinders and mapmakers.

THE PUEBLO INDIANS OF THE SOUTHWEST

In the great Southwest, the Americans found Spanish-Mexican settlements and Indians of an entirely different sort from any they had known.

The Spanish explorers who came north from Mexico had named the natives Pueblo Indians because they were living in *pueblos,* the Spanish word for villages. These Pueblo Indians were never wanderers like the Plains Indians. They were a farming people, raising corn and wheat, and such vegetables and fruits as squash, muskmelon, and watermelon. They raised gourds, too, using the hard outer shells for their dishes and cooking utensils.

From the clay of the desert, which they mixed with ashes, the Pueblos made the sun-dried bricks to which we still give the Spanish name of *adobe*. Each brick was shaped by hand and then dried in the sun. In the dry climate, buildings made of such bricks lasted for hundreds of years. Some of the early village houses are still standing to prove what good builders these Indians were.

There were only a few houses in a village, but each of these was very large and was the home of many families. They were flat-roofed, with one roof rising behind another, so that from a distance they looked like a flight of very wide stairs. In the early days these houses had no doors, but only openings in the roofs, with ladders reaching down into the rooms and from one house to another. This way of building was chosen for safety. If a band of warriors from some wandering tribe came to attack, the families would be safe inside, waiting there with their goats and other animals. Inside the house were the community oven, where the baking was done, and the spring from which to draw water.

CALIFORNIA ON THE SPANISH FRONTIER

The land known as California was claimed by Spain, but it was far away from the important Spanish American cities. For a long time Spanish governors in Mexico did not pay much attention to this northern region, though there were Spanish settlements in Lower California. Then they began to fear that Russia was taking too much interest in California. Word came that Russian fur traders had established themselves on the Aleutian Islands and were moving down the Alaskan coast. In 1769 it seemed wise to the Spaniards to do some exploring and strengthen their claims. They knew that the settlement of colonies was always the best proof of possession.

The region was almost wholly unknown. Two men sat down and pieced together such information as they could gather and studied a very old map. One was Don José de Gálvez, an active and able Spanish official who was planning the undertaking. The other was Father Junípero Serra, an equally capable explorer-priest.

With the map before them the two men chose the sites for three mission stations and gave them names belonging to the saints. Then Father Serra, who was a Franciscan, spoke.

"Don José," he said, "you have named these three. Is there to be none in honor of our father, St. Francis?"

"If St. Francis desires a mission," replied Don José with a smile, "let him show us his harbor."

An expedition went north, two parties traveling by ship and two on land. They founded their first mission at San Diego. Then Gaspar de Portolá, who was in charge, started north by land on an exploring trip. Because his map was wrong, he went far out of his way and became completely lost. He turned west, hoping to reach the ocean, and came out all at once on a height from which he could look out on a large and beautiful harbor. This was given the name San Francisco, in honor of St. Francis.

To this newly discovered harbor came, in 1776, a remarkable Spanish explorer and pathfinder, Juan Bautista de Anza. He had found a land route from Mexico to the region that is now Arizona, then from there to California.

His first trip, from Mexico to Arizona, was made in 1774, with twenty soldiers, with Indian guides, and with cattle for food. When he went back to Mexico he began to enlist persons for a colony, and a year later he started out with them. His march is one of the most successful colonizing trips in all history. It was not an easy way by which he came, over the Colorado desert and across the mountains. Yet, starting with nearly two hundred and fifty persons, some of them women and children, he brought them all except one safely to California. After selecting the site for a settlement at San Francisco, De Anza returned to New Spain.

Father Serra founded nine missions before his death, and twelve others were started later. The Franciscan missionaries carried on both educational and religious work. Indians on the coast had little knowledge of agriculture or the other arts of civilization. The Franciscans trained them

in useful work, teaching them to raise grain and fruit, to care for cattle and horses, to build, spin, weave, do blacksmithing, and carry on other community undertakings. Each mission had its church, its Indian village, its shops and orchards and cultivated fields, and its wide pasture lands. From the towers of the beautiful church buildings the mission bells sounded over the countryside, calling the people to work and prayer. A road built by priests and people connected the twenty-one missions, which were about a day's journey apart.

With the passing of Spanish rule, the day of the mission in California and the Southwest came to an end. By the time settlers from the East came to this country, the mission Indians were scattered, and many of their buildings were falling down. There was left, however, a memory which both Indians and white men held dear.

One of the gifts which the Spaniards brought to the Southwest and to California was the horse. Horses were taken to California by both Father Serra and the Anza colony. In that pleasant country they multiplied rapidly. Cattle, too, came into the Far West and the Southwest by way of Mexico. By the time the Americans arrived from the East there were large numbers of Spanish cattle in California as well as in Arizona, New Mexico, and Texas. Spanish occupation of these regions did much to prepare the way for the Americans who, from 1820 on, began to move into these lands.

In North America each region keeps the mark of the people who first settled it: the Dutch in New York, the French in Quebec and on the inland waterways, the Puritans in New England, and so on. All these settlers brought and kept some of their own ways, which became part of their American way of life.

The Southwest and California have never wholly lost their Spanish inheritance. It shows in the names of their cities and in the style of their buildings. In the lands along the old Spanish frontier there are native peoples, too, whose way of life still shows traces of the times before the white men came.

In the early 1840's hundreds of Americans from the East, still on the move, were eager to pour into the West, but they did not know how to go. They needed maps of the routes, and information about what they would find along the way. They were not Mountain Men, who could pioneer in any wilderness, but brave, adventurous Americans, ready to open up the continent if they could be shown the way.

A young army officer, John Charles Frémont, had prepared himself to do just that service. He became a surveyor, a map-maker, and a geographer. When a call came in 1842 for a man to survey a route to the Northwest, Frémont was ready. When he left St. Louis on his way up the Missouri River, he took with him as guide one of the best scouts in the country, Kit Carson. Beaver trapping was not paying as well as it once had, and this experienced Mountain Man liked the prospect of such a trip as

Frémont proposed. It is not surprising that the two men became fast friends.

Christopher Carson had been in and out of the wilderness since he was fifteen years old. He knew the Western lands as few men did, and could talk several Indian languages. Frémont brought to the partnership a skill which no Mountain Man had. He was a scientist. He could put what he saw on a map, and that map would be so carefully drawn and so accurate that others could follow his route without a guide.

Frémont came back from the first of his expeditions with such a map and with the information that the road leading toward the Rockies and on to Oregon was wide enough, as far as the mountains, for a big wagon. The parties traveling along it, he said, could easily get buffalo meat by a little hunting, and could find pasture and water for their mules. Many of the settlers who started along the Oregon Trail did so because they trusted Frémont's word and could follow his mapped route.

Frémont's second surveying trip was longer and more ambitious. With a larger company he went west in 1843, meeting Carson in Colorado. They reached the Great Salt Lake and explored all the region north of it as far as the Columbia River. It was important for Americans to know these regions thoroughly, for England and the United States were disputing over their rights to Oregon. There were chances of trouble with Mexico, too. Frémont decided to go home by way of California, which was still under Mexican rule.

Mountain climbers still marvel at the winter journey which Frémont and his party took across the Sierra Nevada. These high, unexplored ranges were covered with deep snow and ice. Kit Carson knew that there was a pass

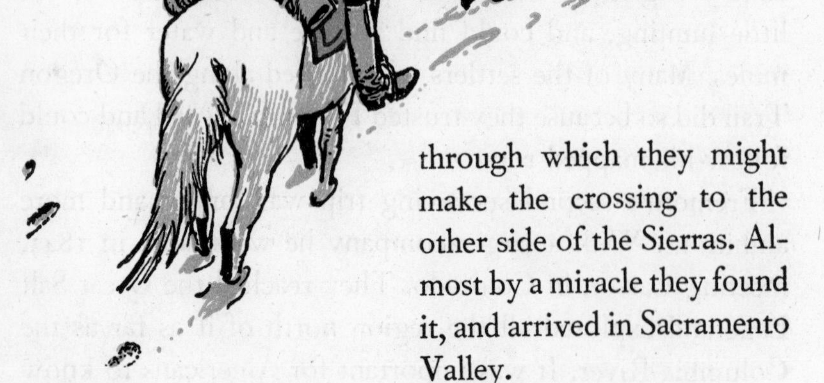

through which they might make the crossing to the other side of the Sierras. Almost by a miracle they found it, and arrived in Sacramento Valley.

Frémont went again to California in the following year, and took a leading part in its conquest by Americans in 1846. When California was admitted to the Union, he was elected one of its first Senators. For years he was known to the country as the "pathfinder" of the West.

By a treaty with Spain in 1819, the United States acquired Florida. But the lands long claimed by Spain in the Southwest were still part of the great Spanish empire until Mexico won her independence in 1821. Then they became Mexican territory. Mexico suffered because one military man after another gained the office of President and ruled as dictator. This made trouble in dealings with other countries. The history of Texas gives a picture of the rapid changes in that region.

As a Spanish province for many years, Texas had very few inhabitants. There were not more than four thousand Spanish Americans living within its borders at the time Mexico won independence from Spain. Before that time, a Connecticut man, Moses Austin, went on horseback from Missouri into Texas and liked the country so much that he asked the Spanish governor at San Antonio for a grant of land there. One way of settling a new country was for a man to get a very large piece of land by promising that he would bring a certain number of families to settle on it. The governor said that he would think the matter over, and Austin went home. By the time the permission came he had died. In the same year the Spanish governor departed for Spain, because Mexico had become independent. So ended the Spanish chapter of Texas history.

Moses Austin had a son, Stephen F. Austin, who was twenty-eight years old when his father died. He got permission from the new Mexican government to carry out his father's plan of colonization and brought down three hundred families. He was an energetic and enthusiastic person and a good advertiser. He went up and down the Southern states, telling everyone of this wonderful new country with its wide prairies and its rich soil. Every kind of crop, he said, would grow there. Soon fully a thousand families had come over into Texas. By 1835 twenty-five thousand Americans were living there.

The Mexican government became disturbed over this large number of independent foreigners from the rich republic to the north. In 1827 President John Quincy Adams had tried to buy Texas for the United States, but without success. After 1830 the Mexican leaders began to shut the door on new Americans who wanted to come, and they put new rules and taxes on those already there. Austin tried to have Texas made a separate state within the Mexican republic. He went to Mexico City to carry the protests of Texans as to the way they were being treated. The Mexican President, the dictator Santa Anna, kept him as a prisoner for a year.

When Austin returned home from this imprisonment, he found that the Texan leaders had determined to break away from Mexico. They were going to set up an independent Texas which should belong neither to Mexico nor to the United States. In 1836 they fought a sharp and bitter war with Mexico. Texans remember with pride the bravery of a small company of Americans who held their fort, called the Alamo, until they were massacred to the last man. "Remember the Alamo!" became the watchword of the rest of the Texan fighters. Under General Sam Houston they were victorious, and General Santa Anna was taken prisoner.

The Mexican flag came down, and a new flag with a single star, the "Lone Star flag," was run up. General Houston became President of the new republic. Most of the Texans wanted to have their republic admitted as one of the United States, but the American Congress was unwilling. To admit Texas meant almost certain war with Mexico, which still hoped to get her province back. There was

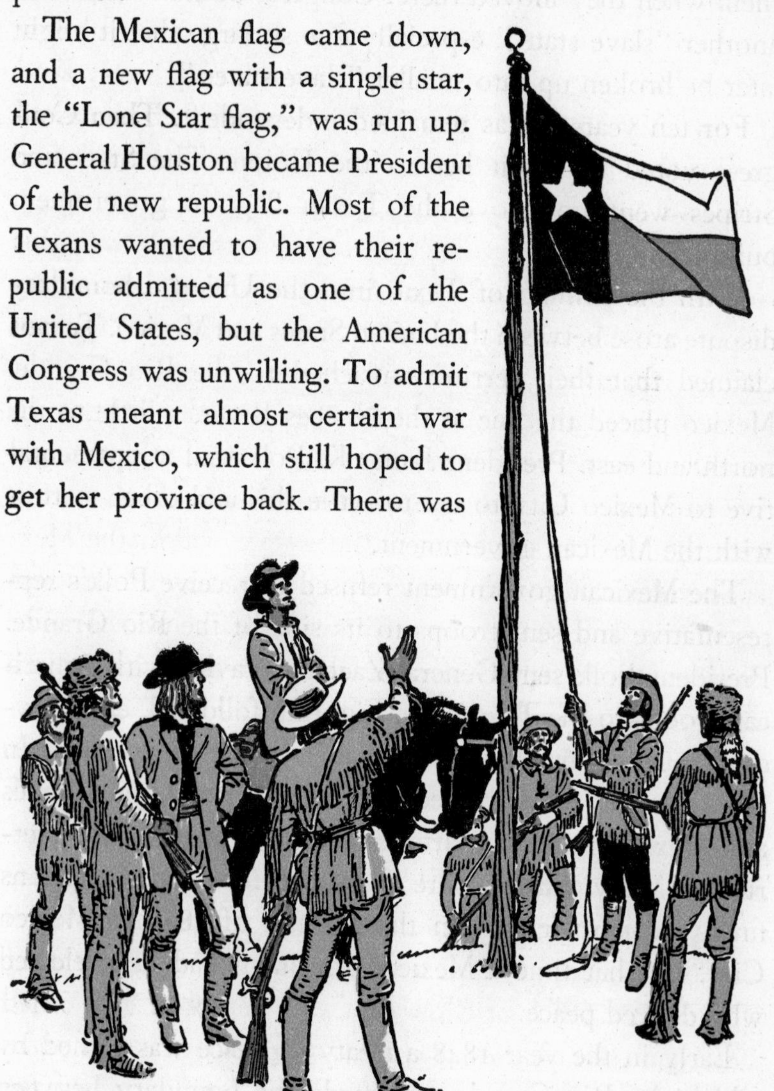

another objection. The people who had settled Texas were mostly from the South, and had taken their slaves with them when they moved there. Congress hesitated to admit another "slave state," especially one so large that it might later be broken up into smaller "slave states."

For ten years Texas remained independent. Then Congress voted to admit her to the Union. The Stars and Stripes went up above the Texan flag on government buildings.

With the coming of Texas into the Union a boundary dispute arose between the United States and Mexico. Texans claimed that their territory reached to the Rio Grande. Mexico placed the line at the Nueces River, a little to the north and east. President James K. Polk sent a representative to Mexico City to try to settle this and other matters with the Mexican government.

The Mexican government refused to receive Polk's representative and sent troops to its side of the Rio Grande. President Polk sent General Zachary Taylor with American troops to the Texas side. Fighting followed, each government insisting that troops had invaded its country. In 1846 war was officially declared between the United States and Mexico. American armies advanced into Mexican territory. Many battles were fought before the Americans finally won their way in the autumn of 1847 to Mexico City. By that time a Mexican President had been elected who desired peace.

Early in the year 1848 a treaty of peace was signed by which the Rio Grande was made the boundary between the two countries. Meanwhile there had been fighting in California, also. The terms of the treaty of peace included the purchase of California and New Mexico by the United States for fifteen million dollars. A smaller purchase a few years later rounded out our Southwestern border. The states of California, Arizona, New Mexico, Utah, Nevada, and parts of Colorado and Wyoming were made from these two additions to our territory.

MORMON PIONEERS IN UTAH

Other Americans on the move were families who belonged to a Mormon church founded in New York State in 1830. The members moved to Illinois, where they were not welcome because of some of their beliefs and practices. Their leaders then resolved to cross the Mississippi and journey to the Far West. There they hoped to find freedom and peace. Their leader, Brigham Young, set out in the spring of 1847 to find a place for settlement. With his party of one hundred and forty-three, he arrived on July 24, 1847, in the valley of Great Salt Lake. This day is now commemorated in Utah as Pioneer Day.

The people set up their tents and began at once to plow the hard, dry soil. In two months five hundred and eighty wagons arrived and over two thousand oxen. By the end of the year four thousand settlers were in the valley, and they continued to come in great numbers for years.

The journey across the plains was hard. Many of the Mormons, especially the immigrants from other countries who joined the church, were poor. They could not afford wagons and horses or oxen for the transportation of themselves and their goods. Then, too, it had been found that oxen and horses increased the danger of Indian attack, since the Indians wanted the animals.

Mormon leaders invented a two-wheeled handcart. It was about the width of a wagon and had a box three or four feet deep set on a frame. Sometimes the box was open; sometimes there was a high canvas cover. A cart could carry a load of three to five hundred pounds. The load included flour and other provisions for the journey, and seventeen pounds of baggage for each person in the group to which the cart belonged. Thousands of Mormons made the thirteen-hundred-mile journey to their future homes taking turns in dragging these handcarts. A handcart caravan could move forward only about twenty miles a day.

The Salt Lake valley had been considered a desert. Dams were built across small streams and the area was flooded. Brigham Young chose a site for a city and planned irrigation for the farms. Soon the valley was made fertile, Salt Lake City was begun, and other towns were started. When the first arrivals had reached the place in 1847, the region was owned by Mexico. In 1848, at the close of the Mexican War, it became a part of the United States.

ON TO OREGON

Great Britain and the United States both had claims to the great northern region west of the Rocky Mountains known as the Oregon country. For thirty years the matter was left unsettled. Then the coming of large numbers of settlers over the Oregon Trail made it necessary that the boundary be fixed.

The men who went as missionaries to the Indians were the leaders in the planting of settlements. In 1834 Jason Lee started a Methodist mission in Willamette Valley, which was the first permanent American settlement in that region. Two years later Marcus Whitman, with his wife Narcissa and another missionary couple, crossed the Rocky Mountains and started missions near the present site of Walla Walla, Washington. Whitman represented a Congregational board of missions which had its headquarters in Boston. When, a few years later, there was danger of losing the support of this board, he made a famous winter trip back East, four thousand miles in all, to beg that the missions be continued. These successful missions and a Catholic mission under the leadership of Father De Smet made the region known in other parts of the country.

It took courage for settlers to make the dangerous journey of four or five months to reach their new homes. Great caravans of covered wagons, usually drawn by oxen or mules, met at Independence, Missouri, and started in one great wagon train. The leaders of the expedition were on horseback. At night the wagons were formed into a great hollow square or circle, within which the animals were placed. Each man, sleeping under his own wagon, was ready to defend his family against Indian attack.

In 1843 a thousand persons crossed the plains and mountains to settle in the Northwest. By 1846 there were six thousand Americans in the region. In that year England and the United States made a treaty, drawing the boundary line for the Oregon country at the 49th parallel. The boundaries of the United States, north and south, were now fixed.

GOLD IN CALIFORNIA

California became part of the United States on February 2, 1848. Nine days earlier, a man named James Marshall went to his sawmill on the south fork of the American River in the Sierra Nevada to shut the gates and empty the standing water. The mill had not been working right, and Indian laborers had been picking rocks out of the stream.

As Marshall and his foreman walked along, they saw on the ground ahead of them a bit of rock which shone like gold. Marshall picked it up, looked at it, and later gave it to his small son, telling him to ask his mother to test it to see if it was gold. She dropped it in her soap kettle. Next morning she cut her soap, and at the bottom of the kettle there lay grains of bright gold.

Four days later Marshall rode into the fort of Captain John Sutter, who owned all the upper Sacramento Valley and ruled the region from his big fort and trading post. When the two were alone, Marshall opened a cloth and poured from it an ounce and a half of yellow powder. Together they weighed it and put it to every test they knew. With each test they became more sure that it was gold. They decided to keep the secret until they were ready to make it known, but the news spread.

When the word came to San Francisco and the other Pacific ports, men dropped whatever they were doing and rushed for the valley where this gold was to be found. Crews left their ships, clerks left their stores, and laborers ran from their fields. All Sutter's land was dug over, and more gold was found there and in the valleys near by. The governor came out to see the mines and sent an official report to Washington.

"There is more gold," he wrote, "in the country drained by the Sacramento and San Joaquin rivers than will pay the cost of the war with Mexico a hundred times over."

The President reported the discovery to Congress in his message of December 5, 1848, and a gold rush began. Sixty ships loaded with gold seekers left Atlantic ports for the Pacific coast early in January. Soon Boston, New York, Baltimore, and Philadelphia were sending fifty and sixty ships a month. The news went all over the world.

THE UNITED STATES: *The Westward Movement*

Up to this time the frontier had been moved steadily westward, first to the Ohio Valley, then to the Mississippi, then farther west. Now all this was changed. There was a leap to the Pacific coast. Vessels went from Atlantic ports south around Cape Horn and up past South America. Mexicans pushed up from the south. Settlers from Oregon poured down. The land trails laid out by Pike and Frémont and Kit Carson were filled with people coming west.

The hardships of the journey caused many to drop out along the way or to turn back, but still the "Forty-niners" came. Eighty thousand people poured into California in that year of 1849. The gold was there, and many people found it. Others turned to trading and storekeeping and building houses and boats, making a living by doing business with the hundreds of immigrants. More than gold had been found. The American people had discovered their own country, which stretched from coast to coast.

They became acquainted with neighbor countries, too.

by Land and Water Across the Continent

To shorten the long sea route around South America they tried crossing at Panama, going on mules across the rough country to the Pacific coast, where steamers waited to take them north. They also went by way of Nicaragua.

Such travel brought all these regions closer together. A movement of people which would naturally have taken thirty or fifty years happened in two or three years. Once more Americans were on the move. When they settled down, great regions which had never before been occupied by white men had thriving towns and cities.

SEAFARING AMERICANS

The westward movement of Americans took place by sea as well as by land. Americans have always been seafaring people. By the year 1800 New England sea captains had already sailed around Cape Horn and into the Pacific Ocean.

The first vessels to go into these far waters were whaling ships, or whalers, as they were called. At that time oil for lamps and wax for candles came from whales. In colonial days whaling was carried on chiefly in the North Atlantic. But long before the covered wagons of the pioneers were making their slow way across the continent to the Pacific coast, whalers were going in and out of the western ports of both South and North America. After the War of 1812 the number of such ships increased rapidly.

New Bedford on the Massachusetts coast was the world's center of the whaling industry. Here ships were built and fitted out with needed supplies. In 1846 there were more than seven hundred

American whaling vessels at sea. Much exploration was done by the Yankee whaling captains during their two-year and three-year voyages. In their search for new whaling grounds they discovered and claimed for the United States tiny Pacific islands, little dreaming that those islands would prove tremendously important a hundred years later as landing places for American airplanes.

The Hawaiian Islands, first visited by English and American explorers before 1800, became a headquarters for whaling vessels. In a single year four hundred of these ships came into the harbor of Honolulu for repairs and supplies. Missionaries from the United States were sent to these islands to convert the natives to Christianity. In 1826 the United States made a treaty of peace and friendship with the native rulers of Hawaii.

The United States government took pains to support the whaling industry and to arrange for the safety of its men. In 1853 four ships of the United States Navy, under the command of Commodore Matthew C. Perry, entered the harbor of Tokyo with a letter from the President of the United States to the Emperor of Japan. This letter stated that the United States wished to arrange for friendly treatment of American seamen who were shipwrecked in Japanese waters, and to get permission for all American ships to obtain water, fuel, and provisions at one or more ports. Japan had long kept itself apart from the world, closing its ports to foreign trade. In 1854 the permission asked by the United States was granted. Japan was opened to the world.

The United States developed a big merchant marine. Between 1850 and 1860 its vessels afloat were reckoned as a third of the world's total number of merchant vessels. Sailing packets were strong, sturdy vessels for carrying passengers, mail, and freight. They went back and forth across the Atlantic on a schedule of dates announced in

advance, as the dates of steamship sailings are announced today. These vessels were the chief link between the Old World and the New World. They carried hundreds of immigrants to the United States and Canada.

Clipper ships brought beauty and excitement to sea travel. These long, narrow wooden vessels with a wide spread of sails on their tall masts were built for speed. There was need for speed. Merchants wanted tea brought swiftly from China. During the California gold rush, clipper ships took eager men around Cape Horn to the Pacific coast. There was competition for speed records, with races across the Pacific and the Atlantic. The clipper ship was the pride of the seas between 1843 and 1868.

The trade with China made fortunes for New England merchants and brought to the people along the Atlantic coast a knowledge of strange ports and foreign ways of life.

Sea captains from the United States did much business, too, in the nearer ports of Brazil and Argentina, and on the west coast of South America. An energetic New Englander, William Wheelwright, took the first steamships into Pacific waters in 1840. They were used in coast trade from Chile to Panama.

THE PURCHASE OF ALASKA

Vessels carrying fur traders went from the Atlantic into northern Pacific waters along with the whaling ships. There they found ships of other nations. Russia had laid claim to Alaska, which lies across Bering Strait not far from Siberia. In Alaska the Russians obtained large quantities of valuable sealskins. British ships, also, were in these waters. England and the United States both made treaties with Russia which gave their citizens the right to engage in this fur trade.

From time to time there was talk at Washington of trying to buy Alaska. In 1867 the opportunity came. An ambassador was sent by Russia to discuss the matter. He and the United States Secretary of State, William H. Seward,

The Alaskan Peninsula

came to a quick agreement on price, and the United States purchased this huge region for a little more than seven million dollars. The people of the United States had little interest in this new possession, which at that time could be approached only by water or by crossing Canadian territory. The newspapers promptly named it "Seward's icebox," declaring that the government had thrown away money to get a land of rock, ice, and snow. Popular interest in the territory rose, however, near the end of the century when the news of Alaskan gold drew thousands of Americans to the north. Then the development of this region as a place of homes and towns began.

AN EXPANDING NATION

In the years from 1800 to 1870 the people of the United States moved their frontier from the Ohio and Mississippi valleys and the Great Lakes steadily westward until it reached the Pacific Ocean.

Early in the century the Louisiana Purchase added a vast territory to their possessions. The newly invented steamboat, railroads, and canals increased travel and trade.

Meanwhile explorers were opening up the great new western possessions, which were enlarged by territory won in the Mexican War. Scouts went first to look over the land. Then small groups of pioneers followed to explore and settle, and after them came large numbers of people. At every stopping place along the routes people stayed and settled, while more adventurous ones soon moved on. Gold found in California drew many people to the Pacific coast. Sea captains explored far north to Alaskan waters and went across the Pacific to trade with the people of the Orient. The Hawaiian Islands were used as midway stations for American vessels going north and west. The purchase of Alaska from Russia added a great unknown northern territory to the lands of the United States.

Americans showed themselves to be a restless, energetic, freedom-loving people. Many new states were created from the western territory and were added to the Union. When the Congress of the United States met in Washington, it included representatives from North and South and East and West who lived hundreds of miles apart and had widely different interests.

Talking Together

1. Describe the advantages and disadvantages of the different routes from the East to California in 1850.

2. San Francisco began as an important town and developed into an important city. Why was this to be expected?

3. If you had been a member of a pioneer family trying to decide whether to settle in California or Oregon, where would you have urged them to go?

4. Perhaps some of the boys will tell the class which of the many different kinds of expeditions they would have joined and why. Would girls have been on any of these expeditions?

Interesting Things to Try

1. The pioneer period offers many good subjects for a frieze such as: (a) a gold-mining boom town; (b) different ways of traveling west; (c) a Mississippi flatboat going down the river; (d) adventures of the Lewis and Clark expedition; (e) a caravan of covered wagons making and breaking camp.

2. Any one of the many people of this period who had thrilling adventures and unusual experiences would make a good subject for a report; for example, John C. Frémont, Kit Carson, Sacajawea, Stephen Austin, Sam Houston, and others.

3. Perhaps a committee will volunteer to make a map showing how we grew from the United States of 1783 by adding the Louisiana Purchase, 1803; the Florida purchase, 1819; Texas annexation, 1845; Oregon Territory, 1846; Mexican Cession, 1848. Cut up the map along the boundaries of each new addition. The committee might tell the story of each new addition as the map is joined, piece by piece, on the bulletin board.

4. In 1935, pioneers went to settle in the Matanuska Valley in Alaska. Would they have met the same difficulties as our early pioneers in the West? Ask your librarian to help you find material about the Matanuska Valley settlement.

Let's Read

America Today and Yesterday, by Homer F. Aker, Eugene Hilton, and Vanza N. Aker. Use the index to find material about the people in this unit.

Children of the Covered Wagon, by Mary J. Carr. You will enjoy the adventures of Jerry and Jim on the Oregon Trail.

Heroes on Your Stamps, by John Gregory. Stories of the many men whose pictures are on the stamps of the United States.

The Boy Scouts Yearbook of Patriots and Pioneers, edited by Franklin K. Mathiews. You will find this an exciting collection of stories.

Willow Whistle, by Cornelia Meigs. This is a delightful story of pioneer days in the Middle West.

Little History of the United States, by Mabel M. Pyne. Most of the history here is told in pictures rather than words.

War Paint and Powder Horn, by Vernon Quinn. These are stirring tales of the old Santa Fe Trail when Indians were enemies.

More Ways to Illustrate Oral Reports

When you make an oral report, there are still other ways to illustrate it besides the cartoons, posters, graphs, charts, and maps already mentioned.

1. Collect materials for an exhibit. Explain them in your report.
2. Post pictures on the bulletin board and show how they illustrate your talk. Many times pictures tell a better story than words.
3. Make an illustrated booklet for the library reading table to include additional material that you do not have time for in your talk.
4. If you have a projector you can illustrate your report with lantern slides that you have made.

Can you use any of these suggestions in making a report on any of the people mentioned in number 2 under "Interesting Things to Try"?

Quiz Yourself

I. Copy these groups of events on your paper. Arrange in order of time by putting 1 in front of the event that happened first, 2 in front of the second, and 3 in front of the third.

A. ( ) Discovery of gold in California
( ) Oregon boundary fixed by treaty
( ) Purchase of Louisiana

B. ( ) War of 1812
( ) Lewis and Clark expedition
( ) Purchase of Alaska

C. ( ) Thomas Jefferson is elected President
( ) Mexico becomes a nation
( ) Texas becomes a separate nation

II. Here are some statements about five of these persons: Sacajawea, Frémont, Houston, Jefferson, Carson, Key, Serra, and Pike. Number your paper from 1 to 5. After each number write the name of the person about whom the statement is true.

1. Author of "The Star-Spangled Banner"
2. A guide for Lewis and Clark
3. Mapmaker and geographer of the West
4. First American explorer of the Southwest
5. Most famous of the "Mountain Men."

III. Number your paper from 1 to 3. After each number write the letter of the choice that best answers the question.

1. What was the western boundary of the United States in 1800? (a) Appalachian Mountains, (b) Rocky Mountains, (c) Mississippi River, (d) Pacific Ocean.
2. Which of the following routes extended southwestward from St. Louis, Missouri? (a) Cumberland Road, (b) Oregon Trail, (c) Wilderness Road, (d) Santa Fe Trail.
3. Which of these was a part of the western boundary of the Louisiana Purchase? (a) Appalachian Mountains, (b) Mississippi River, (c) Pacific Ocean, (d) Rocky Mountains.

VIII DEMOCRACY GAINS IN THE AMERICAS

THE AMERICAS IN 1810. *Russia, Spain, and Portugal had sold or lost all their possessions on the American continents before the end of the nineteenth century.*

DEMOCRACY GAINS IN THE AMERICAS

From 1800 to 1870 the people of the Americas became more and more independent. The spirit of the pioneer was still active in every nation. There were different problems in different regions. But in all the Americas people were working toward the same ideal of more democracy.

SOUTH AMERICANS FIGHT FOR FREEDOM

After the success of the United States in winning independence, the patriots of the Spanish colonies in the Americas grew restless. Their sufferings under the rule of Spain were much greater than those which the northern colonists had endured under English rule. The Spanish kings sent out viceroys and governors who managed the affairs of each country as they saw fit, often with little care for the interests of the colonies. The wealth of the country was in Spanish hands, and the colonies were not permitted even to trade with one another. The desire for freedom was in the air. If the people of North America could win it, the South Americans felt they could do the same.

The words of the Declaration of Independence were often quoted by South American patriots. Some of these men came to the United States and met our leaders. One such visitor was Miranda, who went from our shores to England, where he spent many years planning and working for South American independence. Other patriots went to Europe, where they found other young men talking about the rights of the common man. One of these patriots was Simón Bolívar, the great hero of South America.

BOLÍVAR, THE LIBERATOR

Simón Bolívar was born in Venezuela in 1783, the year in which the American Revolution ended. His father died when he was only three years old, and his lovely young mother found the handsome, dark-eyed youngster a difficult child to manage. There is a story of her asking advice of an old family friend who said that the boy was "like a horn of gunpowder."

Overhearing this remark, little Simón shouted: "Then be careful not to come near me. I might explode."

He did "explode" later, with a passion for South American freedom.

As a boy, Simón had an outdoor life, riding with his private teacher all over the big family estates in the mountains. Before he was twelve years old, he learned to ride wild horses, to lasso a bull, and to shoot straight. From this teacher he learned, too, about the ideas of freedom which were growing in the world at that time.

Simón was proud of his family and proud of being a Venezuelan, but as he grew older, he found out that the sons of the ruling Spanish officials looked down on him because he had been born in America. Those boys, like their fathers, called all native Americans "Creoles." In North America, in colonial days, boys could hold their heads high and glory in being Virginians or natives of Connecticut or some other colony.

In all the Spanish colonies, from Mexico to Argentina, a boy of native birth could never hope to hold high office. He could not be as free to do what he pleased as were the sons of Spaniards who had come to the New World only a few months or years earlier. A Creole boy could not travel from one South American colony to another without getting permission from a Spanish official, and such permission was usually refused. There were plenty of reasons for a proud, quick-tempered lad like Simón to be angry at the way his people were treated.

Young Bolívar went to Spain to be educated, as was the custom for wealthy boys of the colonies. There he met other South Americans who were eager for revolution, and found again the old teacher who had been with him during his boyhood in Venezuela. It was while he was on a walking trip in Italy with this teacher that Bolívar made the pledge which every South American schoolboy of today can repeat.

As he stood on a hill outside Rome, looking over the city, he turned to his companion and said: "I swear before you, I swear by the God of my forefathers, I swear by my forefathers and by my native country, that I shall never allow my hands to be idle, nor my soul to rest, until I have broken the chains which bind us to Spain."

Bolívar went back to Venezuela to work with other young patriots for independence, and was there when news came that Napoleon had put his brother on the throne of Spain. That was the spark which set all South America on fire for freedom. When the news came to Venezuela, the people rose in their wrath.

"Down with the Frenchman!" they shouted in the streets. "We will not have him rule over us."

Miranda came back to Venezuela to lead in the fight against the Spaniards. The colonists sent the Spanish governor home and set up their own congress. On July 5, 1811, Venezuela declared itself independent of Spain. "These provinces," the declaration said, "are, and ought to be, from this day forth, in fact and of right, free, sovereign, and independent states." Argentina and Chile had taken their first steps toward independence in 1810 by refusing to accept royal governors.

In the long and bloody wars that followed, Bolívar took the leadership in the north, winning for himself the title of "Liberator," by which he is always known. Five republics, Venezuela, Colombia, Ecuador, Peru, and Bolivia, which was named for him, count him their Liberator.

South Americans remember every happening in the life of Bolívar. The people talk of amazing marches over the lofty, snow-covered Andes, by means of which he surprised the enemy and won victories. They tell how all sorts of men, native Indians and riders from the plains, aristocrats and military officers from England and Europe, were ready to follow this young general with his burning eyes, his eager talk, and his purpose to win. Sometimes they remember him as poor, defeated, and in exile, and again as riding in triumph into a city after a great victory.

The war was long. The Spaniards sent one trained army after another. They were determined to put down this revolution and keep their American empire. But in the end they had to yield. General Bolívar and his fellow officers kept on fighting till the whole north was theirs.

The South American Republics

Meanwhile another great general was leading armies of patriots in the south. In Argentina, Chile, and Peru, General San Martín is held in high honor as the "Savior of the South."

José de San Martín was born in 1778 in a province which is now within the boundaries of Argentina. He was the son of the Spanish governor of that region. His father was called back to Spain, and young José began at the age of eleven his training as a Spanish soldier. When the Wars of Independence began, he went back to the country of his birth with twenty years of experience in army life. He was ready to take command of troops, and before long he was planning the war.

General San Martín undertook to do a very bold thing. He did not wait in Argentina for the Spaniards to come over from their strong center in Peru and attack. Instead, he planned to take armies over the snow-covered Andes into Chile, on the west coast, and then up to Peru by sea. Only a bold man could have made such a plan. Only a very wise and skillful military leader could have carried it out.

San Martín built up his army slowly, working for three years to gather the cannon and powder and supplies for his great march over the Andes. On the day when the first troops were to start, he took the soldiers to the church, and there they had their banners blessed before they started. Their march is considered one of the greatest in history.

San Martín helped to free Chile from Spanish control. Then he went north to Peru, while Bolívar and his army were coming south. Bolívar and his generals took the leadership. The final victory, at the Battle of Ayacucho, on December 9, 1824, was won by a leader from the north. But General San Martín had done his part long before by freeing the south. There he is called the "Saint of the Sword."

The end of Spanish rule was for these South American colonies only a beginning, as the end of the American Revolution was only a beginning for the United States. But in the wars certain things had been accomplished. Just as soldiers from different North American colonies had come to know one another by fighting side by side against the British, so in South America the movement of armies

from one province to another had made the people of the different regions known to one another. The South American provinces did not unite to form a United States, but set up separate governments. These independent republics in the north, south, east, and west began to trade with one another and with the outside world.

REVOLUTION IN MEXICO AND IN CENTRAL AMERICA

The Mexican people revolted against Spain at the same time that the Wars of Independence were going on in South America. One of the leaders in Mexico was a white-haired Creole priest, Father Miguel Hidalgo. When the moment for revolt came, he rang his church bell to call the people of his village together. There, on September 16, 1810, before listening Indians and white men, he raised the famous cry: "Long live independence! Long live America! Death to bad government!"

Another man almost equally honored in Mexico is General José Morelos. He led in the fighting and gathered the congress which made in 1813 its declaration of independence. Here, as in South America, the war was long and bloody. The fighting here was less against Spanish armies than it was a war between Indians and the white men who were loyal to Spain.

In Central America the break with Spain came without violence, because there were no Spanish troops in that region. The declaration of independence in Central America was made in September, 1821, and the Spanish governor of the five districts returned to Spain.

BRAZIL WINS INDEPENDENCE

The great movement for independence spread to another vast region of South America. In Brazil, which had always been under Portuguese rule, it was a young emperor, heir to the throne of Portugal, who took the lead. Some years earlier, the Portuguese royal family had come to Brazil for safety when Napoleon's army invaded Portugal. In 1821 King John was able to return to his own country, but his son, Pedro I, chose to stay in the land where he had spent most of his life. Brazilians remember the day in the year 1822 when the young prince decided to help his adopted country to become free.

Prince Pedro was out hunting when letters from the king, his father, were brought to him. In them he was ordered home. But the Brazilian patriots had been urging

him to stay. He read the letters and made his choice. On the banks of a little stream, the Ypiranga, he drew out his sword, waved it in the air, and shouted: "The time has arrived. Independence or death! We are separated from Portugal."

Brazil remained an empire for many years, but it was an independent empire. Under Dom Pedro's son, Dom Pedro II, there was more progress and more peace than in some of the neighboring South American republics.

THE MONROE DOCTRINE

The United States was friendly to the desire of other American peoples for independence. Its leaders gave encouragement to the new Spanish-American republics as soon as they declared their freedom. Statesmen felt it to be a cause of rejoicing that Spain was losing control of these regions. Brazil's independence was also approved by the government in Washington.

European nations did not give up easily their hope of controlling territory in the New World. Russia owned Alaska and was interested in the Pacific Northwest. In 1823, during the South American Wars of Independence, James Monroe, who was then President of the United States, sent a famous message to Congress. He said that European nations were not in the future to plant colonies on the American continents. He also said that any interference with American republics would be considered by the United States to be an unfriendly act.

This message, which meant briefly "hands off the Americas," came to be known as the Monroe Doctrine.

GROWTH OF THE UNION

People began soon after 1800 to talk about the United States as the "Union." The word reminded them of the way the nation was made up from the separate colonies. As the country grew, new states were admitted every few years to the Union. Then the people living in these states sent Senators and Representatives to sit in Congress with the leaders from the older parts of the country. People from every region came together in Washington.

Soon it became plain that people from different sections of the country had very different ideas. This was nothing new. In earlier days each colony had been different from

its neighbors to the north and south. Now the differences were between larger sections of the country. People began to talk about the East and the West, the North and the South.

The people in the different sections were interested in different ways of living and working. The businessmen of the North had their factories and their shipping. Many persons left farms and went to work in the factories. There were large towns as well as cities. Northerners wanted laws which would help them in their trade and their industries. Their wants were different from those of the Southerners. In the South there were many plantation owners with hundreds of slaves raising cotton. The South was still chiefly agricultural. The pioneers of the new West had their special wants, too. They were often impatient with

the people from the older and more settled parts of the country. In Washington, leaders from all sections tried to come into agreement.

From Tennessee there came to Congress in 1796 a young backwoodsman, Andrew Jackson. Tennessee was at that time a new state, a western state as compared with the states along the Atlantic seacoast. Young Jackson was a tall, lank fellow, blue-eyed, with reddish-brown hair. He stayed in Congress for only a short time, but came to public notice again in the War of 1812. As a major general in the United States Army, he led his troops to victory and became a popular hero. His soldiers called him "Old Hickory" because he was, they said, as strong and tough as a hickory tree. General Jackson also fought successfully against the Indians.

Andrew Jackson was a bitter fighter in politics as well as in war. He was one of the people and defended their rights. When he became a candidate for the presidency, the people of the West supported him. He was a man in whom they believed. In 1828 he was elected President. Working people from all over the country went to Washington to watch him take the oath of office.

Jackson was one of the first national leaders to say that the new Western lands should be given freely to the people, not sold for public profit.

During Jackson's presidency the question came up as to whether a state could leave the Union because it did not like certain laws. The state which considered making this move was South Carolina. Jackson declared this could not be done. At a public dinner he spoke for the Union, declaring, "It must be preserved!"

A New England statesman of this period was Daniel Webster. He served in Washington as Senator from Massachusetts for many years and was one of the country's leading orators. The galleries of the Senate chamber would fill with visitors when it was known that he was going to speak. His voice, once heard, was never forgotten. It sounded through the Senate chamber like a trumpet. Webster won fame as a defender of the Union.

Senator John C. Calhoun of South Carolina spoke often in the Senate for the whole South as well as for his own state. He felt that each state had rights which it must preserve. Each state was a part of the Union, but it should decide certain things for itself. He feared the growing power of the North.

Henry Clay of Kentucky, another statesman of the time, tried to keep the peace between North and South. When Senators from Northern states and Southern states disagreed, he would suggest a plan which all could support. He was known as the "Great Peacemaker."

North and South differed more and more about admitting slaves into new territories. Many people of the South felt that there should be as many slave states as free states so that Southern interests would be protected against the powerful North. Many Northerners wanted to stop the spread of slavery. They had never needed slaves in their factories or on their farms, and they wanted only free labor in the new lands.

In 1820 the number of Senators from states having slavery was just the same as the number of Senators from states which did not have slaves. Then Missouri asked to be taken into the Union as a state permitting slavery. Bitter debate followed in Congress. There was danger to the Union. Henry Clay helped to work out a compromise in which each side yielded something for the sake of harmony. It was agreed that Maine should be cut off from Massachusetts and admitted to the Union as a free state at the same time as Missouri. Then the number of free states and slave states would be the same. It was also agreed that no other slave state could be taken into the Union north of the parallel of 36°30′ which forms the southern boundary of Missouri.

This agreement, passed by Congress, was known as the Missouri Compromise. It lasted until 1850. Then the question came up as to other new Western lands. The Mexican War was just over. Vast new regions had been added to the United States. Gold had been found in California. Settlers were ready to go into the new lands. Should these become slave states or free states? Calhoun, Webster, and Clay, who had all grown old in the service of their country, debated the matter in Congress. Another compromise was made, and things went on peacefully for a short time.

During the years since the Missouri Compromise the question of whether slavery was right or wrong had been much debated. A group of Northerners called Abolitionists were against slavery. They thought it right to give help to slaves who had run away from their masters. Southerners felt that such help to escaping slaves was an attack on the rights of owners to their own property.

The whole question came up again in 1854 about the territories of Kansas and Nebraska. Should they be slave states or free? Senator Stephen A. Douglas proposed that the territories decide for themselves, and such a law was passed by Congress. This law destroyed all that had been accomplished by the Missouri Compromise. Both North and South were again roused over the two questions of slavery and states' rights.

ABRAHAM LINCOLN SPEAKS

Then a new voice was heard. Abraham Lincoln of Illinois became a candidate for election to the office of United States Senator. He was little known beyond the borders of his state, but the country began to listen to him.

Lincoln was born in Kentucky on February 12, 1809, the son of frontier parents. His father was Thomas Lincoln; his mother, Nancy Hanks Lincoln. Their home was a cabin on a small farm. In 1816 the family moved to southern Indiana, hoping to find better opportunities than they had in Kentucky. But the mother died in 1818, and Thomas Lincoln went back to Kentucky. There he married a widow with three children and brought them to Indiana. Abraham's stepmother was an ambitious woman, who encouraged her tall young stepson to study and make an effort to do well for himself. The boy was fond of reading.

Although he had little chance to go to school, he taught himself by reading what books he could get—the Bible, *Aesop's Fables, Robinson Crusoe, Pilgrim's Progress,* and Weems's *Life of Washington.*

By the time Abraham Lincoln was seventeen years old, he was six feet, four inches tall. He was a good companion, well liked by everyone, and known as a fine storyteller. He was a hard worker, too, able to do every job that went with frontier life.

When Abraham was twenty-one, his father moved to Illinois. There the young man made his home. He studied

law, held one small political office after another, served as a soldier in an Indian war, and practiced law in Springfield, the capital of Illinois. Country people and men and women without money took their troubles to him, for he was kind and wise. More often than not, he could win their cases before the court. He always helped them, and they liked and respected him. In 1842 he married Mary Todd. He was elected to the national House of Representatives for a term, and was known as a leader in the West.

This was the man who in 1858 decided to run against Stephen A. Douglas, then seeking re-election as Senator from Illinois. Lincoln was a member of the new Republican party. Douglas was a Democrat. The two men met in a series of debates.

Douglas, known as the "Little Giant," was short, broad-shouldered, with a fine head and a pleasant voice. He was a very good public speaker. Lincoln was tall and awkward, but his face showed good humor, generosity, and intelligence. In his speeches he explained very skillfully why the new law about slavery in the territories would not work. He also made it clear that he believed the Union must be preserved.

LINCOLN BECOMES PRESIDENT

Douglas won that campaign and went back to Washington as Senator. But Lincoln had become known. All over the country his speeches were read. Men said that a leader had come out of the West. He was chosen in 1860 as the Republican candidate for the presidency, and was elected in November.

The month after Lincoln's election the South Carolina legislature carried out its view of states' rights. It declared that the union "between South Carolina and the other states, under the name of the United States of America, is hereby dissolved." Before Lincoln was inaugurated, six more states—Georgia, Alabama, Florida, Mississippi, Louisiana, and Texas—had withdrawn from the Union.

On March 4, 1861, Abraham Lincoln was inaugurated as President of the United States. He declared in his address that it was still his hope that war would not come.

The states which withdrew from the Union formed a government, calling themselves the Confederate States of

America, or the Confederacy. They seized at once several forts within their borders. On April 12, 1861, they fired on Fort Sumter near Charleston, South Carolina. President Lincoln called for seventy-five thousand volunteers to defend the Union. Four more states—Virginia, North Carolina, Arkansas, and Tennessee—then joined the Confederacy. It had already adopted its own constitution as a separate nation, and had chosen Jefferson Davis as its president. War had begun.

WAR BETWEEN THE STATES

The war lasted for four long years. In many battles and campaigns the bravery of the men on both sides was shown. In this War Between the States all were fighting for what they believed to be right.

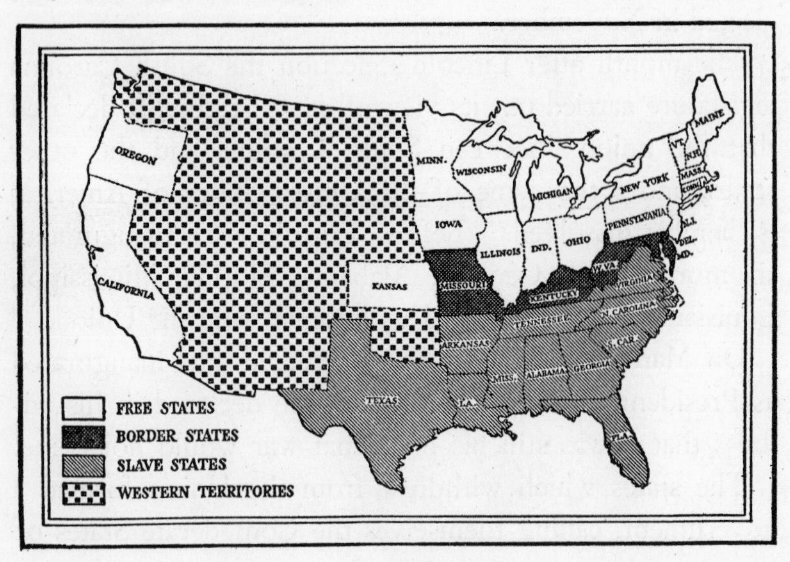

The Confederacy won a first great victory at Bull Run. There General Thomas J. Jackson, called "Stonewall" Jackson because his men "stood like a stone wall," turned back a large Union army by skillful use of his own smaller number of troops. The Northern armies suffered steady defeats at first. They tried again and again without success to invade Virginia and capture Richmond, the capital of the Confederacy.

On the sea, Union ships blockaded Southern ports, so that there should be no trading with the outside world, and no buying of cannon or other supplies from abroad. Gradually this blockade became fairly successful. Admiral Farragut took New Orleans and worked his way up the Mississippi River. A new leader, General Ulysses S. Grant, took other river forts, cutting off the western Confederate states from the rest of the South. Then Grant besieged Vicksburg, Mississippi, for six months and finally took it.

After these victories, Lincoln made Grant commander in chief of the Northern armies. Grant sent General Sherman to march through Georgia in order to cut the Confederacy in two. He himself took charge of the army in Virginia. He fought a stubborn, hammering campaign, of which he wrote to one of his generals: "We will fight it out on this line if it takes all summer."

Meanwhile General Robert E. Lee, the South's ablest leader, had led his army into Pennsylvania in 1863. The most critical battle of the entire war was fought at Gettysburg, where, after three days of heroic fighting on both sides, the Southern army was driven back.

In Virginia, the two armies continued the struggle in a series of battles in which many thousands of men were lost on both sides. Grant could call for more men and get

them from the North. Lee's army became smaller and smaller because there were no more men in the South to fight. At last in April, 1865, Lee's troops were surrounded, and he was forced to surrender.

The two generals met at Appomattox in a private house. They had fought side by side as young men in the Mexican War and now talked of those days. Grant wrote out the terms of surrender. Lee said that they were generous, and remarked that most of the horses in his army were owned by the officers.

"Let them keep them," said Grant. "They will need them for the spring plowing."

The Confederate officers were permitted to keep their arms, too, and the soldiers were given rations of food. They needed them, for they were half starved.

When the news of the surrender came to the Union army, the men began to cheer. Grant told them to stop. "The war is over," he said. "The rebels are our countrymen again."

As Lee returned to his camp, the soldiers crowded around him. They could not believe he had surrendered. He bade them a sad good-by. "I have done the best I could for you," he said.

Robert E. Lee was a brilliant soldier, a cultured gentleman, and a man of the greatest nobility of character. Southerners, in the army and out, adored him. Northerners admired and respected him.

Lincoln, as President during the war years, was a wise and able leader. Those who worked with him were slow to appreciate his greatness. He suffered much from lack of support by many of the leaders of his party in Washington. But these men came to see how wise he was. People called him "Honest Abe" because he was always fair and open in his dealings. He moved slowly, but when the need came for action, he was ready.

One of his important acts was the issuing of the Emancipation Proclamation. This act declared that from January 1, 1863, all slaves living in sections in rebellion against the United States would be free. He had long believed in freeing the slaves, but believed also that the owners in the South should be paid for the loss of their property. Amendments to the Constitution within a few years abolished slavery completely in the United States and made all Negroes citizens. This was another big step toward democracy in the Americas.

Lincoln was re-elected in 1864. At his second inauguration, when the long war was at last drawing to a close, he made a noble and moving appeal to the people of the country:

> With malice toward none; with charity for all; with firmness in the right, as God gives us to see the right, let us strive on to finish the work we are in; to bind up the nation's wounds; ... to do all which may achieve a just and lasting peace among ourselves and with all nations.

Lincoln was always kindly and generous in his spirit. He was never bitter against the South, even though it was his duty to lead the war against its armies. He was protecting the Union, and he looked forward to the time when war should end and all should be united once more.

A few days after the surrender at Appomattox, on the night of April 14, 1865, President Lincoln was shot, as he sat in a theater, by John Wilkes Booth, an actor who had always sympathized strongly with the South. The President was carried to a house across the street, and there he died the following morning, leaving the whole country shocked and grief-stricken.

One of his Cabinet officers said, as Lincoln drew his last breath: "Now he belongs to the ages."

The years have proved this saying true. The honor given to Lincoln has increased with the years.

A CHAPTER OF MEXICAN HISTORY

During the years when the United States was struggling to remain a Union, other nations of the Western Hemisphere were making progress toward democracy.

Mexico had become independent of Spain in 1821. That was the period of the Wars of Independence in South America when Spain lost all its colonies on both continents. But as the years went on, European rulers often looked with longing eyes at the rich New World. They did not give up easily the hope of regaining control of some part of it. An Indian president of the Mexican republic had to lead his people, during the 1860's, in defense of their independence when it was threatened by the French emperor, Napoleon III.

This Indian leader was Benito Juárez. Born in 1806 in a tiny mountain village, he was early left an orphan. He tended his grandfather's sheep on the hills until he was twelve years old. Then he set out for the nearest town, thirty miles away, seeking an education and a chance to better himself. At that time he could neither read nor write, nor did he speak Spanish, but only his Indian language. In the town he had great good fortune. A kindly priest took him into his home and taught him. Soon he was ready to go to the church school and later to the higher public schools.

Juárez became a lawyer. He was highly respected in his province for his fair decisions and his kindness to the poor people who sought his help before the courts. He soon became active in national affairs and worked with other Mexican patriots to put out of office the ruling dictator, Santa Anna. When this was accomplished, Juárez was given high office in the new government and wrote for Mexico a democratic law called by his name. Modern Mexico celebrates February 5 as Constitution Day in honor of the adoption in 1857 of a constitution which contained the Juárez Law.

Civil war followed these patriot reforms, and Juárez, as President of Mexico, led the people through terrible years of fighting. The nation failed during those years to pay huge debts which the earlier governments had left behind. While Juárez was trying to get his people back to prosperity, French troops were landed on Mexican soil. Napoleon III made the excuse that he was simply trying to collect debts which were owed to France. Soon, however, with the support of many wealthy Mexicans who had opposed Juárez, he tried to set up an empire in place of the republic. He sent an Austrian archduke, Maximilian, to rule in Mexico City. President Juárez had to move his government north to a province which bordered on the United States. But always the Mexican patriots held him to be his country's rightful head.

Maximilian's rule was short. During these years the United States was fighting its War Between the States. It was, therefore, too much occupied with its own affairs to pay much attention to the troubles of this neighbor republic, although the sympathies of the leaders were with President Juárez. At the close of its own war, the United States

gave notice to France that it objected to having foreign troops on North American territory. Napoleon III began to call his army home. President Juárez returned to Mexico City. Maximilian surrendered and was put to death.

This was the last attempt of a European power to take control of the territory of any nation of the Western Hemisphere.

A WISE EMPEROR IN BRAZIL

When Brazil freed itself from Portugal and became an independent nation in 1822, its patriots chose to keep an emperor at the head of the widely scattered group of states. His son, Pedro II, born in Brazil, was called to the throne in 1840 at the age of fifteen. From then until 1889 he ruled Brazil wisely and well.

Under his lead the ports of Brazil were opened to foreign trade, and railroads were built. Industries were started, and education was improved. Dom Pedro II did much for the arts and sciences. He traveled in Europe and the United States, and made his country respected abroad. During the years of his leadership the population of Brazil increased rapidly, for immigrants were welcomed in this mighty land, which had room and opportunity for all.

In 1889 Brazil chose to become a republic, as it would have done much earlier if the emperor had not been so well liked and wise in his dealings with his Congress. Emperor Pedro and his family were forced to depart for Portugal. While modern Brazil celebrates each year the beginning of its republican form of government, it honors on another national day the emperor who ruled wisely for almost fifty years.

CHANGES IN SOUTH AMERICA

While Brazil was being led by one man for this long period, most of the other South American republics were having frequent changes of leadership.

After the close of the Wars of Independence in 1824, each of the republics began its independent national life. Each had much open land, to which, as the years went by, came immigrants from overseas. Each had wealth in natural resources, which men from Europe, Great Britain, and the United States came eagerly to develop. Railroads were built, cattle were raised on the plains, and hides and meat were shipped to other parts of the world. Mines were worked in the mountains, and their products went overseas.

As often happens in rapidly growing countries, one strong man after another took control of the government. Sometimes these leaders did well for the people; sometimes they did not. Always patriots who cared for the rights of the people were working for the good of their countries. There were wars over boundaries. There was sometimes civil war between two groups. But gradually the people were getting better schools for their children and a better living for those who worked with their hands. A national spirit was growing in each country.

CANADA, FROM COLONY TO DOMINION

North of the United States, Canada was spreading westward until it stretched from the Atlantic to the Pacific. It was also receiving thousands of new settlers from the British Isles and Europe.

Canada celebrates July 1 as the birthday of the nation. On that day in 1867 it ceased to be a colony and became a dominion, independent in many ways and yet still a part of what is now called the British Commonwealth of Nations. It honors a great leader, John A. Macdonald, and the men who worked with him to bring about this change.

John A. Macdonald was born in Glasgow, Scotland, in 1815. He came across the ocean with his family when he was only five years old. His father found life in the new country difficult, and the family was always poor. In later years Macdonald said that because of hardships he had no real childhood. At fifteen it was necessary for him to give up school and go to work. Yet he kept on educating himself by constant reading, and became a lawyer. Before he was thirty he began his public life by being elected to the legislature of his province.

Canada was growing fast. Thousands of immigrants from the British Isles were coming to settle its open lands. These newcomers flocked into the provinces of the Midwest and the Far West.

The old ways of government were proving unsuccessful for the widely separated regions. There was an east Canada and a west Canada, and far out on the Pacific coast there was a region called British Columbia. Macdonald, who had become a national leader, dreamed of Canada as a federation of independent states within the British Empire, and led the way in making his dream come true.

In 1864 a conference was held in Quebec to which came delegates from the Eastern provinces of British North America. These delegates made a plan for their government which was promptly approved by the Canadian Parliament and then taken to London. That was a new method. For the first time in history a colony was taking the lead by presenting to its mother country a constitution by which it desired to be governed. The British Parliament gave its approval. By the British North America Act, the Dominion of Canada came into existence on July 1, 1867. Ottawa became the capital. Other provinces joined the Dominion later.

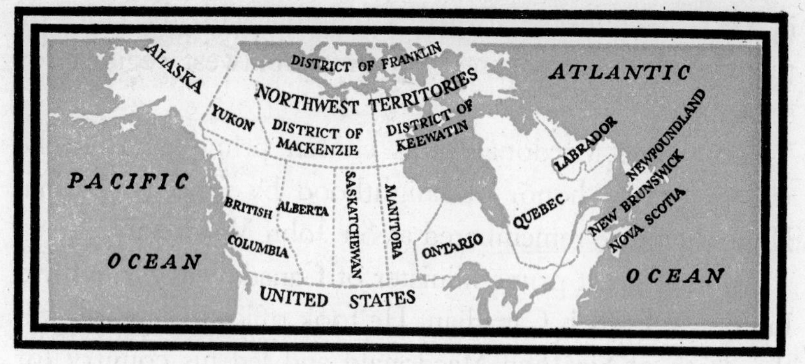

THE DOMINION OF CANADA

The right of self-government was the central idea of the Dominion plan. Not only were the people to choose and carry on the government; each of the provinces was to be free to keep its own ways and manage its affairs according to its desires. But all would work together in matters which had to do with the whole nation.

Within the Dominion were French-speaking provinces and English-speaking provinces. Both languages were made official. Both were to be used in the new Parliament. From that day to the present every official paper of Canada has been written in both French and English. Thus Canadians have shown to the world that people with different traditions and languages can work together in a single nation.

John A. Macdonald became head of the new government, with the title of prime minister. He had long planned for a united Canada which should stretch from ocean to ocean. Under his leadership the Canadian Pacific Railway was built across a thousand miles of prairie and five hundred miles of mountain country. When it was completed in 1885, it connected British Columbia with the cities of the East and also opened up great midwest regions for settlement.

Soon after Macdonald was chosen prime minister, he was given the honor of knighthood by Queen Victoria. He is therefore remembered as Sir John Macdonald.

Another great prime minister of Canada was Sir Wilfrid Laurier, a French Canadian. He took office five years after the death of Sir John Macdonald and led his country for fifteen years. Macdonald had come to Canada as a child. Laurier's ancestry went back to the days of the first settlers. His first Canadian forefather had come across the seas from Normandy in the year 1641. Laurier was born two hundred years later, in 1841. Macdonald had grown up in poverty and struggled to get an education. Young Laurier received an excellent education, first in a French-Canadian school and then in an English-speaking school. He was thus particularly well fitted to lead all parties in the government.

Sir Wilfrid was popular with both French and British Canadians. He guided the fortunes of his country during a period of rapid growth, when the Dominion was becoming a strong and powerful nation.

DEMOCRACY AND INDEPENDENCE

During the nineteenth century all the Americas made gains in national independence and democracy.

South Americans were thirty-five years behind the colonies of North America in declaring and winning their independence. In a series of Wars of Independence which lasted from 1810 to 1824, the Spanish colonies from Venezuela and Colombia in the north to Argentina and Chile in the south won their freedom. During the same period Mexico and Central America freed themselves from Spanish rule, and Brazil declared its independence of Portugal. All these colonies began to act as independent republics.

Before the United States became a completely united nation, differences between East and West, North and South had to be settled. War came between the states of North and South, which ended in a military victory for the North. Abraham Lincoln, who was President in those dark years, stood always for the ideal of the united nation with liberty and justice for all.

Other nations of the Western Hemisphere were also winning victories for democracy. Mexico fought a war for its freedom and adopted a democratic constitution. Brazil became a republic. Canada became a Dominion with territory reaching from the Atlantic to the Pacific.

Talking Together

1. Why did the people in the North, South, and West of the United States develop different ways of working and living?

2. The settlers who came to this country and the Indian tribes they found here spoke many different languages. How did it happen that the language of the United States became what it is today?

3. In how many ways is your life different from Abraham Lincoln's when he was a boy?

4. Can you explain the meaning of the following words: patriot, Creole, foreign, liberator, candidate, boundaries, debated, independence, Dominion?

Interesting Things to Try

1. You might like to make a special "Who's Who" of the leaders in the quarrel between the North and the South; or a "Who's Who in Latin American History." You will want to get more material from other books.

2. On large outline maps of North and South America, show in different colors the territory claimed by European countries in 1800, and also the territory independent of European countries. Do the same for the year 1850. Be very careful to color correctly the territory of the United States at those dates.

3. Make a time line to show the important dates in this unit. Use one color for the dates and labels for South America and Mexico, another color for the United States, and a third for Canada.

4. Since Abraham Lincoln is today one of our greatest national heroes, try one or more of these activities: (a) make a mural picturing the most important events in his life; (b) dramatize scenes from his life; (c) make a reading book about him for the fourth grade; (d) arrange a sand-table scene of his birthplace; (e) display pictures on the bulletin board; (f) tell interesting stories about him to your class; (g) plan an assembly program based on these ideas and others of your own.

Let's Read

Canada, My Neighbor, by Harold B. Clifford. Two children who visit Canada learn about its history and present-day life.

They Live in South America, by Alice Dalgliesh. The author writes very interestingly about countries in South America she visited by airplane.

America's Building, by G. E. Freeland, E. E. Walker, and H. E. Williams. If you are interested in the leaders of the North and South, read pages 155–179.

The Story of the Other America, by Richard C. Gill and Helen L. Hoke. Pictures as well as words tell a delightful story.

The Story of the American People, by Mary G. Kelty. The story of slavery and the trouble it caused is well told on pages 459–512.

More Ways of Making Reports

A number of suggestions have already been made about ways to add interest to oral reports. Here are still other suggestions:

1. Tell anecdotes, little interesting stories; for example, the story of how Abraham Lincoln walked many miles to return a few pennies.
2. Make up some conversation between two persons; for example, the scene between Bolívar and his teacher outside Rome.
3. Broadcast to the class through a loud speaker from a microphone in an adjoining room, using part of some famous speech by Webster or Lincoln.
4. Prepare a dramatization, such as a scene in Lincoln's life.
5. Get several others to take part with you in a panel discussion or "town meeting." Choose a subject for discussion with two sides. Choose an even number of members of the panel for each side, and another member to act as chairman. The panel should sit at a table at the front of the room. Members of the class may address questions to the panel when the discussion is thrown open.

Quiz Yourself

Something is wrong with each of the following statements. On a separate sheet copy the sentences, leaving out or correcting the part in each that is not true.

1. Among the heroes of South America are Bolívar, Miranda, Juárez, and San Martín.
2. Abraham Lincoln, born in Kentucky, was a surveyor when he became important enough in politics to be elected President of the United States.
3. Brazil freed itself from Spain, had an emperor who ruled for many years, built many factories and railroads, and finally became a republic with a president.
4. Andrew Jackson of Tennessee became President of the United States after he had been a congressman and a general in the War Between the States.
5. Simón Bolívar was born in Venezuela, went to school in Spain, was known as a Creole, became President of Argentina, and helped free the whole north of South America from Spanish rule.
6. Some of the Confederate States of America were Georgia, Louisiana, Texas, Maine, Missouri, Tennessee, and Virginia.
7. The people in the different South American colonies came to know one another as they fought for their liberty, started a United States of South America, and traded with one another and with other countries in the world.
8. Among the generals leading armies for the Union were U. S. Grant, Jefferson Davis, and William T. Sherman; leaders of the Confederate forces were Robert E. Lee, "Stonewall" Jackson, and Admiral Farragut.
9. Canada celebrates July 1 as a holiday because on that day in 1867 it elected a president and became a Dominion within the British Empire, with each province allowed to manage local affairs.

IX BETTER WAYS OF LIVING FOR ALL

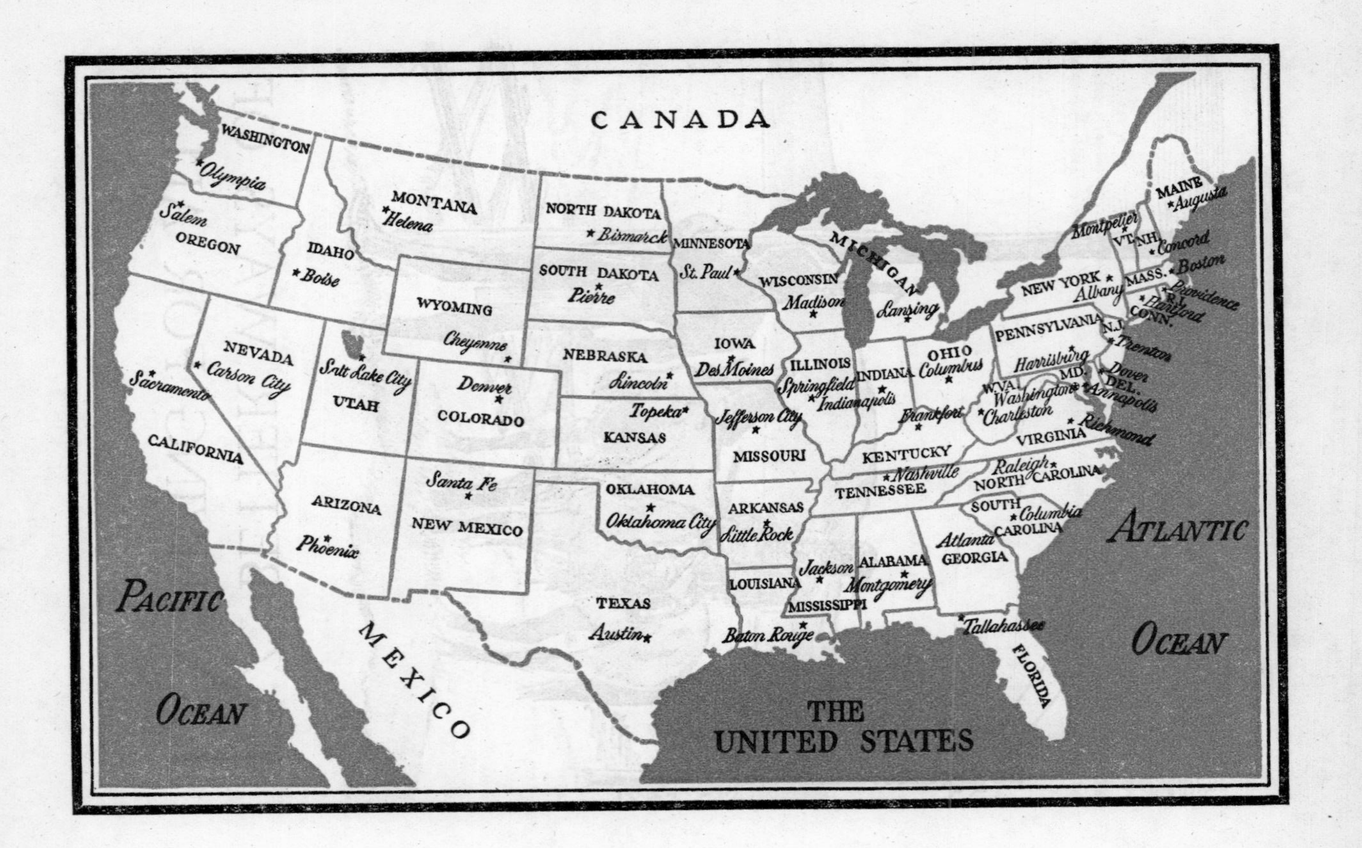
CANADA
WASHINGTON
Olympia
MONTANA
Helena
NORTH DAKOTA
Bismarck
MINNESOTA
St. Paul
MICHIGAN
MAINE
Augusta
Montpelier
VT.
NH.
Concord
Salem
OREGON
IDAHO
Boise
SOUTH DAKOTA
Pierre
WISCONSIN
Madison
Lansing
NEW YORK
Albany
MASS.
Boston
Providence
R.I.
Hartford
CONN.
WYOMING
Cheyenne
NEVADA
Carson City
Salt Lake City
UTAH
NEBRASKA
Lincoln
IOWA
Des Moines
ILLINOIS
Springfield
INDIANA
Indianapolis
OHIO
Columbus
PENNSYLVANIA
Harrisburg
N.J.
Trenton
Dover
DEL.
MD.
Annapolis
W.VA.
Washington
Charleston
Sacramento
Denver
COLORADO
Topeka
KANSAS
Jefferson City
MISSOURI
Frankfort
KENTUCKY
VIRGINIA
Richmond
CALIFORNIA
Santa Fe
NEW MEXICO
ARIZONA
Phoenix
OKLAHOMA
Oklahoma City
ARKANSAS
Little Rock
Nashville
TENNESSEE
Raleigh
NORTH CAROLINA
SOUTH CAROLINA
Columbia
Atlanta
GEORGIA
ATLANTIC
OCEAN
PACIFIC
OCEAN
TEXAS
Austin
LOUISIANA
Baton Rouge
Jackson
MISSISSIPPI
ALABAMA
Montgomery
Tallahassee
FLORIDA
MEXICO
THE
UNITED STATES

BETTER WAYS OF LIVING FOR ALL

When the War Between the States was over, the people of the nation had great tasks ahead of them. They had only begun to occupy the vast areas of land which had come into the possession of the United States during the years from 1800 to 1860.

THE PEOPLE AND THE LAND

Most of the new lands were public lands. They were the property of the nation, which had acquired them by purchase or by treaties with other nations. The government wanted people to settle these regions, but ways had to be worked out for distributing the land.

It was the custom for those who arrived first in a region to choose the pieces of land which they wanted. Each man settled, or "squatted," on his chosen land. Then the government sent surveyors, who drew plans of the region and marked boundaries. When this had been done, there was a land auction. This was the most exciting event in a frontier settlement. Each man in the crowd tried to prove his right to the piece of land on which he had settled. If he could do this, he could buy it from the government at the low price charged for such public lands. Usually "squatters" got their chosen lands. But sometimes a man would lose a piece of land on which he had already dug a well and built a cabin, because someone offered a high price for it. There were often disputes as to which persons came first to the best land.

Many people felt that the government should not sell public lands, even at a low price. Since the lands belonged to the people, they should be given to those who wanted to settle on them. In 1862, when large sections of public land were to be thrown open for settlement, the government passed an act which granted free lands. Anyone might have one hundred and sixty acres of the public lands if he would make a home on them and cultivate them. Such a piece of land was called a homestead. This Homestead Act

was a fair and democratic plan. It opened new lands to rich and poor alike.

Sometimes there were land "rushes" when new territory was thrown open for settlement. Such a rush took place in what is now Oklahoma. On April 22, 1889, twenty thousand people waited on one border of a huge section of land which had been Indian territory and was to be opened that day to white settlers. Guards went up and down the border lines to hold the people back. Finally a United States officer rode to a high point of ground. At exactly twelve o'clock he waved a signal flag. There was the blast of a bugle, and the people rushed across the line, each intent on claiming some part of the new land for his own.

Indians were living on much of the land which the government bought or gained at the close of the Mexican War. Indians never understood the white man's way of buying and selling land. They felt that any land which they used was theirs. Tribes lived on large areas, hunting and fishing in one place and another. Several tribes might claim the same land, using it in different years or even in different months of the same year.

"Sell a country!" exclaimed an Ohio chieftain to a group of pioneers. "Why not sell the air, the clouds, the great sea, as well as the land?"

Another Indian put the same idea in another way. "When you white men buy a farm, you buy only the land. You don't buy the horses and cows and sheep. The elk are our horses; the buffaloes are our cows; the deer are our sheep."

As white settlers moved their frontier farther and farther west. the Indians fought bitterly for their right to roam the plains. But after many battles they were forced to make one treaty after another by which they gave up their lands. In the end the Indians who were left were required to live on public lands which the national government set apart for their use. These land grants were called reservations.

On the reservations efforts were made to train the Indians in the ways of settled life. Such ways were very different from the customs of their wandering existence. Sometimes these efforts were wise; sometimes they were not. In 1924 Indians of the reservations were made citizens of the United States. Today the Indian population is growing.

The national government turned millions of acres of the public land over to the states for free public education. From 1848 on, each new state, when it came into the Union, was given land in each township for public schools. After 1862 the states also received large grants of land for colleges, universities, agricultural schools, and other educational purposes. This was a wholly democratic use of the people's land.

Public lands were also used by Congress to encourage railroad building. Millions of acres were turned over to the companies which were laying tracks in the West. These companies then sold the land to settlers, and thus paid the expenses of railroad building. The owners of the railroads made immense fortunes in this way. They sent agents to Europe to advertise their lands and encourage immigration. The families which came from the East and from Europe took up lands near the railroads, and began soon to ship their farm products to Eastern markets.

In 1844 an invention was made which brought all parts of the United States together by means of quick communication. In 1832 an American portrait painter, Samuel F. B. Morse, coming home after a visit to France, heard talk on board ship of new electrical machines with which a French scientist was experimenting. Morse had studied at Yale College and knew something about scientific matters. He asked many questions, and an idea came to him. If, as was being said, electricity traveled over wires, could not signals be sent from one place to another over a wire by means of electricity? He came ashore with a notebook in which he had drawn rough plans for a telegraph instrument.

Morse gave up his portrait painting and lived in poverty as he worked over his idea. It was six years before he made his first successful telegraph. That was only a beginning. He must next prove to the world what it would do. Six more years passed before Congress voted him the money with which to build a telegraph line from Washington to Baltimore.

On May 24, 1844, Morse, sitting at a table in Washington, clicked off his first public message. He had worked out an alphabet of dots and dashes by means of which he spelled out words. With his finger on a sending key he clicked out the words, "What hath God wrought!" His assistant in Baltimore got the message over the wire. The telegraph had proved itself.

A few years later another American, Cyrus W. Field, started plans for laying a submarine telegraph cable. It was to run under the Atlantic Ocean between America and the British Isles. After many accidents the cable was laid. In 1858 President Buchanan of the United States and Queen Victoria of England exchanged greetings by telegraph. In a few months this cable too failed. It was not until 1866 that a really successful cable was finally laid.

TWO OCEANS LINKED BY RAIL

The first great railroad project to link East and West was begun in the year when the Homestead Act was passed. Congress, with the support of President Lincoln, granted money and land to two companies which were to unite in building a Western railway to connect with Eastern railroads. The Union Pacific Railroad Company was to begin at Council Bluffs, Iowa, and build west. The Central Pacific Company was to build a road east from California.

Seventeen hundred miles of track had to be laid over plains, mountains, and deserts. In its first year the Union Pacific laid only forty miles of track. In five years the Central Pacific covered less than one hundred and fifty miles. There was good reason why the work went slowly. The Central Pacific had to bring material from the East. Iron rails, machinery, and locomotives were transported around Cape Horn or across the Isthmus of Panama. The Union Pacific, as it crossed the plains, used at one time ten thousand laborers and ten thousand horses and mules. On the plains, workers had to have guns always at hand in case of Indian attacks. The Plains Indians knew what the coming of the railroad would mean to them. The buffaloes

would be killed or driven away, and with them would go the Indian way of getting a living.

For years the railroad building went on. As the roads came near together, a race began between the workmen of the two companies. In the month of April, 1869, each group was laying five miles of track a day across what is now the state of Utah. On May 9 the rival crews were in sight of each other all day. They slept that night a few yards from the point where the two tracks would meet. Next day a great crowd gathered to see the last rail laid.

The last wooden tie to be laid where the two roads joined was of California laurel. The rails were fastened to it by spikes of silver from Nevada and Idaho, spikes of gold, silver, and iron from Arizona, and a spike of gold from California. The driving of the last spike touched an electric

wire which carried to the nation by telegraph the news that the transcontinental railroad was completed. Until then the Atlantic seaboard and the Pacific coast had been separated by at least four weeks of travel. They were now only a week's distance apart.

A period of railroad building followed. The Northern Pacific Railroad connected Lake Superior with the Pacific at Puget Sound, and two transcontinental roads, far to the south, crossed to southern California. By 1884 the United States had four coast-to-coast routes, and Canada was completing a transcontinental railroad.

CATTLE AND COWBOYS

The building of railroads made great changes in the Southwest. Texas had long been cattle country. Away back in 1540 Coronado brought five hundred cows along when he led an army into the Southwest on an exploring expedition. From the cattle which he left behind, there developed, during the centuries of Spanish occupation, the breed of Texas longhorns. These animals were found running wild by early settlers from the United States. The miles and miles of open land, with plenty of grass and water, met all their needs.

The settlers started great ranches on which they raised cattle for sale. Cowboys drove small herds of these cattle to nearby markets, but larger markets were waiting. Meat was needed in the Middle West and the East to feed a growing population. After the first transcontinental rail-

road was built, cowboys began to drive the cattle hundreds of miles to points where they could be sold to buyers from the Middle West. "Cow towns," as they were called, sprang up where trail and railroad met. From these towns in Kansas, Nebraska, Montana, and Wyoming, cattle were shipped to packing houses in St. Louis, Kansas City, Omaha, and Chicago.

Cattlemen soon found that they could winter their herds on the Great Plains north of Texas and thus avoid making the long drive from the Southwest. Colorado, Wyoming, and Montana became cattle-raising country. Cowboys rode over the plains where the Indians had long hunted buffaloes.

These skilled and daring horsemen rode the ranges all the year. The ranges were not fenced; so cattle of different owners often wandered far. Twice each year the cattle were brought together in "roundups." At the spring roundup each owner marked, or "branded," his calves with his own mark so that they could always be recognized as belonging to him. At this time and in the autumn cattle were sorted out according to their brands, and the cowboys collected those which belonged in their herds. Sometimes two or three hundred cowboys would come together at one of these roundups, and there would be races and exhibitions of riding and expert roping of cattle. At the fall roundup the cattle to be sent to market were selected. Then the cowboys began the long cattle drives across plains and hills and rivers to the railroad.

When they started they would have trouble keeping their great herds together. After a few days the cattle would become used to falling into line behind leaders. But there was always the danger of a stampede. If the leaders would not cross a stream or were alarmed at night by a sudden noise or by a storm, the whole herd might start running and scatter far and wide. Cowboys could often quiet the cattle by singing. They made up songs as they rode, and these songs have become part of the American literature of the West.

Cattle drives ended when ranges were fenced with barbed wire, which was invented in the 1860's. The open range ended, too, and the modern stock farm began.

MACHINES FOR FARMERS

In the old days a farmer had only his muscles and those of his animals on which to depend for necessary labor. For opening up new country and cultivating great sections of prairie, machines were needed. American inventors met the need.

In 1831 Cyrus McCormick, a young Virginian, drove a machine drawn by four horses into a field of standing wheat, ready for cutting. The machine reaper cut six acres in one day, and cut them well. This was six times as much as any man could do by hand.

McCormick patented his machine in 1834, but he built only a few reapers during the next ten years because he did not have money for materials. He worked hard, however, perfecting his machine. Then he went into the West, and riding on horseback across the prairies, he saw rich land lying unused. Farmers told him that they planted only small crops because larger ones could not be harvested. When he talked of his reaper, they were eager to own one. That year he got one hundred and fifty reapers built in one factory and one hundred in another, and sold them all. At last he could start his own factory in Chicago.

By 1851 he was building a thousand reapers a year, and the farmers of the prairies were calling for more. Two men

working with a reaper could do ten or twelve times the work of two men using hand tools. McCormick became rich through the sale of his machines, and the Western lands were turned into farms far more rapidly than anyone had dreamed they could be.

Other men were building farm machines, too. A grain binder was invented which could be used with a reaper, binding the grain as it was cut. Threshing machines were another American development. Corn planters, cutters, huskers, and shellers were invented. All of these mechanical devices were ready to be used on a large scale when the gasoline engine was invented and could furnish power to run them.

The gold discovered in California in 1848 speeded the settlement of the Far West. Another important discovery of underground wealth was that of oil in Pennsylvania. Even in colonial days settlers were acquainted with oil, or petroleum, which lay in some places near the surface of the ground. Indians used this heavy liquid as medicine, and the colonists followed their example. It was known, too, that this oil would burn, but it gave off a dull, smoky flame and had a bad smell when burning.

A few men, however, kept experimenting with oil. One such group asked a scientist to make a study of the region in Pennsylvania where oil showed itself. He reported that there were large amounts underground, and that this petroleum could be put to many uses. Encouraged by this report, the men decided to hire someone to search for this hidden liquid. One of them had the bright idea of using a hollow drill, like that used in getting underground salt.

Colonel E. L. Drake took charge of the enterprise. He got Uncle Billy Smith, an old man experienced in drilling deep salt wells, to work for him. Uncle Billy and his two sons started in May, 1859. Drilling was slow. By August the drill had gone down only seventy feet and was being pushed inch by inch through solid rock. Drake and his group of businessmen were running out of money and fearing that they must give up the venture.

Then, on August 28, oil began to rise in the pipe. When Colonel Drake arrived the following morning, the old man and his sons had several barrels filled with oil to show him. Colonel Drake at once connected a pump which he had ready. This was the first oil pump ever used, the forerunner of thousands upon thousands of oil pumps today. Oil to fill eight barrels was brought up that day, and still it kept coming. By October the well was producing twenty barrels each day.

Soon petroleum was discovered in one state after another, ready to supply the fuel for the Machine Age.

Iron, too, was needed for this Machine Age. It had been found in small quantities in colonial times and immediately put to use. Before 1850 the iron mountains of the Lake Superior region in Michigan and Wisconsin were discovered, and later those of Minnesota. Soon a great iron and steel industry came into being.

Gold and silver were found in the mountains of Nevada and Colorado. As the news spread, thousands of persons rushed west. In the single year of 1859 one hundred thousand people journeyed on horseback, by wagon, or afoot to the Pike's Peak region of Colorado. In later years the finding of copper and other minerals drew people to Washington and Oregon, and to Montana, Idaho, New Mexico, and Arizona.

Most of these people did not find the quick wealth for which they hoped. But they stayed and started farms and towns. They came to see that much of the wealth of the country was in its grass lands for raising animals and its rich soil for farming. As railroads opened up the country, people rushed to occupy it.

BELL AND THE TELEPHONE

Americans have always been inventors. Pioneers had to be clever at making new things and thinking up new ways of doing things if they were to live with any comfort in a new country. But invention did not stop when pioneering stopped. Many new inventions began to change the daily life of people in the United States.

Alexander Graham Bell, a Scotchman who lived in Boston, Massachusetts, studied the telegraph and wanted to improve on it. He had spent his life studying how sounds were made, and was head of a school for the deaf. There he was having great success in teaching pupils who had never heard a sound to speak words which could be understood.

The telegraph carried signals, not word sounds. Words were translated into short and long signals, or "dots and dashes," and then clicked over the wires. When a message was received, it was translated back into words. Bell asked himself whether machines could be built which would send the actual sound of words over wires charged with electricity. He became so much interested in the idea that he gave up his school and began to experiment.

The task which he had set for himself was tremendous. An assistant who worked with him at this time said:

> Bell would often awaken me in the middle of the night, his black eyes blazing with excitement. Leaving me to go down to the cellar, he would rush wildly to the barn and begin to send me signals along his experimental wires. If I noticed any improvement in his apparatus, he would be delighted.

At last, on a June day in 1875, a sound was carried over one of the wires. Bell worked for ten months more, and in March, 1876, his hopes were rewarded. He had made a sending machine which was like the parts of the throat and mouth used in speaking, and a receiving apparatus like a human ear. He spoke words into his sending machine. They were carried over the wire and heard in a distant room by his assistant. The telephone had been invented.

It was at first hardly more than a mechanical toy. But even the first telephones were immensely popular. In 1880 there were fifty thousand of them in use in homes and

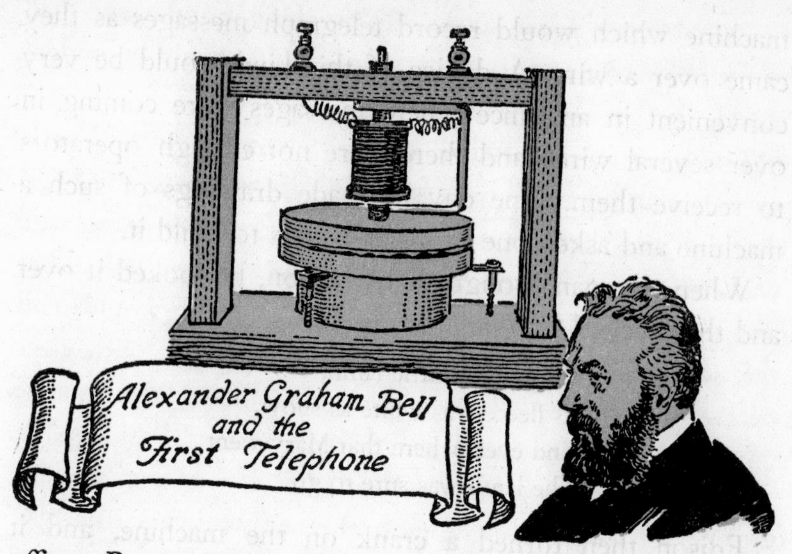

offices. By 1890 great improvements had been made in the instruments, and the number in use had increased to two hundred and fifty thousand. By that time a person could talk from Boston or New York to a city in the Middle West. Other inventors besides Bell worked on the telephone to bring it to perfection.

EDISON AND THE PHONOGRAPH

In 1877, one year after Bell produced his telephone, Thomas Edison invented a machine which could make a record of sounds and then repeat them. He called this machine the phonograph.

Thomas Alva Edison was thirty years old at this time. He had been a telegraph operator and had studied both the telegraph and the telephone. His idea was to make a machine which would record telegraph messages as they came over a wire. A device of this kind would be very convenient in an office where messages were coming in over several wires and there were not enough operators to receive them. One day he made drawings of such a machine and asked one of his assistants to build it.

When the man brought it to Edison, he looked it over and then recited into it:

> Mary had a little lamb,
> Its fleece was white as snow,
> And everywhere that Mary went
> The lamb was sure to go.

Edison then turned a crank on the machine, and it began to recite the lines back to him.

"I never was so taken aback in my life," Edison said of that moment.

All the men in the laboratory were standing around watching. They never knew what queer thing Edison would invent next. They laughed and then were silent with wonder at what had happened. They tried the machine again and again. One man after another shouted or talked or sang into it, and then turned the crank to hear it repeat the sounds.

The next day Edison took the little machine under his arm and went to the office of the *Scientific American* in New York. To the editor's astonishment he began to repeat the words, "Mary had a little lamb . . ." Then he turned the crank, and his voice came back. Work in the office ceased. People crowded in from other rooms to see

and hear. Newspapers came out next morning with an account of the wonder, and soon Edison was receiving letters and telegrams from all over the world. Everyone wanted one of the new machines.

From that little phonograph came the elaborate machines which now record speech and music. It was one of the great inventions in a century of inventions.

EDISON, MASTER INVENTOR

Edison became the greatest inventor of his time. During his long life of eighty-four years he took out patents with the government which showed him to be inventor of more than eight hundred separate devices.

Much of his work had to do with lighting. Two years after he invented the phonograph, he made an electric light bulb which became the model for all such bulbs.

Charles F. Brush had already made a big lamp which was being used in street lighting, but there was need of a small lamp which could be used in homes and offices. Edison managed, after many experiments, to pump most of the air out of a glass bulb and to put inside it a thread which would carry electric current and glow with light. In 1879 he succeeded in making a bulb which burned for forty hours. That little lamp proved that electricity could be used for home lighting.

Edison worked for months to make lamps which would burn for long periods of time. When this was accomplished, there was the job of manufacturing them at a low price and in large numbers. Then Edison set up an electric light system in New York City, with a central station and wires running from it along streets and into houses. In those houses the bulbs were placed, and they gave out light steadily. People could hardly believe that electricity could be turned to such practical use. Edison was always eager to have his inventions serve as many people as possible.

When people began to want telegraphs and telephones and electric lighting, there had to be a great deal of electric current. A great many dynamos must be kept constantly turning to produce this current. The dynamo, which is a machine for producing electric current, had been invented early in the nineteenth century. It was the master machine for all electrical devices. But it was a machine. Like all machines it must be kept moving. It was found that dynamos could be run by water power. Waterfalls, with their tremendous force of falling water, could be used to turn the dynamos.

Power plants were built beside waterfalls. Then the electric current could be carried a short distance or a long way to the places where it was needed. In many parts of the United States there was a wealth of water power, which was soon put to use to turn dynamos.

Electric power was added to steam power to keep the many new machines working. A machine is a dead thing unless there is some sort of power to keep it going. Without such power lights go out, automobiles stop, and factories are silent.

THE GASOLINE ENGINE AND THE AUTOMOBILE

The invention of the gasoline engine made possible the automobile. When oil was discovered in Pennsylvania, inventors went to work to get from the heavy liquid a light, convenient fuel. By refining processes, they got gasoline.

An engine using gasoline for fuel could be small. A steam engine, with coal for fuel, was too big and heavy to be put into a carriage for use on a highway.

Gasoline engines were made in Germany and France between 1860 and 1880 and placed in vehicles. One was brought to America and shown at the World's Fair in 1893. Already American inventors were at work on such machines. Charles Duryea and his brother Frank, young mechanics, made gasoline-driven carriages as early as 1892. Henry Ford finished his first gasoline engine and tested it on the road in 1893. Elwood Haynes, R. E. Olds, and others soon put vehicles of their own making on the road.

The first "horseless-carriage" race was run on Thanksgiving Day, 1895. A Chicago newspaper offered a money prize, and six machines set out in a snowstorm over the road from Chicago to Evanston, Illinois. Only two finished, and the Duryea machine won easily.

As the demand for automobiles increased, manufacturers began to compete in producing new models. Henry Ford chose to build a low-priced car and figured out factory methods for building in quantity and keeping prices down. Within a few years there were hundreds and then thousands of American automobiles on the road.

FROM IRON TO STEEL

Machines need iron and steel for their parts. Long before the invention of the automobile a new process was discovered for turning iron into steel. It prepared the way for the modern Machine Age. The new way was discovered about the middle of the nineteenth century, by William Kelly in the United States and Henry Bessemer in England. It was astonishingly simple.

Before iron can be of any use, the ore which comes from the mines must be purified. Waste matter must be removed. Kelly found that this could be done by melting the ore and forcing cold air through the hot metal. The process was like blowing air bubbles through a glass of water with a straw. Tremendous heat was first applied. Then cold air was blown into the melted iron, which churned and sizzled and roared. Black smoke shot up into the air, and then red flame and thousands of sparks. For ten or fifteen minutes these fireworks continued. Then the flames died down. Within the kettle or furnace there remained steel. The waste matter had been driven out of the iron, and the pure metal was ready for use.

Great mills were built in which steel could be produced by this Kelly-Bessemer process rapidly and cheaply by the ton, instead of slowly by the pound. Pennsylvania had the coal for feeding the giant furnaces, and the Lake Superior region supplied the iron ore. When iron and coal were brought together, America could have almost unlimited steel for use in making railroad tracks, machines, ships, and skyscrapers.

Machines changed the way of life of thousands of people in the United States. Before the coming of machines people worked in their homes or in small village shops. Women wove cloth on their own looms, and shoemakers fitted each customer with shoes made by hand.

The sewing machine, invented by Elias Howe in 1846, led to the making of clothes in factories. Shoe machinery took the making of shoes out of the small shop. Great printing presses made possible the modern newspaper. These and many other inventions took workers from their homes and gathered them daily in factories or mills or other big establishments.

The United States became an industrial country as well as an agricultural one. The machine changed the way in

which great numbers of people earned their living. Before the coming of the machine most people in the United States worked for themselves. With the coming of machines, many people went to work in factories for wages, and they had to live near those factories. As towns and cities grew, these people could not have enough land around their houses for the raising of their own food. They bought food and clothing and paid rent, all with the money which they earned by running machines.

The factory owner gained a great deal of power over his workers. He decided what wages he would pay and how many hours a worker should spend at his job. If a worker was not satisfied, he could leave. But often he would find other factory owners were paying the same wages and expecting the same number of hours of work. The only way for workers to improve the conditions under which they worked was to organize labor unions.

LABOR UNIONS

There were labor unions in the United States almost as soon as there were employers with groups of workers. One of the first was a union of carpenters in Philadelphia. They organized because they objected to working "from sunup to sundown." In summer this meant a working day of from twelve to fifteen hours. They demanded a working day of ten hours and stopped work until their employers agreed to it. This was one of the first strikes to take place in the United States.

The coming of the Machine Age brought about the organization of big labor unions. Businesses were becoming big. Railways, steel mills, automobile factories, and other business enterprises were employing thousands. These organizations were run by companies of stockholders. No man could know all his employers. A single worker had no chance to talk over difficulties with those who could remedy them. But leaders of a union could speak for the members of that union. They could press for shorter hours of labor, better wages, and better places in which to work.

One of the first big unions was the Brotherhood of Locomotive Engineers, founded in 1863. Other trade unions followed, and in 1886 many unions were brought together as the American Federation of Labor. Men and women of separate trades were organized into district groups, or "locals," which managed affairs in their own regions. The leader of the federation was Samuel Gompers, who had come to New York from London when he was thirteen years old and had worked in a cigar factory. He was head of the trade-union groups for many years.

Labor unions worked always to improve the life of the workers. They succeeded in having the working day shortened. The unions always stood for shorter hours, especially for women and children. Often they worked with the government and were helped by laws passed by Congress.

Farmers also felt the need of organization which would bring the people of a region together to become acquainted and talk over their problems. They formed the Grange, which admitted women as well as men. Each local group

had monthly social and educational meetings. By 1873 there were Granges in almost every state of the Union. They were especially strong in the Middle West.

PEOPLE FROM MANY LANDS

From 1840 on, a flood of people from every country of Europe poured into the United States. Some came to escape oppression by harsh governments. They had heard that in America every man was free. Most of them came from countries where there was great poverty. They had heard that in America there was plenty of food, with the chance to earn a good living. Railroad companies and manufacturers had sent their agents into every part of Europe with advertisements of the rich lands that were waiting for newcomers. There were tales of gold and silver to be found and of opportunities of many kinds.

Between 1870 and 1880 more than five million immigrants landed in the eastern parts of the United States. For fifty years they continued to come in great numbers. America was to every new arrival a "Promised Land," a land of opportunity.

The newcomers did much for the country. At first most of them moved quickly to the northern and western regions. They went into the newly opened lands and became farmers. They laid the tracks of the transcontinental railroads. They went into the mines and dug the coal and the copper and the iron. They worked in the forests, cutting lumber. They brought their strength and used it as it was needed.

They brought their own ways, too, their customs and their music and their arts. The United States was richer for their coming. Their children went to the public schools and learned what it means to be citizens of a republic.

GAINS FOR WOMEN

Many women were interested in winning better opportunities for girls who wanted to go beyond the lower schools. Emma Willard of New York wrote and lectured up and down the country to get better education for both girls and boys. Mary Lyon in Massachusetts started a school for girls which was like the colleges for boys. It became Mount Holyoke College. It was made possible by gifts from ministers, farmers, lawyers, doctors, and mothers who wanted their daughters to have a chance for higher education. From it and other schools young women went out as teachers in the pioneer settlements of the Ohio Valley and regions beyond.

A few colleges began to open their doors to young women as well as young men. Girls and boys had studied together in school, but not in college. Oberlin College in Ohio, from the year of its opening in 1833, invited women

to study with men and receive the same degrees at graduation. Coeducation spread rapidly in the new West and more slowly in the East.

Women were becoming more active in public life. Away back in 1848 in a little chapel in Seneca Falls, New York, there was held a convention of brave and determined women. They came together to discuss the need for securing rights for women. One of their demands was that women be given the right to vote. That was a bold demand in those days. At that time women had few rights over their property after marriage, and even lacked the right to control their children's welfare.

Two leaders of the group who met were Lucretia Mott and Elizabeth Cady Stanton. Others who soon began to work with them were Lucy Stone and Susan B. Anthony. Miss Anthony went from city to city speaking to large audiences.

In 1869 Wyoming gave women the right to vote. Colorado, Utah, and Idaho followed. Year by year other states joined this pioneer group. Anna Howard Shaw and Carrie Chapman Catt were leaders of a younger company of women who took up the fight. In 1918, President Woodrow Wilson expressed his approval of the cause and recommended an amendment to the Constitution of the United States which should give the women of the nation the right to vote. Congress gave its approval, and in 1920, by vote of thirty-six states, the Nineteenth Amendment became the law of the land.

MICHAEL PUPIN, BOY IMMIGRANT

In 1874 a fifteen-year-old lad, Michael Pupin, came off a ship at New York with only five cents in his pocket. He was a Serbian, and he wanted to become an American. He could speak no English and had no relatives in this country.

The immigration officers asked him if he knew anyone here. He shook his head, and then his face brightened. Yes, he knew of three Americans—Franklin, Lincoln, and Harriet Beecher Stowe. In his faraway European home Michael had heard the story of Franklin's bringing down electricity with his kite during a thunderstorm. He had learned of Lincoln as the hero of freedom, and had read a Serbian translation of *Uncle Tom's Cabin.* The immigration officers let the boy enter the country.

Young Pupin earned his living first by shoveling coal in a mine, then by driving mules on a farm, and next by working in a biscuit factory. All the while he was learning English and reading and studying. In six years he was ready to be admitted to Columbia University. There he did well in his classes while working long hours outside to earn money for his board and room. He found time to enter into college sports, became popular with his fellow students, and was elected president of his class in his third year.

During all this time Michael Pupin was looking forward to the day when he would become an American citizen. Youths born in the United States took their citizenship as a matter of course. To this Serbian-born lad, American citizenship was a high honor and privilege. In June of 1883, nine years after he came ashore as a penniless stranger, he was admitted to citizenship. On the following day he graduated from Columbia University.

Pupin chose electricity as the subject which he wanted most to study and became a science professor at Columbia and a famous inventor. One of his inventions did much to improve the telephone. During a long life he did great service for his adopted country. In 1923 he wrote the story of his life in the well-known book called *From Immigrant to Inventor*.

JACOB A. RIIS, REFORMER

Another immigrant who arrived in New York about the same time as Pupin was from Denmark. Jacob A. Riis was a young man of twenty-one, well educated and able to speak English when he landed. For several years he went from one kind of work to another, trying to get and hold jobs which would keep him alive. He saw that immigrants were coming to this country so fast that there was no proper place for them to live. More and more of the newcomers stayed in the East, living in towns and cities and working in factories and mills. The port cities were particularly crowded, and many workers lived in wretched houses.

When Riis became a reporter on the *New York Sun*, he wrote stories to make his readers know of these conditions. He told them that thousands and thousands of their neighbors were living in dark, crowded rooms with not enough food for their children's health. His book *How the Other Half Lives* woke people up to the need for reform. When Theodore Roosevelt became Police Commissioner of New York City, he worked with Riis for better houses for workers and for parks and playgrounds in crowded sections.

"If I were asked," said Roosevelt years later, "to name a fellow man who came nearest to being the ideal American citizen, I should name Jacob Riis."

JANE ADDAMS, GOOD NEIGHBOR

An Illinois woman, Jane Addams, saw the same needs of the workers in Chicago and left her own beautiful home to live among poor people from other lands and be a neighbor to them. From college she had gone abroad. Next she studied at the Women's Medical College in Philadelphia, then decided to spend her life in social work. She and a friend bought a fine old home on the edge of the foreign district of Chicago. It was about to be torn down or made over into a tenement house into which many poor families could be crowded. The two young women brought their own furniture and made of it a home such as they would have had in the residence district of Chicago. Then they opened the doors and invited their neighbors to come in.

Families from thirty-six different countries were living near by. Most of them spoke only their own language, although the children were learning English in the public schools. At first they came shyly, not knowing what to make of this invitation. Miss Addams started a nursery where mothers could leave their babies when they went to work. A kindergarten followed, and then clubs for children and for older people. Hull House, as it was called, became the center for a great neighborhood.

Jane Addams worked for better laws to improve living conditions. The houses in which many of the workers lived were a disgrace to any city. Many children who should have been in school were working long hours in crowded factories. Miss Addams fought for better tenements, for better milk for children, and for laws which should protect women and children. Her work did not stop with Chicago or with Illinois. She became active in organizations which were working to get the vote for women and in movements for world peace. In 1931 she was awarded a Nobel peace prize.

BOOKER T. WASHINGTON, NEGRO EDUCATOR

Workers from foreign lands were not the only ones needing help. In the South there was the problem of how the Negroes might be educated and helped to become good citizens.

Soon after the close of the War Between the States, Booker T. Washington, a young Negro, was working at a salt furnace in Virginia. None of his fellow workers could read or write, but this boy, who had been a slave and had been set free, longed for education. He saw children carrying spelling books to school and begged his mother for one. She managed to save money to buy him a Webster blue-backed speller, from which he learned the alphabet and how to read words. In 1872, when he was fifteen years old, he heard of a school at Hampton, Virginia, where Negro boys were being educated. He went there and was cordially received and given a chance to stay and earn his way through the school.

Some years later, citizens of Tuskegee, Alabama, came to Hampton and asked for a teacher to start a Negro school. Booker Washington was chosen to go. He opened the school with himself as the only teacher. One day he invited his boys to come on a Saturday afternoon for a "chopping bee." They came, not knowing what project was ahead. They found themselves cutting trees and preparing lumber for a school building. Some objected that this was not schooling. Their new teacher told them that this was the only way to get schooling. They must earn it for themselves.

Booker T. Washington built a great school for Negroes and was its head for many years. He believed in work as the road to success for his people, and in giving them a

practical education to fit them to make better use of the land and become leaders in their communities. Students from his school at Tuskegee and the school at Hampton went all over the South as teachers.

THEODORE ROOSEVELT, PRESIDENT

A man who was working to better the living conditions of people was Theodore Roosevelt. Few men have crowded so much useful activity into their lives as did he. He was born in New York City in 1858. He was not a strong boy, but he early made up his mind to make himself strong by training and developing his body. With this purpose he went west, after graduating from Harvard College, and lived for a time on a ranch in North Dakota. There he spent long days on horseback, exploring the mountains and hunting wild animals. As he lived with cowboys and ranchmen, he came to know the West as few Easterners did.

On his return home Roosevelt became active in public life. He held important offices in his home state of New York. It was at this time, when he was Police Commissioner of New York City, that he worked with Jacob Riis to give the children playgrounds and parks. He became Assistant Secretary of the Navy, then Vice-President, and then President from 1901 to 1909.

Roosevelt came to the office of President with the purpose of giving what he called a "square deal" to all citizens. He wanted everyone to have equal opportunities, no matter what his race, no matter whether he was rich or

poor, a recent immigrant, or a member of a family which had been settled in America for many generations. He tried as President to see that everyone received this "square deal."

One of Roosevelt's first acts in office was to urge the saving of the forest lands of the nation. Trees had been cut down as settlers moved into new country. That was necessary, but as time went on, the people had grown careless and wasteful of the forests. Lumber was cut recklessly and often great woodlands were swept by fire.

Roosevelt got Congress to set aside as national property great tracts of forest land, and directed that many of these lands were to be public parks and playgrounds for the people. He also started great irrigation projects. The United States owes much to this policy of conservation, begun by earlier Presidents and carried forward vigorously by Theodore Roosevelt.

All over the world the United States became known through Mark Twain and his books. *The Adventures of Tom Sawyer* and *The Adventures of Huckleberry Finn* gave lively pictures of his boyhood on the banks of the Mississippi River. Samuel Clemens borrowed from the river the name which he put on the title page of his books. As a small boy he listened while the sailors on the boats took soundings to find out how deep the water was. A man threw out a measuring line with a weight on one end and bits of leather or cloth tied to it at points six feet apart. "Mark twain!" he would call when the line

showed twelve feet, or two "marks" of depth. Young Samuel would say the words over to himself, and later he chose them for his writing name.

Mark Twain lived in Hannibal, Missouri, from the time he was four years old. He rode on river boats and watched them at wharves loading and unloading freight. For three years he was a river pilot himself, and later wrote about that experience in a book called *Life on the Mississippi*. He went out to Nevada for a time and told, in a book named *Roughing It*, of his hunt for a silver mine and the exciting life on the frontier. All his books gave vivid pictures of the democratic, free life lived in America, especially in the new West. Most of his stories were full of humor and became very popular because they made people laugh.

Samuel Clemens traveled abroad many times, and wrote an amusing book called *The Innocents Abroad*. In 1907 he was given a degree by the University of Oxford. While in England he was entertained by the king and queen. He was called the "king of American writers," but people of England, as well as his own countrymen, regarded him as representative of American life.

ADVANCES ON MANY LINES

In the years from 1860 to 1910 the United States grew up. The nation discovered its natural wealth and developed it. The Western lands were taken up by settlers. Railroads and farm machines helped in the occupation of great areas of open land which were turned into farms and became the food-producing regions of the nation. Inventions such as the telephone, the phonograph, the electric light, and the automobile changed the daily life of the people.

New industries led to the employment of large numbers of men and women in factories and mills. Immigrants poured into the country from the British Isles and from Europe. The changing ways of life created bad living conditions in places where people were crowded together in city districts or near steel mills or coal mines. Public-spirited leaders sooner or later came forward to better these conditions, for there were always people who kept before them the ideals of democracy and worked toward them.

An American way of life grew out of the different ways of life of many peoples. It became known to many parts of the world through the books of Mark Twain and other American writers. In the nations to the north and south of the United States, the American way of life was also being worked out in government and in the life of the people.

Talking Together

1. Discuss the ways in which each of the following helped to unite our country into one great nation: railroads, telephone, telegraph, radio, farm machinery, automobile, airplane, and books.

2. Long before the automobile, airplane, and radio were invented, someone suggested that the United States Patent Office ought to be closed because all the important machines had been invented and patented. Discuss the disadvantages if this suggestion were followed now. Look in *The World Almanac* to find out what sort of inventions were made last year.

3. What are some of the inventions that you use, or have the benefit of, that your parents did not have when they were your age? You may have to ask them.

4. Have you ever seen or known any Indians? Where and how do Indians live in the United States today? For added information, one member of the class might write to the Commissioner of Indian Affairs, Department of the Interior, Washington, D.C.

5. Do all workers belong to labor unions? Are there labor unions in your community? Why are there unions in some communities and not in others?

Interesting Things to Try

1. Make a time line from 1790 to the present year. What scale will you use? On the time line put, at the proper places, the dates and names of important inventions. Find the dates in the encyclopedia or *The World Almanac* for inventions for which no dates are given in this book.

2. "The Story of Machines" would make a good starting point for an assembly program. Divide the class into groups to prepare class programs on some part of this subject. One group may choose to dramatize the story of a great invention, such as the telegraph. Another may prefer to show in pictures the development of the complex farm machinery of today from the forked-stick plow of

primitive man. Still another group may present scenes from the life of an inventor, such as Edison. From the class programs choose the most interesting to present as an assembly program.

3. From railroad maps in a geography book and the description given in this unit, make a map showing the route of the first railroad that joined the east and west coasts. Label it 1869. On another map show four coast-to-coast routes in the year 1884.

4. Plan a frieze in three parts, illustrating the prairie wagon, stagecoach, and railroad as means of transportation across the prairies. Put in the date for each section of the frieze.

5. Since the first oil well was drilled in Pennsylvania in 1859, the petroleum industry has become one of the greatest in the country. From an encyclopedia or other sources make a list of the many kinds of products now obtained from petroleum. The number will surprise you.

6. Make a poster called "The United States: A Land of Many Peoples." Divide it into three columns. In the first, list the names of important persons, past and present, who were not born in this country but who became famous here. In the second column give the reason for their importance. In the third, give the country of their birth.

7. Some members of the class may wish to make a poster headed "Famous Women of the United States." Divide it into two columns. In one column give the names of the famous women, and in the other the reason for their importance.

A Special Report

The story of each invention and inventor mentioned in this unit would make an interesting oral report. Let the class make a list of the inventions and inventors about which they would like to know more. Then let each pupil choose the subject on which he would like to work. Reports may be made individually or as a group or committee project. Use as many as possible of the different ways that have been suggested for making reports interesting. A skillful person could use them all. Are you skillful?

Let's Read

Machines and the Men Who Made the World of Industry, by Gertrude Hartman. Machines have built a magic world for us. Here is their story from the cotton gin to the airplane.

Great Moments in Science, by Marion Lansing. The story of early inventions like the clock, the telescope, and the camera, as well as later inventions.

The Story Book of Iron and Steel, *The Story Book of Oil*, *The Story Book of Things We Use*, three books by Maude and Miska Petersham. Very easy reading with very interesting pictures.

The Cowboy Book, by William C. and Helen S. Pryor. Thrilling stories and colorful pictures of the life of a cowboy.

Travel by Air, Land, and Sea, by H. H. Webster. Delightfully told stories of transportation, from the earliest beginnings of ships and railroads down to the present.

Living in the Age of Machines, by Howard E. Wilson, Florence H. Wilson, and Bessie P. Erb. "Transportation Time Line," page 6, is especially interesting.

Quiz Yourself

Why not make up your own "Quiz Yourself" this time? Here are some suggestions:

1. Prepare a "Best Answer" quiz program, with each pupil writing the first part of a sentence and then giving four choices of ways to complete the sentence. Make the choices difficult so that the selection of the right one will not be easy.
2. A committee of three or more could make an "Order of Time" quiz. Look at "Quiz Yourself" in Units IV, VI, and VII for suggestions.
3. Another committee could make a "Matching Test" in which pupils would be asked to match the names of men with a list of their achievements. You will find an exercise like this in Units I and II.

X WIDER HORIZONS CHALLENGE AMERICANS

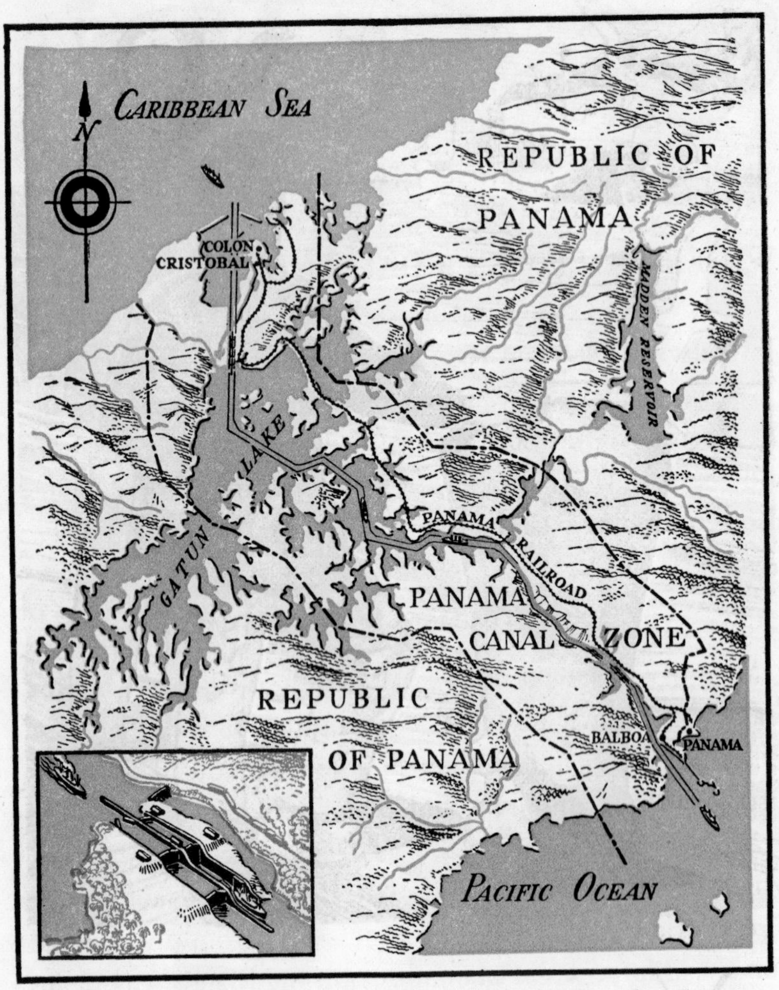

PANAMA CANAL AND THE CANAL ZONE. *The Canal runs through a strip of land ten miles wide called the Canal Zone, which is controlled by the United States.*

WIDER HORIZONS CHALLENGE AMERICANS

Between 1800 and 1900 the people of the United States were chiefly busy about their affairs at home. As the century came to an end, they were engaging more and more in world trade. At that time the United States also acquired new lands in both the Atlantic and the Pacific.

CUBA'S STRUGGLE FOR INDEPENDENCE

Most of this new territory was acquired when the United States was drawn into Cuba's struggle for independence. Cuba had been under Spanish rule since the days of its discovery by Columbus, but its leaders had long desired freedom. Cubans fought a Ten Years War against Spain, which ended in their defeat. Later, patriots again started a revolution. By this time businessmen from the United States had large sugar plantations on the island. Americans watched the struggle with great interest, but the government at Washington held back from taking part in it.

Then a tragic event occurred. A United States warship, the *Maine*, was blown up by an explosion in Havana harbor. This happened in 1898, while the Spanish government was attempting to end the war by offers to the Cubans of increased independence. Two New York newspapers which were strongly anti-Spanish insisted at once that Spain was responsible. There was great excitement in the United States, and within a few weeks Congress recognized the independence of Cuba and demanded that Spain withdraw from the island.

The war with Spain which followed lasted less than three months, with the United States winning an easy victory.

The first dramatic event of the war occurred thousands of miles from either Cuba or the United States. Spain had long held possession of the Philippine Islands in the far Pacific. Commodore George Dewey, who was in command of the United States fleet in the Pacific, sailed into Manila Bay and destroyed the few out-of-date Spanish war vessels which defended it.

In the Atlantic, ships and troops from the United States won victories at Santiago, Cuba, and also in Puerto Rico, and soon the war was over.

NEW ISLAND TERRITORIES

By the peace treaty which followed, Spain withdrew from Cuba. In the Pacific Ocean the United States came into possession of the Philippine Islands, and also of Guam, an island sixteen hundred miles east of Manila, and tiny Wake Island, lying between Guam and the Hawaiian Islands. It also gained the important island of Puerto Rico in the Caribbean Sea.

Cuba did not become a part of the United States. For a time it was under United States military control, but in 1902 it became a full-fledged republic. Three times during the years that followed, the United States, because of trouble on the island, took a hand in Cuba's government. Since 1934, however, the republic has been completely independent.

More than eight million people of several races lived in our new island possessions in the Caribbean Sea and the Pacific Ocean. The government at Washington did not seek to rule permanently over these people. In 1917 the Puerto Ricans became American citizens with considerable local self-government under a governor appointed by the President of the United States. The people of the Philippines were promised independence when they should become ready for it. This promise was carried out, and the Philippines became entirely independent in July, 1946.

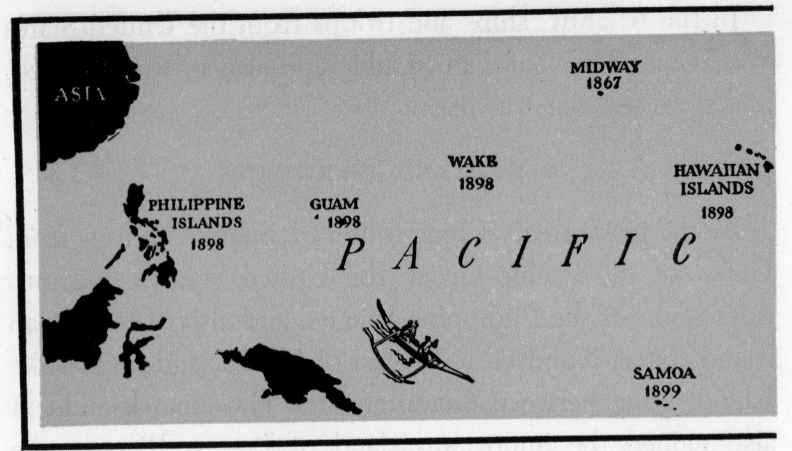

United States Possessions in the Pacific

American sugar planters living on the Hawaiian Islands had long urged that the islands be annexed to the United States. There was some opposition by native Hawaiians, but in 1898 the islands became American. Hawaii was soon declared a territory, and its citizens acquired American citizenship.

The Midway Islands, belonging to the Hawaiian group and lying fourteen hundred miles northwest of Honolulu, had been occupied by the United States in 1867. In 1905 an American submarine cable station was placed there.

Our ships had often visited the Samoan Islands in the Pacific. In 1878 trade and harbor rights were gained for American vessels. Germany and Great Britain also wanted naval bases there. In 1899, by an agreement between the three powers, the United States took over some of the islands. These, known as American Samoa, became the naval outpost of the United States in the South Pacific.

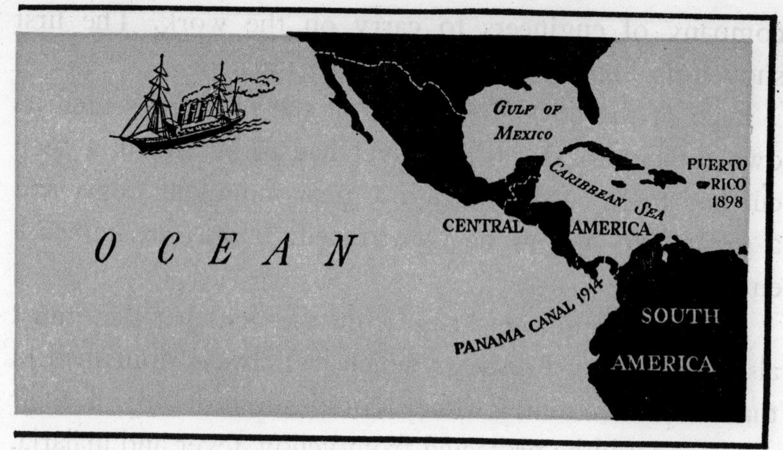

AND IN THE CARIBBEAN REGION IN 1900

BUILDING THE PANAMA CANAL

The United States found itself in 1900 a world power with territory in both the Atlantic and Pacific oceans. The need of a canal across the Isthmus of Panama as a short cut between the oceans was plain.

Talk of a waterway across this narrow neck of land began almost as soon as Balboa discovered the Pacific Ocean. But the building of such a canal was a tremendous undertaking. The project was once attempted by French engineers but they could not carry it through. The expense was too great, and yellow fever took the lives of hundreds of the workmen.

After the Spanish-American War the United States, under the energetic leadership of President Theodore Roosevelt, undertook the task. Colonel George W. Goethals of the United States Army was placed in charge, with an able company of engineers to carry on the work. The first shovelful of earth was thrown up in 1904.

Each of the thirty-four miles of the route presented its own difficulties. A rushing river had to be tamed, a deep cut had to be made through a great mountain ridge, and a great lake had to be constructed. It was an immense enterprise.

American engineers knew from the first that they must also battle against diseases which had always flourished in that tropical country. They could succeed only if their workers could be protected from yellow fever and malaria. Fortunately, for the first time in history such protection was possible.

In Cuba a great discovery had been made. For many years a Cuban physician, Dr. Carlos Finlay, had insisted that yellow fever was carried from person to person by a certain mosquito. People had laughed at the idea. But medical officers of the United States Army who came to Cuba after the Spanish-American War were willing to give this theory a test.

Major Walter Reed led in a series of experiments. American soldiers gallantly risked their lives by allowing themselves to be bitten by the suspected mosquitoes. Some men died; others lived. When the tests were completed, Major Reed was able to announce to the world that yellow fever was carried in one way, and one way only—by this particular mosquito.

Major William C. Gorgas, a United States Army surgeon, went to work to rid the city of Havana of this insect by

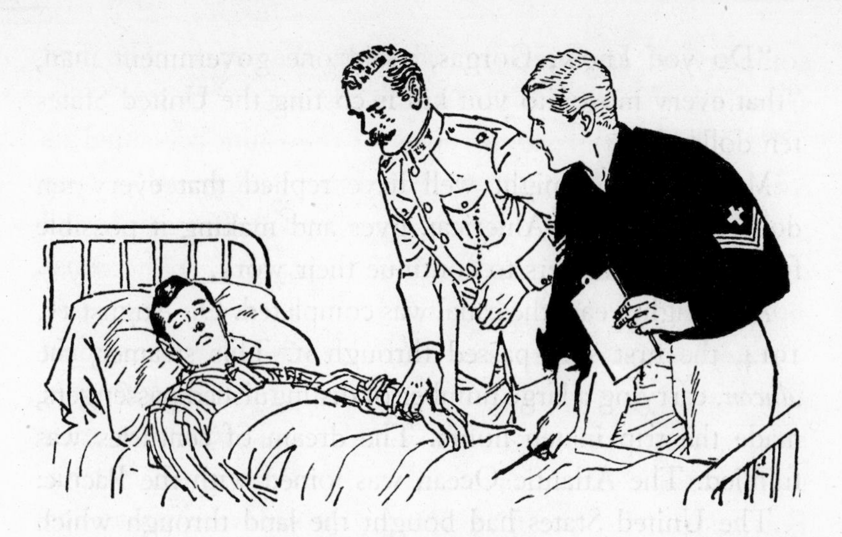

destroying its breeding places. The mosquito lays its eggs in standing water. An army of workers cleaned up the city and removed every pool of standing water. Oil was sprayed on creeks and swamps. In a remarkably short time yellow fever disappeared.

This victory was important to both North and South Americans. For more than two hundred years the disease had swept through the port cities of the Atlantic coast. It could now be prevented. Another mosquito was found to be carrying malaria from man to man. Another victory was in sight.

The victory over disease made possible the building of the Panama Canal. Colonel Goethals invited Major Gorgas to come from Cuba to Panama. Gorgas sent men into the jungles on both sides of the canal route to hunt for and destroy mosquitoes. He did not have enough money or helpers, and officials still doubted the results.

"Do you know, Gorgas," said one government man, "that every mosquito you kill is costing the United States ten dollars?"

Major Gorgas might well have replied that every ten dollars was saving American lives and making it possible for the canal builders to continue their work.

After eight years the canal was completed. On August 15, 1914, the first ship passed through it. This steamer, the *Ancon*, carrying a large number of distinguished passengers, made the trip in ten hours. The dream of centuries was fulfilled. The Atlantic Ocean was joined with the Pacific.

The United States had bought the land through which the waterway was cut, and has controlled this Canal Zone ever since. The canal itself is open to the ships of other nations. It served at once to increase trade between the west coast republics of South America and the eastern ports of the United States. It thus became useful in bringing the people of the two continents together as well as in increasing world trade.

FROM WIRELESS TELEGRAPHY TO BROADCASTING

Knowledge and new inventions, trade and big events were changing life for people in all countries of the world.

For years scientists studying electricity knew that there were mysterious waves traveling through space and tried to find out more and more about them. But years passed before it occurred to anyone to make practical use of them for telegraphing messages. Then a young man, twenty-one years old, experimented with them. He was Guglielmo Marconi, son of an Italian father and an Irish mother. At his father's home in Bologna, Italy, he succeeded in sending messages from one room to another with no wires to carry them. He went to England and showed British postal officials what could be done. There he was granted a patent, and in 1901 he proved that a wireless signal could be sent across the Atlantic Ocean.

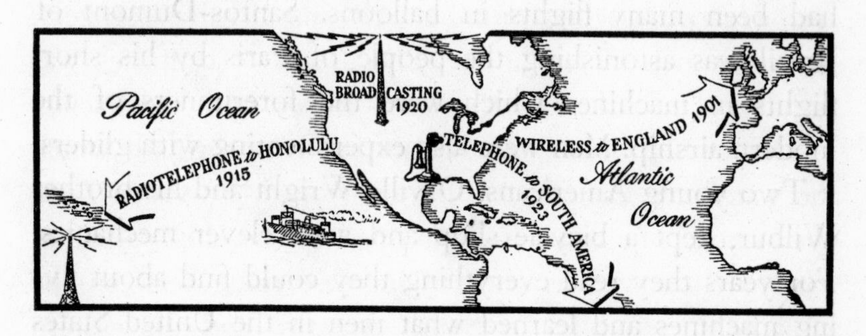

Then wireless, or radio, leaped into use. In 1903 a message of greeting was sent across the Atlantic Ocean from Theodore Roosevelt, President of the United States, to the King of England. People remembered their amazement when President Buchanan and Queen Victoria had exchanged messages by cable in 1858. Wireless was a still greater wonder. It was especially valuable in reaching ships far out at sea.

The first signals sent by wireless were weak and could be barely heard. Successful communication was made possible by the invention of a vacuum tube by Lee De Forest in the United States. By its use signals were magnified many, many times.

The radiotelephone soon followed. In 1915 the sound of spoken words was carried without wires from a point near Washington, D.C., to Honolulu. In 1920 radio broadcasting began.

AIRPLANES AND THE WRIGHT BROTHERS

The year 1903 was a great year in aviation. Earlier there had been many flights in balloons. Santos-Dumont of Brazil was astonishing the people of Paris by his short flights in machines which were the forerunners of the modern airship. Men were also experimenting with gliders.

Two young Americans, Orville Wright and his brother Wilbur, kept a bicycle shop and were clever mechanics. For years they read everything they could find about flying machines and learned what men in the United States and Europe were inventing. For years they made gliders and coasted in the air with them. At last they were ready to mount a little homemade gasoline engine on one of their gliders. They planned to start their machine on a sloping track and then lift it into the air.

On the advice of the United States Weather Bureau they had chosen Kitty Hawk, North Carolina, for their experiments. Here the winds were likely to be blowing at sixteen to twenty-five miles an hour. There were sloping sand dunes for take-offs, and the ground was soft for landing. Here they had coasted hundreds of times in their gliders.

On December 17, 1903, they tried out their new machine at Kitty Hawk. On the first attempt it stayed in the air twelve seconds, covering a distance of one hundred feet, flying ten feet above the ground. On the fourth attempt the machine stayed in the air for fifty-nine seconds and covered a distance of 852 feet. That flight marked the beginning of the age of the airplane.

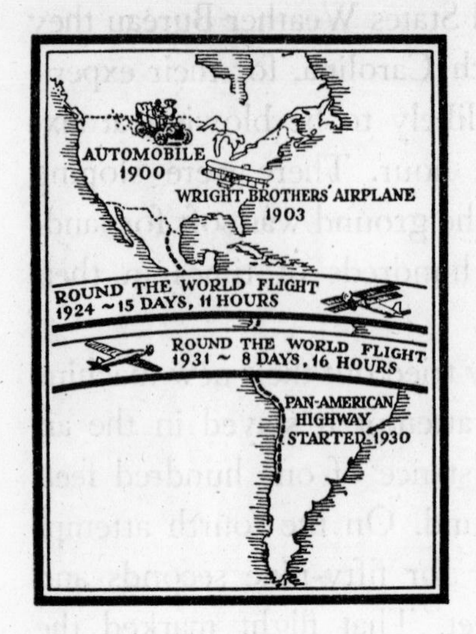

CONQUERING DISTANCE

Inventions were bringing people of all regions and countries closer together. Railways, telegraph, and telephone had begun the process. The automobile, invented just before 1900, came into wide use within twenty years. Radio and the airplane continued this conquest of distance. In 1924 two United States Army airplanes went slowly and laboriously around the world. They were in the air for fifteen days and eleven hours. But the necessary stops between flights made the time of the tour nearly six months. This was a great event for that time. But only seven years later, two American fliers, starting in the United States, encircled the globe in eight days and sixteen hours. The world seemed to be growing smaller year by year.

PROGRESS IN WAYS OF LIVING

Before and after World War I, there were various kinds of progress in the daily life of people in the United States. Some gains were the result of new inventions and machines. Others came through the government or the efforts of public-spirited citizens.

The United States Post Office expanded its services for the benefit of persons living outside towns and cities. Rural free delivery of mail was established in 1896, and soon there were more than eight thousand rural routes. People living on farms were able to receive daily newspapers and so keep in closer touch with the world. The farmer could hear quickly from his markets. Lonely families looked forward to the daily visit of the postman. Parcel-post service, begun in 1913, added to the comfort of country people as well as to the convenience of people in cities.

Good roads and the use of automobiles caused changes in rural schools by bringing children of big districts together. The little school at the crossroads of a farming community was replaced by a larger, better-equipped school building, to which children were brought many miles in motorbuses.

In New York and other big cities many children of immigrants came to school not knowing the English language. Not only were they taught to read and write, but they were trained in American ways. As they studied and played with American-born children, they quickly learned to be loyal American citizens.

People like Jane Addams and Jacob Riis worked to protect children by laws. Many children of poor parents worked in factories or in their homes. A garment manufacturer would often give out jobs in the making of clothes to be done in the tenements where families lived, and little children would labor for long hours at these tasks. After the harm done by such work was made clear, states and cities required parents to send their boys and girls to school until they were old enough to work without injury to their health. Laws were also passed in many states which forbade employers to keep boys and girls at work for more than an eight-hour day. School officials and social workers tried year by year to give all children a chance for a good education.

In 1900, five hundred boys in Macoupin County, Illinois, were given selected seed corn to plant. They were told to be ready to exhibit their product at the next farmers' county institute. This was the beginning of Four-H clubs for boys and girls. The name Four-H comes from the tests set up for head, hand, heart, and health. The club symbol is a four-leaf clover with an *H* on each leaf. Corn clubs were also organized in Ohio. Soon such clubs raised other farm and garden products. By 1909 there were boys' and girls' rural clubs in twenty states. In 1914 the Department of Agriculture at Washington took official notice of these clubs and arranged to help them, as state agricultural stations were already doing. Today hundreds of thousands of boys and girls all over the country belong to these busy, helpful groups.

There is a pleasant story of the way the Boy Scout movement came to this country from England. William D. Boyce, a Chicago publisher, while visiting in London got lost in a London fog. A boy came up to him, saluted, and said, "May I be of service to you, sir?"

Mr. Boyce replied, "If you can show me how to get to this address, I shall be very much obliged."

The boy saluted again and said, "Follow me, sir."

When they reached the place Mr. Boyce was looking for, he pulled out a coin and offered it to his guide.

"Sir," said the boy, "I am a Scout. Scouts do not take money for such services."

Mr. Boyce was much interested in what the boy told him about the Scouts. They went together to the office of Sir Robert Baden-Powell, founder of the Boy Scout organization. Mr. Boyce brought back to this country the story of what the Scouts were doing and told it to a friend in Washington. Together they started in 1910 the Boy Scouts of America. Girl Scouts and Campfire Girls were soon organized.

All these clubs for young people grew rapidly. They have shown what an important place boys and girls have in the life of the community and the nation.

From about 1890, the different nations of the Western Hemisphere were having more and more dealings with one another. Questions are bound to arise between neighbors which they must settle together. Trade between their citizens brings problems. There are often questions about boundaries between countries. The peoples of the twenty-one American republics and the Dominion of Canada discovered that many of their interests were the same. They also learned to settle differences by peaceful means.

CANADA AND THE UNITED STATES

For more than a century there has been an unguarded frontier between Canada and the United States. Both nations are proud that there are no fortifications on their coast-to-coast boundary line. Each looks upon the other as a friendly neighbor.

The two countries have frequently had questions to settle about their inland waterways and the oceans to the east and west in which they both have an interest. Rivers cross from Canada into the United States. Atlantic and Pacific fishermen go north and south of the ocean boundary line. More than once a threat of war has arisen over such matters, but leaders in both countries have managed to reach agreements. The people of both countries have a will to peace. Their governments are therefore able to work together with increasing friendliness.

South American republics have had many questions to settle among themselves. There have been many disputes over boundary lines between their territories. Within the Spanish empire in South America it was never important to draw such lines. But when separate republics were formed, some of the border lines between them lay in unexplored wilderness. If rich deposits of minerals were found in such territory, each nation promptly claimed ownership. There was also frequent trouble over ways to the sea. Inland nations fought to keep from being shut out from trade by sea with distant countries.

While there have been wars over such boundary disputes, there have also been outstanding peace agreements. One of these was between Argentina and Chile. The disputed border lay high in the Andes. There was angry discussion between the two governments. However, they finally agreed to have their claims settled by arbitration. That is, each nation agreed to state its case to a committee of men of other countries and to accept the decision of that committee as final.

A long period of delay followed, and excited leaders in both countries were pushing preparations for war when the decision came. Arbitration had settled the dispute.

In thankfulness for peace, a great statue, known as the "Christ of the Andes," was erected in 1904 on the boundary line in the high mountains between the countries of Chile and Argentina. Cannon which would have been used in war

were melted to supply the bronze for the statue. Beneath the figure of the Christ there has been placed, within recent years, a bronze tablet with these words, spoken at the time the statue was dedicated: "Sooner shall these mountains crumble to dust than Argentines and Chileans break the peace sworn at the feet of Christ the Redeemer."

THE PAN AMERICAN UNION

For more than a century representatives of the twenty-one American republics have come together now and again in conference. "Americans are spread over all climates but should form one family," said a Honduran statesman in 1822 as he urged a Pan American conference. From Mexico and Chile, and from Portuguese Brazil there also came in those early years the desire for such unity. The first conference was held in 1826. It was called by Simón Bolívar, the South American Liberator. People of the southern countries like to remember that Pan Americanism had its beginnings in Spanish America.

The first conferences did not have important results, but in 1890 real progress was made. Delegates from eighteen countries came together in Washington, D.C. They planned an organization which grew into the Pan American Union. The date of its beginning, April 14, is now known as Pan American Day and is celebrated in both North and South America. At first this Union was hardly more than a group of committees, but its influence has increased. Through its work information is exchanged between member countries, and important meetings are arranged. Since 1890 several Pan American conferences have been held in different countries.

At the Pan American Conference in 1923 the first international telephone service between the two continents was begun. In 1925 plans were made for a Pan American Highway to stretch from Alaska to the tip of South America, uniting all the countries. Each nation was to build its own section. Work on this great roadway was started in 1930, and some sections are now in use.

Scientists of different nations have worked together within the Pan American Union for public health. Students have been encouraged to go back and forth between North and South American colleges and universities. In many, many ways the bonds between the peoples of the Americas have been strengthened.

War made the American people aware as never before of their relation to the people of other countries.

In 1917 the United States entered the war now known as World War I, which had then been going on in Europe for three years. This war, begun by the assassination of an Austrian archduke in June, 1914, drew most of Europe into conflict within a few weeks. Germany and Austria took up arms against Russia and France. When the Germans in-

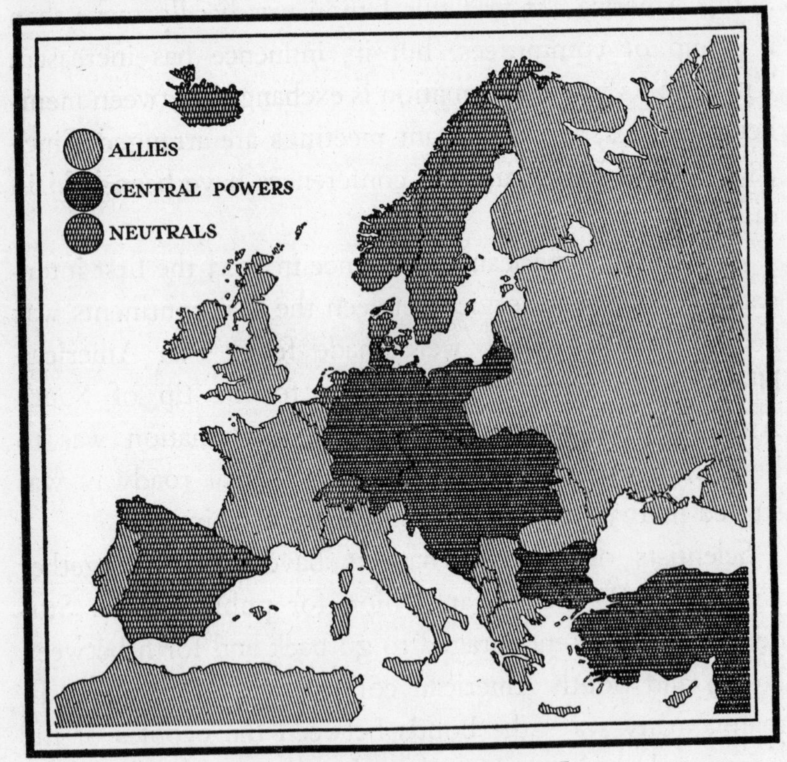

EUROPE IN WORLD WAR I

vaded Belgium, Great Britain entered the war. Other European nations joined on one side or the other, and Canada, Australia, and other British dominions took part as members of the British Empire.

The United States did not want to join in this war. Woodrow Wilson, then President, made every effort to keep the nation out, and also to bring about peace between the warring nations. But American ships sailing to British and European ports were attacked. The sinking of American vessels by German submarines finally brought the United States to declare war on Germany in April, 1917. This placed the nation on the side of England and France and their allies. Soon thousands of American soldiers were on their way to France. Within a year and a half the nation sent nearly two million men overseas. Under the command of General John J. Pershing these soldiers fought beside the troops of England and France.

After many terrible battles Germany and the nations fighting on her side were defeated. Fighting ended on November 11, 1918, when an armistice was declared.

WOODROW WILSON AND THE LEAGUE OF NATIONS

An armistice is a peace which lasts until the terms for a treaty of peace can be arranged. Representatives of the victorious nations gathered in Paris in 1919 to make the final treaty. President Wilson himself went to Paris to this conference. He had in his mind plans for a peace treaty which should go beyond the ending of this war and should

set up a League of Nations. It was his hope and belief that a league which brought all the nations together in conference would help to prevent future wars.

Woodrow Wilson had long been a student of the ways of government. He had been both college professor and college president, and then the governor of the state of New Jersey. In 1913 he had become President of the United States, and had been re-elected in 1916. He had been a very able war leader. Now he was eager to work for permanent world peace.

He had a difficult experience at the Paris conference. Each nation was concerned with itself, what it had suffered, and what it hoped to gain from the treaty. But Wilson finally succeeded in having his plan for a League of Nations made a part of the peace treaty. This treaty he brought home with him. It was necessary for the Senate of the United States to give its consent. Then Wilson met bitter disappointment. The Senate refused its approval. Some of its members feared that the United States would be drawn into European affairs and even into future wars if it entered the proposed League of Nations. They felt that the United States should not agree to go to war if the boundaries of any member of the league were crossed by an enemy army.

While President Wilson was urging the people to support his plan, he became seriously ill. The time for action passed. The League of Nations was formed, but the United States did not become a member. President Wilson never recovered his health, but died in 1924 at the age of sixty-seven. Today he is honored as a man who looked into the future and saw what was needed. He knew that wars would come unless the nations of the world united to prevent them.

In the years that followed the end of the war the United States did not stand wholly apart. It did much for the relief of starving and suffering peoples of Europe through an organization headed by Herbert Hoover. Americans helped to organize a world League of Red Cross Societies. United States Presidents made several moves for world peace. Some of its most honored citizens worked often with the committees of the League of Nations on international health and labor problems.

All Americans except the Indians are immigrants or the descendants of immigrants. For many years the United States kept its doors wide open for those who wished to come in from Europe. The only limits on immigration had to do with the health and character of persons who wished to enter. In the years immediately following World War I enormous numbers of people entered the country. The nation was richer for their coming. But many Americans were disturbed because of the great number of newcomers. In 1920 one eighth of the people of the United States were foreign born. There were no more wide, empty

lands waiting for settlers as there had been in the past. Large numbers of the recent immigrants were crowded in great cities or in communities near the mines or mills where they were employed.

People began to fear the results if more thousands came to join these foreign-born groups. Again and again it was proposed that a limit should be put on the number admitted. Members of labor unions favored such limits. They wanted to keep wages and the standard of American living high. The newcomers could be hired at low wages. Because they were paid so little, they were forced to live as American workers were not willing to live.

One President after another had refused to sign laws which limited immigration. They felt that America should continue to be the land of opportunity for all who wished to come to it, as it had been for three hundred years. But after World War I such laws were passed.

THE UNITED STATES CLOSES ITS DOORS

In 1921 and 1924 Immigration Acts set limits to the number of immigrants to be admitted in a single year. For each country there was a number, or quota, which would be received. The quota was figured as a certain part of the total number of people from that country who were living in the United States in a particular year. Thus the doors of America were only partly closed.

Immigrants from Canada, Mexico, countries of Central and South America, and the islands of the Caribbean Sea were not to be under this quota system. However, other acts were passed which set some limits as to who should be admitted from these lands.

The doors of the United States had long been closed against free immigration from the countries of the Orient. For a time after the discovery of gold in California in 1848, Chinese laborers were welcomed. Hundreds of them helped to build the railways of the West. But as white laborers came from the Eastern states, there was competition between the races, and trouble began. Then agreements were made between the United States and China, and acts were passed by Congress which shut out Chinese laborers, though Chinese teachers, students, merchants, and travelers were admitted. An arrangement was also made with Japan which limited the coming of Japanese laborers to the Western coast. People of these nations were indignant when the United States, in its Immigration Act of 1924, excluded all Asiatic peoples from its quota system. Relations between the United States and the nations of the Pacific were made more difficult by this act.

A CHANGING WORLD

With the discovery of America the world suddenly grew larger. Soon two new continents were added to the map. A few years later Magellan's voyage proved that the world was round and larger than anyone had dreamed. But as the twentieth century opened, the world began to seem smaller; and it has seemed to grow smaller ever since.

Changes have never come so fast in all the long history of the world as in the past forty or fifty years. A man who is now sixty years old has seen amazing changes in daily living since he was a child. He was full grown before automobiles appeared on the streets. He has seen the telephone and the radio come into common use. The beginning of moving pictures is within his time. So are airplane travel and the swift crossing of oceans on huge modern ships.

During the nineteenth century the people of the United States were busy about their affairs at home. As the century came to an end, they were engaging more and more in world trade. The United States acquired new lands in both the Atlantic and Pacific oceans. A few years later, it had to take its part in the First World War. It had become a world power, but it held back from taking its place as an active member of a world family of nations. Its people had still to learn the lessons of a world which was growing smaller every year.

Talking Together

1. How many different radio stations can you hear on your radio? Where are they located? How far are these places from where you live? Radio gives you entertainment and information. Name two popular programs that furnish entertainment and two that give information about what is happening in the world.

2. How many of the forty-eight states of the United States border on Canada? Can you name them from east to west? Which states of the United States border on Mexico?

3. "The Airplane Makes the World Grow Smaller" is a good topic for discussion. How much can you contribute to show that this is true?

4. Choose two persons mentioned in this unit. Make a true statement about each and see if the class can name the person.

Interesting Things to Try

1. Immigration makes a good subject for a graph. In *The World Almanac* find the number of people who came to this country in different years and prepare a graph using these figures.

2. Since all Americans who are not Indians are immigrants or descendants of immigrants, it would be interesting to know how many different countries are represented in this way in your classroom. Each pupil might list the country or countries which his ancestors left to come to America. Then a combination list could be made for the class as a whole.

3. For a week clip out every reference to Canada from the newspapers which come into your home. Choose a committee to sort the clippings and to arrange the most interesting on the bulletin board. What new things did you learn about Canada in this way?

4. Have the president of the class write to the Association of American Railroads, Transportation Building, Washington, D.C., asking for free pictures and booklets.

5. Choose a committee to interview the postmaster to find out all

the different kinds of services furnished by the post office to the people of your community.

6. Make a time line to show the territorial growth of the United States from 1783 down to the present time.

7. Choose committees to make illustrated booklets about the different possessions of the United States. Each booklet should contain a map and tell something of the history, the products and industries, the people, and the government of the possession. What kinds of reference books will you use?

Increasing Your Vocabulary

The author of this book has tried to write the story of the Americas chiefly in words which you already understand. New words have also been used; first, because you need to meet new words in order to add to your vocabulary, and second, because special words are sometimes needed to explain correctly historical happenings.

When you come to a word in this history that you do not know, you may do one of several things—

1. You may skip it and not bother about it.
2. You may ask an older person what it means.
3. You may try to think what the word means by the way it is used in the sentence or paragraph.
4. You may use a dictionary and choose the meaning that seems to fit best the way the word is used in the book.

A pupil who is at all interested in increasing his vocabulary would never use the first way given above. Neither would he use the second way until he had tried the third and fourth ways.

Some boys and girls have a larger vocabulary than others. Look up the words below on the pages where they are used. What will you do about the words you do not understand?

	Page		*Page*		*Page*
anti-Spanish	384	expanded	395	allies	403
enterprise	388	inland	399	descendants	406
forerunners	392	arbitration	399	quota	407

Let's Read

Up Canada Way, by Helen Dickson. This colorful little book makes you acquainted with the Canada of today.

Widening Trails, by William H. Johnson. Use the index to locate information about the Philippines and the Panama Canal.

America Then and Now, by Edna McGuire. Here you will find more stories about people and events in the unit you are studying.

Wonderful Wings: The Story of Aviation, by I. Leon Maizlish. The story of the airplane is told from earliest times to now.

My First Geography of the Pacific, by Arensa Sondergaard. Pictures help to tell the story of the Pacific Islands.

The World's Messengers, by H. H. Webster. You will find an interesting story of radio on pages 91–128.

Quiz Yourself

What are the names of the places described below? Write them on a separate sheet of paper, not in this book.

1. A country whose 4000-mile southern boundary has no forts for defense against its foreign neighbor.
2. A group of islands that became part of the United States.
3. An island republic to which the United States has been a helpful neighbor.
4. An island which largely governs itself but whose governor is appointed by the President of the United States.
5. The place where experiments were carried on which proved that a certain kind of mosquito carried yellow fever germs.
6. The country in which the first experiments were carried on with wireless, or radio.
7. The countries on whose boundary line was erected a famous statue to mark the establishment of peace between them.
8. The place where a French company had failed but where American engineers succeeded in doing a job that established a new route for world trade.

XI AMERICANS IN THE WORLD COMMUNITY

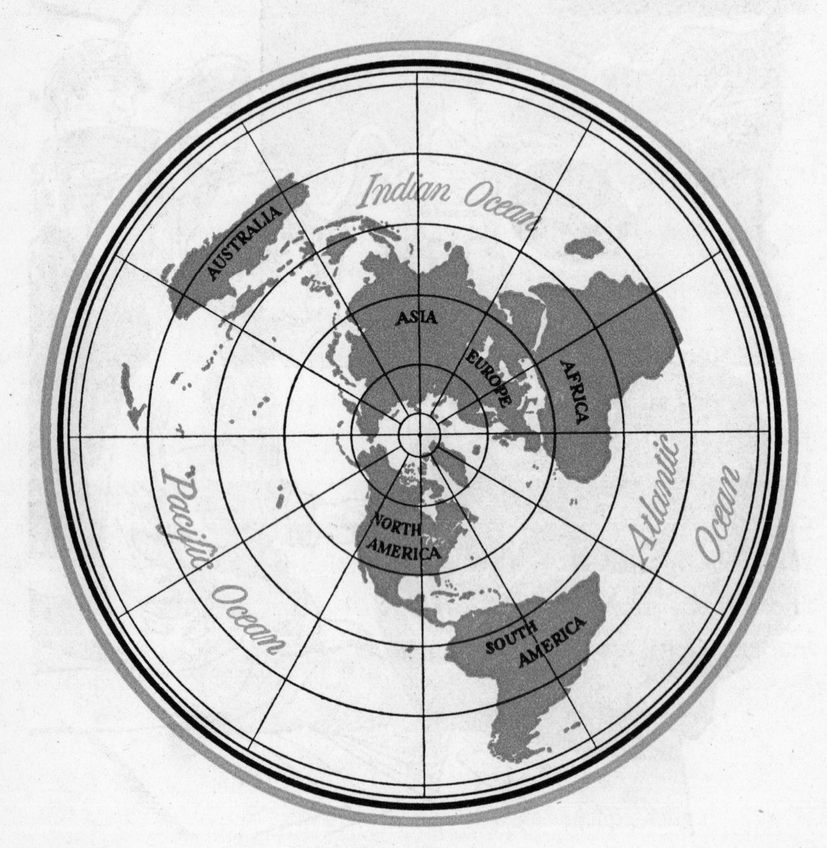
Indian Ocean
AUSTRALIA
ASIA
EUROPE
AFRICA
Atlantic Ocean
Pacific Ocean
NORTH AMERICA
SOUTH AMERICA

ONE WORLD

AMERICANS IN THE WORLD COMMUNITY

The story of events which are happening day by day is a different kind of story from that of the past. People speak of present and recent happenings as "current events." One event follows rapidly on another as if caught up by the current of a swift-flowing stream.

No one is far enough away from the events of his own time to see them as he can see the happenings of long ago. But he can have a most exciting experience as he observes current events. He is watching history in the making. It is being described in the newspapers and over the radio and shown in moving pictures. Often he actually sees the leaders of his country who are taking active part in it.

A CHANGING UNITED STATES

Anyone can read modern history by looking about him in his own community. In every town and city there have been changes within the last ten or twenty or twenty-five years. The fine public buildings are modern. There is probably a new post office, and surely a new schoolhouse.

Many of the stores and office buildings on the main street are new. American architects have been clever in meeting the needs of changing, growing communities. Buildings of recent years have more windows to let in light. They have been planned so that every foot of space is used. They are arranged in attractive groups. "If a building is true to the purpose for which it is built, it will have its own beauty," the architects say. Americans have a right to be proud of the improvements made by modern builders.

In the center of even a small town there will be signposts which show that its main street is part of a national system of highways. Good roads have been built throughout the country to take care of the millions of automobiles. States have planned together and with the Federal government to connect all parts of the country. In almost every region landing fields are being constructed for airplanes.

Besides these local improvements there are in many parts of the country great public works, such as bridges and dams across rivers. Since the beginning of the twentieth

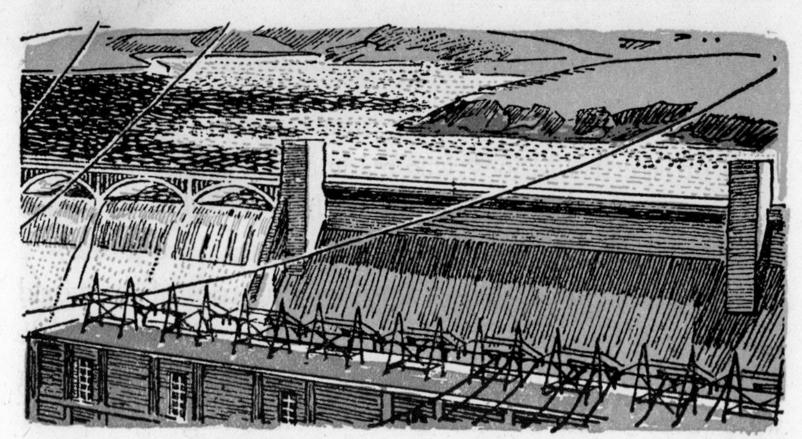

century the United States has undertaken many such projects for the benefit of the people. Chief among these have been the projects for flood control. Great destruction has always been caused by the overflow of some of the great rivers. Modern engineers saw that the flood waters could be turned to good use if they were controlled and distributed where water was needed.

President Theodore Roosevelt led the way in plans for flood control. He saw that the Federal government must work with the states, for the course of a river might lie in several states. In his time the Roosevelt Dam in Arizona and the Arrowrock Dam in Idaho were built to hold back flood waters, which could then irrigate wide areas. President Herbert Hoover, who had been an engineer, saw work started on the Hoover Dam, sometimes called Boulder Dam, on the Colorado River. Much of the water stored here is used for electric power. The states of Colorado, Arizona, Nevada, New Mexico, and California are all benefited.

From 1920 on, the United States enjoyed a period of great prosperity. Money was made easily and spent freely. People congratulated themselves that World War I was over and life could be normal and peaceful once more.

But in the United States and other countries of the world trouble was coming. The war had nearly ruined the trade and business of European nations. Poverty and suffering were widespread. In the United States large groups of people were not sharing in the general prosperity. Farmers complained that the prices which they were getting for their crops were too low. The Federal government was making efforts to remedy this situation.

In 1929 prosperity abruptly stopped. A business depression began, which had been in the making since the end of World War I. This condition of business was world wide, but it came with great suddenness in the United States. In October there were serious losses in the New York Stock Exchange, which is the country's central money market. The trouble spread to all parts of the country. Business slowed down, and the effect was felt in banks large and small, in little country stores, on farms, and in shops and factories.

FRANKLIN D. ROOSEVELT AND A "NEW DEAL"

In 1932 it was time for a presidential election. By that time the affairs of the country were in great confusion.

Factories were shutting their doors. Millions of men were unable to get work. Banks were closing. Franklin D. Roosevelt, a distant cousin of Theodore Roosevelt, was the presidential candidate of the Democratic party. He promised what he called a "new deal" for the American people. He won the election by a big majority.

He was fifty-one years old at the time. In his youth he had had all the privileges which wealth could give. He was graduated from Harvard College in 1904, and became a lawyer in New York City. There he chose to enter political life. He was elected to the New York legislature, then served during the First World War as Assistant Secretary of the Navy, and was becoming an important figure in the nation when he was taken ill. He had a severe attack of infantile paralysis which left him crippled. Many a man would have felt that his public life was ended. But Franklin Roosevelt fought his way back to health, and served two terms as governor of New York.

This was the man who came to the White House in Washington in March, 1933. He and the Congress working with him began at once to carry out his promise of help to the people and the nation. The government promptly put large numbers of men to work on public projects, such as the building of roads and public buildings and other necessary town and state projects. The CCC, or Civilian Conservation Corps, was started for young men from seventeen to twenty-three years old. They lived in camps

and worked in forests, making trails and roads, planting trees, and preventing forest fires.

Huge flood control and power projects were undertaken. In the years of World War I the Federal government had built a dam and a chemical plant at Muscle Shoals on the Tennessee River. This undertaking was expanded into a project for the development of the entire river valley in order to make use of its resources for the benefit of the people. First came the building of dams and reservoirs for flood control and water power. The river was widened and deepened for the use of boats. Water power furnished electric power, so that electricity could now be used by all inhabitants of the great valley.

Another part of the New Deal plan had to do with reform of laws and the improvement of social and business conditions. Congress adopted plans for protecting persons against unemployment and for old-age pensions.

THE GOOD NEIGHBOR POLICY

On the day when he became President in 1933, Roosevelt made an important declaration. "In the field of world policy," he announced, "I would dedicate this nation to the policy of the good neighbor—the neighbor who resolutely respects himself, and because he does so, respects the rights of others." Nations south of the United States had often felt that this country was not a good neighbor. They feared lest it use its power to interfere with their independence.

Slowly, during President Roosevelt's long term of office, the people of these nations came to feel that the United States really intended to be a good neighbor. Pan American conferences were held from time to time to discuss matters which concerned all the Americas. Students went back and forth between the colleges and universities of the various countries. Engineers, doctors, agricultural experts, went from the United States to be of aid in countries where they were desired. Radio programs and the exchange of letters by children of different countries helped toward inter-American understanding.

Europe at the Opening of World War II

BEGINNINGS OF ANOTHER WORLD WAR

In 1939 war came again to Europe. Within two years this war spread over most of the globe. Like all wars it had been long in the making. Its causes went back to the First World War and even further.

The defeat of Germany in 1918 was followed by peace terms which were intended to make the conquered nation pay heavy war damages. By the Treaty of Versailles its overseas territories were taken away, and it was forbidden to arm itself for war. Large debt payments were ordered.

In the years that followed, other nations passed trade laws which made it difficult for Germany to sell abroad the goods which would have helped in making the required payments. Its people went through a period of great poverty and distress. They were restless and unhappy and felt that their nation had no hope. They were, therefore, ready to follow any leader who promised better things.

In Italy there were also poverty and dissatisfaction. Its people felt that they had not been fairly treated after the war in the distribution of territory, although they had fought on the side of the Allies.

THE RISE OF DICTATORS

A new kind of government grew up which was the opposite of democracy. In a democratic country the people are the real rulers. Any powers which their government has are given by the people. Certain rights and liberties are guaranteed to every person.

In Italy and Germany there grew up an idea of the state as all-powerful. Citizens belonged to the state. It had the right to tell them what they should do and how they should think. This theory of national life is called Fascism. It leads quickly to the rule of strong men who love power and seek to control the state. These men become dictators.

Fascism appeared first in Italy when Benito Mussolini came into power in 1922. He began to organize the life of the nation on Fascist lines. He and his followers gained their opportunity because of the unhappiness and poverty of the people. They promised to do much for the future of Italy.

In Germany, Adolf Hitler, a veteran of the First World War, organized a revolutionary party and seized control of the government. He had a plan of Fascism and added to it another idea, that of a superior race. He announced that

Germans belonged to this race and should rule the world. He said that peoples of other races in Europe had no rights in the future order which he planned for Europe, nor in the world order which was to come. He and his followers were called Nazis.

Japan became a Fascist state of a different sort. Certain Japanese beliefs led naturally to this form of government, for the people had always held their emperor to be a divine ruler with all power in the state and over his people.

FASCIST NATIONS BEGIN THE ATTACK

The rulers of Italy, Germany, and Japan looked out on the world and felt that they had too small a share in its wealth and its territory. They resented the power and wealth of the democratic nations which prospered at home

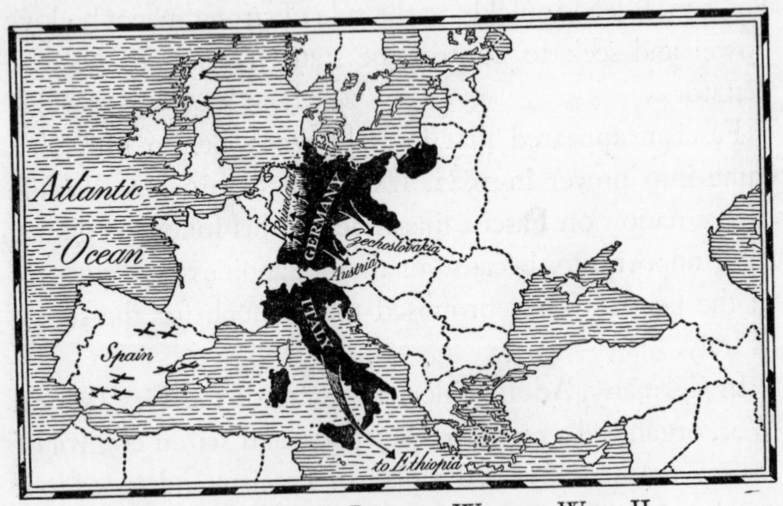

FASCIST MOVES BEFORE WORLD WAR II

and had colonies abroad. They wanted more territory and more share in world trade. They began to call themselves the "have-not" nations and to speak of Great Britain, the United States, and other great nations as the "have" nations. Their next step was to move out and acquire more territory and more wealth.

At first each Fascist nation acted alone. In 1931 Japan invaded Manchuria, declaring that it needed space into which people could move from its crowded islands. This land Japan had long wanted to own, for it is rich in minerals. Four years later Italy sent armies into Africa and took possession of Ethiopia. Germany was moving into the Rhineland provinces in which it had been forbidden since the First World War to keep any soldiers. The three nations gradually began to work together as their leaders saw that their interests were in many ways the same.

JAPANESE THRUSTS INTO CHINESE TERRITORY

When civil war broke out in Spain, both Italy and Germany sent aid to Fascist groups which were trying to get control there. In 1937 Japan sent an invading army into North China. In 1938 Germany sent troops into Austria and then into Czechoslovakia. In March, 1939, the Spanish republic fell, and Spain became a Fascist state under the leadership of General Franco.

As Americans looked on at these events from 1931 to 1939, many could not believe that they had any part in them. In Great Britain, France, and Russia there was increasing concern, but the people of the United States felt very far away. Our government made certain protests when weaker nations such as Manchuria were invaded. But few people realized that a new kind of state had come into being which was directly opposed to democracy and aimed at world conquest.

WAR IN EUROPE

Soviet Russia tried to draw England, France, and other European nations into a plan to stop the moves of Germany, but they were not ready. Finally, however, Great Britain and France united to halt Germany in its course. When Germany invaded Poland in September, 1939, France and England declared war. Russia, meanwhile, had signed a ten-year peace pact with Germany. Russia joined in invading Poland and required of neighbor Baltic nations that they give it certain military and other rights in their territory. Germany moved swiftly to the north and west.

Denmark, Norway, Holland, Belgium, and France were attacked and forced to yield. Italy and Japan joined forces with Germany to form a group known as the Axis.

The United States was still trying to keep out of actual war, but it continued to give aid to the nations fighting against Germany, and especially to England, which stood almost alone against the Axis. In June, 1941, Germany broke its pact with the Soviet Union and invaded Russia. Japan had by this time carried its war into other parts of the Orient besides China.

WAR BECOMES WORLD WIDE

Then, on December 7, 1941, Japanese airplanes suddenly attacked the United States at Pearl Harbor in Hawaii. On that very day leaders of the United States government were working in Washington and Tokyo with Japanese leaders to keep peace with Japan. At Pearl Harbor several thousand men in the armed forces were killed or wounded, American warships were sunk, and large numbers of airplanes were destroyed.

The United States promptly declared war on Japan, as did also Great Britain. China made its declaration of war against Japan on the following day. Japan had actually been carrying on war against China for four years. Within three days the United States was also at war with Germany and Italy.

Meanwhile the Japanese were moving fast. During that same week which followed the attack on Pearl Harbor they made attacks on the Philippines and on the British possessions of Hong Kong and Malaya. Hong Kong fell on Christmas Day. Manila, capital of the Philippines, was taken eight days later. World War II had become a global war, with Japan rapidly gaining ports and islands which gave her control over a huge portion of the Pacific.

Canada was already in this company of warring nations because of its relation with Great Britain. Before the attack at Pearl Harbor the American nations to the south had united with one another and with the United States for defense of the Western Hemisphere. At Pan American conferences they had made plans for unity of action. After Pearl Harbor the republics of North and South America began, one after another, to take part in the war. Some declared war at once; others began soon to help in other ways. As time went on, their contributions became more and more valuable. They had rich stores of natural resources, rubber, minerals, food, on which to draw. Ports and airports were put at the service of the Army, Navy, and Air Forces of the United States.

AMERICANS ON ALL FRONTS

The first year of war was spent by the United States in preparation. While Army and Navy did all that was possible in defense, the nation prepared for action against its enemies. Young men were called for training for military duty. Factories changed with surprising speed from peace-time work to the manufacture of war materials. Thousands of new plants were set up. Shipbuilding became a chief industry. Airplanes were manufactured with all speed. Citizens did their part in

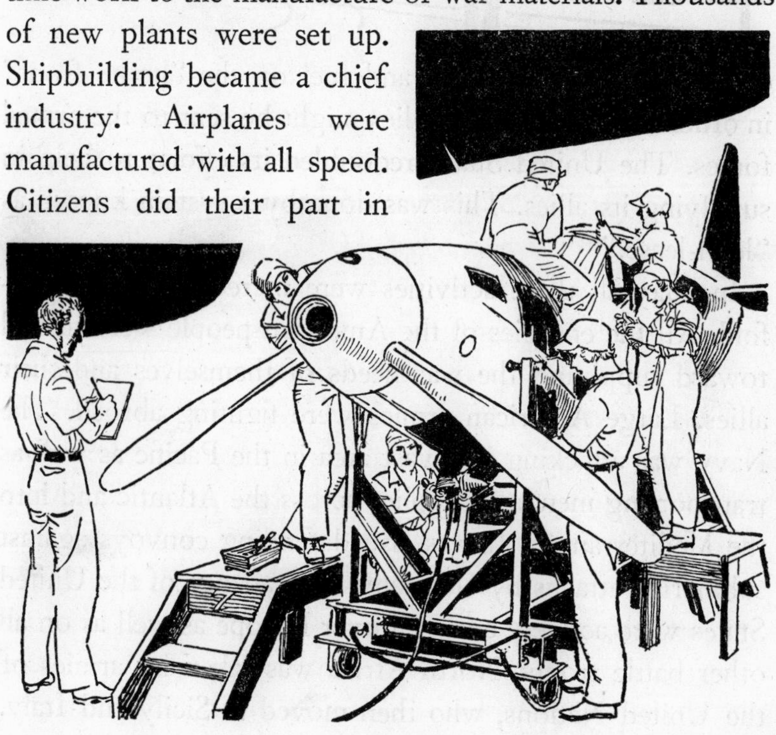

conserving food, clothing, and fuel on the "home front" in order that adequate supplies might be sent to the armed forces. The United States redoubled its efforts to help in supplying its allies. This was done by a system known as "lend-lease."

In 1943 all these activities were increased a thousand-fold. All the energies of the American people were turned toward supplying the war needs of themselves and their allies. Large American armies were fighting abroad. The Navy was attacking in a vast area in the Pacific as well as transporting men and supplies across the Atlantic and into the Mediterranean. It was also defending convoys against submarine attacks by Germany. The airmen of the United States were actively engaged over Europe as well as on all other battle fronts. North Africa was taken by armies of the United Nations, who then moved to Sicily and Italy.

Once again, as so often before, the world was becoming smaller. As airplanes sped back and forth across the oceans, distances seemed less. They were measured in hours rather than in miles. As President Roosevelt or Prime Minister Churchill of Great Britain sat before a microphone and talked to peoples everywhere, the world seemed one neighborhood.

From almost every American family young men went abroad to fight. By the middle of the year 1944 there were seven million members of the armed forces abroad. They and their families at home learned much about the world.

Young men who were sent to distant parts of the world came to know peoples of other races. Fliers, obliged to land in tropical jungles within enemy lines, were often led secretly to safety by friendly natives of nearby villages.

Men training in the British Isles were welcomed in the homes of the English people. Places which had been names on a map became real, not only to the men who visited them but also to their families at home. Wherever American boys went, they made friends with their allies, especially with the children. No part of the world could ever again seem wholly foreign to these widely traveled Americans.

THE FOUR FREEDOMS

Often the question was asked within the United States, "For what is this nation fighting?" The first answer was, "For its life, against enemies that would conquer it." But leaders in this country, as well as those in England and elsewhere, were also looking to the future. Almost a year before armies of the United States began to go overseas, President

Roosevelt made a statement to Americans and to the world of the "four freedoms" for which this nation stood. These were freedom of speech, freedom of worship, freedom from fear, and freedom from want.

Each of these freedoms grew out of America's past, and each was part of its hope for the future of the world. The people of the United States wanted peoples everywhere to possess them. For Americans these freedoms and the way of life which grew out of them meant a democracy.

THE ATLANTIC CHARTER

During the war frequent conferences were held by the leaders of the Allied Nations. President Roosevelt and Prime Minister Churchill met many times. They also had meetings with Marshal Joseph Stalin, leader of Soviet Russia, and General Chiang Kai-shek of China.

At one of these conferences, held in August of 1941 before the United States was attacked by Japan, Roosevelt and Churchill made a declaration of the purposes of their two countries. This declaration was named the Atlantic Charter because the two men met on a ship "somewhere in the Atlantic." Meetings of such important leaders had to be very secret in those days because of the danger from enemy planes and submarines.

The Atlantic Charter gave a picture of a world in which all nations were to live in peace and safety within their own borders. Seas and oceans were to be free for trade. The charter stated that the people of every nation ought to have the right to choose the form of government under which they would live. In the peace which should follow the war there should be freedom for all men everywhere. Such were the hopes of these leaders and their nations for "a better future for the world."

When the Atlantic Charter was announced to the world, the people of the Allied Nations began to look beyond the war toward this better future. They were fighting to defend themselves from being conquered by the Fascist powers, but they were also striving for a world at peace. A month after the Japanese attack on Pearl Harbor, representatives of the twenty-six nations then at war with one or all of the Fascist nations met and agreed to work together as the United Nations. They also pledged themselves to the aims of the Atlantic Charter.

YEAR BY YEAR

Each year of the war had its special dangers. In 1940 and 1941 Great Britain had stood almost alone and had been in the greatest danger of invasion. Her cities were bombed again and again. But the nation stood valiantly, and Germany was unable to invade it.

When the United States came into the war, another danger arose. The Nazis began trying by submarine attacks to sink the vessels which were bringing supplies to England and Russia and also to the Mediterranean. This "Battle of the Atlantic," as it was called, went on for more than two years. Ships traveled with no lights and in large groups for safety. Every effort was made to keep secret the dates when they sailed. But still, many were sunk with great loss of life. However, scientists invented new devices for detecting the approach of submarines. The victory over the submarine was finally won by the building of new ships at a tremendous rate. By 1943 the United States Navy had doubled and become a two-ocean force, active in both the Atlantic and the Pacific. Airplanes were also guarding the sea lanes of travel.

In 1941 the armies of Germany began their invasion of Russia. They attacked on a front which reached from Leningrad in the north to the Black Sea at the south. The Western world watched with the greatest anxiety while the Nazis drove forward toward the three great Russian cities of Leningrad, Moscow, and Stalingrad. At one time it seemed as if the city of Stalingrad was lost, for the troops of the enemy were in its streets. But the Russians would not give it up.

Finally Hitler was forced to withdraw his troops. By their magnificent defense the Soviet armies had saved their own land. They had also given their Western Allies time to build up strong forces.

Over in the Pacific Japanese advances were at last being blocked. Plans to cut off the line of American supplies to Australia had to be given up. The Japanese attack on the tiny island fortress of Midway had been in vain. Japan had been unable to prevent American Marines from recapturing Guadalcanal in the Solomon Islands and taking over a nearly completed airfield.

By the summer of 1944 the Allies were gaining on many fronts. The Russians had driven the German armies back along a line which extended for hundreds of miles. American and British troops had pushed far north in Italy, keeping large German armies active there.

In England great numbers of men were waiting for the day when they should cross the English Channel and invade the continent. Preparations were being made on a scale never before dreamed of. By day and by night a steady stream of airplanes was attacking planned targets in Germany and the countries which its troops had occupied. The airmen were bombing the factories where arms were being made, and the railroads and bridges over which the Germans were trying to move men. It was their task to break up the whole system of transportation and communication in the region where the invasion was to be made.

On June 6, 1944, the invasion began. Thousands of Allied troops were successfully landed by ship and parachute in northern France. General Dwight D. Eisenhower was supreme commander of these invasion forces. On land and sea and in the air the armed forces of the Allied Nations were uniting in a remarkable way.

The Germans fell back, unable to communicate with their advance units and assemble to resist the invasion. But though this first move was successful, nearly a year of heavy fighting followed before the Allied armies came to the Rhine River and Germany. During these months bombing was continued with increasing force, and new armies and supplies were rushed from the United States. The losses of men in the battles were great. The Germans brought out new weapons of destruction. But gradually the Allies were wearing out the enemy on a front which extended from the Mediterranean to the far north. On May 6, 1945, the Germans surrendered. This was the long-awaited V-E (Victory in Europe) Day.

DEATH OF THE PRESIDENT

Franklin Delano Roosevelt, President and Commander in Chief for the United States, did not live to see V-E Day. He died, suddenly, less than a month before the victory which he had done so much to win. With Churchill and Stalin he had made up the "Big Three" who directed the war. He had traveled thousands of miles to meet with these men and with leaders of other nations. He had been President of the United States longer than any other man. All over the world people mourned his death.

Americans remembered his cheerful courage. He had become President in 1933 when banks were closed and twelve million people were unemployed and he had said, "The only thing we have to fear is fear itself." Long before the Pearl Harbor attack he had declared that the United States could not escape if World War II came, and had done everything he could to prepare for it. He had spoken the hopes of the world in the Atlantic Charter and in his message on the Four Freedoms.

In his last inaugural address he had given a memorable message to the nation. "We have learned," he said, "that we cannot live alone. We have learned to be citizens of the world, members of the human community."

THE END OF THE WAR

There had been fears that victory in the Pacific might not come till a year or more after victory in Europe. But events moved fast in that great area. Distances were conquered by the airplanes of the Allies. Ships carried a never-ending supply of arms and food, of airplanes and men to the places where they were most needed.

The Allies won victories in Burma, in China, and in the other lands which the Japanese had conquered early in the war. Gradually the Allies moved in from all sides, tightening the ring within which the Japanese were now defending themselves. United States troops landed on the Philippines, releasing American prisoners and freeing the loyal Filipinos. From their recaptured island bases and from huge aircraft carriers Allied planes could at last begin to bomb cities and military defenses on the home islands of Japan. The next step would be invasion.

Japan was warned that it must surrender or be destroyed. It made no reply. Scientists in the United States had now invented a new kind of bomb. It used a force which man had never before been able to control. Three months after the day of final victory in Europe, Allied airmen dropped two of these "atomic bombs," as they were called, on two

THE WAR IN THE PACIFIC

Japanese cities. The result was terrible. Everything within a large area was destroyed. The government of Japan had known that it could not long continue to fight against the whole world. It now offered to surrender.

V-J (Victory over Japan) Day came on September 2, 1945, when the Japanese military leaders surrendered to the Allies aboard the battleship *Missouri*. But President Harry S. Truman, who had taken office after the death of President Roosevelt, had not waited for that day. When the news of the offer of surrender came, he proclaimed a day of thanksgiving and prayer. On that day millions gave thanks in their churches for the end of the war.

Even before V-E Day the United Nations had begun to plan for the peace which should follow the war. Delegates came together at San Francisco in the spring of 1945 to plan for the future. It was a remarkable gathering of world leaders. They came from all over the globe with one purpose—to create an organization which should "lay the foundation for world peace."

Together they wrote a charter for a United Nations organization, the U.N. Their work was like that of the men who came together in 1787 after the American Revolution to write the Constitution of the United States. But here were delegates from fifty nations. They spoke different languages. They had different ideas about government. But they had one purpose in common. They were determined to do everything they could to keep peace in the world. They were planning an organization within which disputes could be settled before they led to war.

The delegates worked for weeks over this charter. Every word must be finally agreed on by all. Every sentence must say very clearly just what was intended. The delegates did not give up until all were satisfied.

Finally the organization was planned, and the charter which described it was written. Everyone knew that the charter was not perfect. But it was a good beginning, and it was the best on which all could agree. Its hope lay in its first words: "We, the people of the United Nations." The people of the world were uniting to build for the future.

The final day came. The charter had been translated into several languages. For eight hours it lay on the table and the delegates from fifty nations walked proudly forward, one by one, and signed it. They had approved it. Now they were to take it back to their own countries for the approval of their governments.

Governments of those nations did approve the work of their delegates. The charter was accepted, and the United Nations Assembly held its first meeting in London in January, 1946. Many countries asked for the honor of having the world capital located within their borders. It was finally voted to accept the invitation of the United States. At the meeting of the Assembly which was held near New York City, a site within that city was chosen as the permanent world headquarters of the United Nations. While the delegates were making their choice, their chairman showed them an invitation written on parchment from a million New York school children.

"It is the children who understand," said the chairman. "Millions of youths all over the world know, as these American boys and girls know, that the United Nations has begun to build for them a better world."

Only a few centuries have passed since America was a New World, drawing to itself people from many countries. Here they have learned to work together to build a united nation. At times progress has been slow. But the goal of the nation's founders has stood out clearly. Respect for individual liberty has not been lost in the building of a society where all worked together for the common good. Since the days of the town meeting Americans have learned to meet, discuss, and decide on action together. Today the community has become the world. The United Nations Assembly is the world town meeting. It offers the chance for people of all nations to come together and discuss their problems. From their own experience Americans believe that the world can become a united community.

Talking Together

1. Everything that happens is a part of history but some events are more important than others. Do you know of anything that is happening in the United States or in the world today that may be in future history books?

2. Americans went all over the world during World War II. On the blackboard make a list of all the different places visited by relatives and friends of the class during World War II. Find these places on a map of the world.

3. What did President Franklin D. Roosevelt mean when he said, "We cannot live alone"?

4. Have you ever visited an airport? More than one? What airport is nearest your home? What regular airlines use this airport?

5. What is meant by a "have-not" nation?

6. Can you name the "four freedoms"? In what ways would your life be different if you lived in a country without them?

Interesting Things to Try

1. Find a list of the nations which are members of the United Nations. If necessary, write to U.N. headquarters for the names or ask a local newspaper office. On an outline map of the world, color the countries which are members of the U.N.

2. If a signpost shows that a U.S. Highway runs through your community, draw the entire route of that particular numbered highway on an outline map of the United States. Bring to the class any highway maps you can get.

3. On a time line where one inch represents one year, place 1920 at one end of the line and the present year at the other. Put on the time line the important dates and events in this unit.

4. How much does it cost to fly from your nearest airport to New York? To San Francisco? To Mexico City? To Rio de Janeiro? To Moscow? How long will it take to make the trip to each of these places? You will need information from different airlines.

Let's Read

Legends of the United Nations, by Frances Frost. Forty-seven tales from the folklore of members of the United Nations.

Young Franklin Roosevelt, by Rita Halle Kleeman. True stories about the boyhood of President Franklin D. Roosevelt.

Calling South America, by Marion Lansing. Imaginary broadcasts between North and South American schoolboys, with much fresh and interesting information about South America.

Donald Duck Sees South America, by H. Marion Palmer. Donald Duck's rapid and very amusing tour of the continent, illustrated by the Walt Disney Studio.

The Story of American Aviation, by Jim Ray. A well illustrated account of American aviation from the Wrights' first flight.

Checking Your Skills and Habits

Copy this list of questions. Answer each question with a "No," "Yes," or "Sometimes." *Do not write in this book.*

1. Do I take part in class discussions?
2. Do I question statements made by other pupils?
3. Do I help in class planning by contributing suggestions?
4. Do I locate material by using the contents or index of a book?
5. Do I select from a book only the parts relating to my reports?
6. Can I make a simple bibliography?
7. Do I do something more than simply talk when I make an oral report?
8. Do I know how to hunt for information?
9. Do I find out the meanings of words which I do not know?
10. Do I know how to make a simple outline?
11. Can I make a time line?
12. Do I ask good questions about other pupils' reports?
13. Do I listen carefully when others speak?
14. Have I ever brought to class helpful material that had not been asked for?
15. Do I work well with others in a small group?

List of Dates

The list gives dates selected for their importance in New World history. They may be of aid to pupils in making time lines.

A.D.		Unit	Page
1492	Columbus discovered America.	I	18
1493	Spanish colonization began.	I	22
1497	John Cabot reached coast of North America.	I	25
1500	Brazil visited by Cabral.	I	28
1519–1522	First voyage around the world.	II	44
1534	Cartier explored the Gulf of St. Lawrence.	II	58
1565	St. Augustine founded by the Spanish.	II	47
1607	Jamestown founded by the English.	III	75
1608	Quebec founded by the French.	III	97
1619	First representative assembly in English North America.	IV	145
1620	Plymouth founded by the Pilgrims.	III	86
1630	Massachusetts Bay Colony founded.	IV	113
1636	Harvard College founded.	IV	118
1682	La Salle claimed the Mississippi Valley for France.	V	165
1763	End of French rule in North America.	V	176
1775–1783	The American Revolution.	V	186
1776	Declaration of Independence adopted.	V	189
1776	San Francisco founded by the Spanish.	VII	260
1787	The Northwest Ordinance.	VI	222
1787	The Constitutional Convention.	VI	213
1789	Washington inaugurated first President.	VI	215
1793	Eli Whitney invented the cotton gin.	VI	217
1803	Louisiana Purchase.	VII	248
1804–1806	Lewis and Clark expedition.	VII	248
1807	Fulton's steamboat made successful trip.	VI	229

A.D.		Unit	Page
1810–1824	South American Wars of Independence.	VIII	291
1812–1814	War of 1812.	VII	254
1819	The United States purchased Florida from Spain.	VII	267
1821	Independence of Mexico and Central America.	VIII	299, 319
1822	Independence of Brazil.	VIII	299
1823	Monroe Doctrine announced.	VIII	301
1825	Erie Canal completed.	VI	234
1834	McCormick reaper patented.	IX	345
1844	Morse's telegraph was tested.	IX	338
1849	California gold rush.	VII	278
1861–1865	War Between the States.	VIII	312
1862	Homestead Act.	IX	334
1863	Emancipation Proclamation.	VIII	317
1867	Purchase of Alaska.	VII	283
1867	Canada became a Dominion.	VIII	323
1869	First transcontinental railroad completed.	IX	341
1876	Telephone invented by Bell.	IX	350
1879	Electric light bulb invented by Edison.	IX	354
1890	Pan American Union organized.	X	401
1892–1895	First American automobiles.	IX	357
1898	United States acquired Puerto Rico and Philippine Islands.	X	385
1898	United States acquired Hawaii.	X	386
1903	Wright brothers made first airplane flight.	X	393
1914	Panama Canal opened.	X	390
1917	United States entered World War I.	X	403
1920	United States gave vote to women.	IX	366
1933–1945	Franklin D. Roosevelt was President.	XI	419
1939	World War II began.	XI	426
1941–1945	United States in World War II.	XI	427
1945	United Nations organized.	XI	441
1945	First use of atomic energy.	XI	438

List of Maps

Unit I

Unit II

Unit III

Unit IV

Unit V

Index

ā as in dāte
ă as in ăm
â as in fâre
ȧ as in ȧsk
ȧ as in *ȧ*bout
ä as in fär

ē as in bē
ĕ as in mĕt
ȩ as in hȩre
ẽ as in makẽr
ī as in bīte
ĭ as in bĭt

ō as in hōpe
ŏ as in hŏt
ô as in lôrd
ū as in ūse
ŭ as in ŭp
û as in bûrn

th as in thin
t̶h̶ as in t̶h̶en
tū as in pictūre

o͞o as in fo͞od
o͝o as in fo͝ot
ou as in out

A

dāte, ăm, fâre, ȧsk, ȧbout, fär, bē, mĕt, hẹre, makẽr, bīte, bĭt, hōpe, hŏt, lôrd, ūse, ŭp, bûrn, thin, then, pictūre, fōōd, fŏŏt, out

dāte, ăm, fâre, åsk, *a*bout, fär, bē, mĕt, hẹre, makẽr, bīte, bĭt, hōpe, hŏt, lôrd, ūse, ŭp, bûrn, thin, then, pictūre, fōōd, fŏŏt, out

D

dāte, ăm, fâre, ȧsk, ȧbout, fär, bē, mĕt, hẹre, makẽr, bīte, bĭt, hōpe, hŏt, lôrd, ūse, ŭp, bûrn, thin, then, pictụre, fo͞od, fo͝ot, out

dāte, ăm, fâre, ȧsk, *ȧ*bout, fär, bē, mĕt, hẹre, makẽr, bīte, bĭt, hōpe, hŏt, lôrd, ūse, ŭp, bûrn, thin, then, pictūre, fōōd, fŏŏt, out

I

dāte, ăm, fâre, ȧsk, *a*bout, fär, bē, mĕt, hẹre, makẽr, bīte, bĭt, hōpe, hŏt, lôrd, ūse, ŭp, bûrn, thin, then, pictūre, fo͞od, fo͝ot, out

dāte, ăm, fâre, ȧsk, ȧbout, fär, bē, mĕt, hẹre, makẽr, bīte, bĭt, hōpe, hŏt, lôrd, ūse, ŭp, bûrn, thin, then, pictūre, fo͞od, fo͝ot, out

O

P

dāte, ăm, fâre, ȧsk, *ȧ*bout, fär, bē, mĕt, hẹre, makẽr, bīte, bĭt, hōpe, hŏt, lôrd, ūse, ŭp, bûrn, thin, then, pictūre, fōōd, fŏŏt, out

dāte, ăm, fâre, ȧsk, ȧbout, fär, bē, mĕt, hẽre, makẽr, bīte, bĭt, hōpe, hŏt, lôrd, ūse, ŭp, bûrn, thin, then, pictūre, fōōd, fo͝ot, out

U

V

dāte, ăm, fâre, ȧsk, *a*bout, fär, bē, mĕt, hẽre, makẽr, bīte, bĭt, hōpe, hŏt, lôrd, ūse, ŭp, bûrn, thin, then, pictūre, fōōd, fŏŏt, out